KU-485-206

QUILTMAKING
MADE · EASY

DEDICATION

To the memory of my parents. My father, Darcy Ronald Webster, taught me to question received wisdom, and my mother, Margaret Katharine Webster (born Haynes), from a long line of makers, taught me how to make things.

Author's Note.

The projects in this book can be worked either in imperial or in metric measurements. Do keep to one or the other as the instructions will otherwise not work.

QUILTMAKING
MADE · EASY

PAULINE ADAMS

LITTLE HILLS PRESS

ACKNOWLEDGEMENTS

To Barbara Johannah for inventing quick-pieced triangles and eight-pointed stars.

To Georgia Bonesteel and Oxmoor House for permission to show Billings Bonus seam-crossing technique.

To Herta Puls for permission to explain appliqué with greaseproof paper.

To Anne Oliver for inventing appliqué with freezer paper, and to Jean Eitel, the Editor of *Quilt* magazine for permission to explain it.

To Elly Sienkiewicz for permission to explain her method of doing appliqué stems.

To Lucy and Jonty, to Christopher and Claire for patiently waiting for their wedding present quilts, to Simon and Alison for sharing their Log Cabin quilt, and my little grandson, their son Ben, for waiting for his pram quilt.

To Penny Roberts for allowing me to show Penny's Dogwood Trail.

To Tilly Campbell for sharing her Album quilt.

To Mr Blossom of Oaklands Agricultural College, for permission to show the Oaklands Wallhanging.

To Mimram Quilters for permission to show the Welwyn Wallhanging, and for encouragement and teaching practice.

To Alban Quilters, for encouragement and challenges, and Margaret Freeman for permission to show the Chatelaine Mary Jeffreys made for her.

To Peta Breeze for making the Flying Geese barbecue glove, permission to share her Chatelaine, and continued interest, encouragement and informed criticism.

To sharing quilters, known and unknown, for their generosity with techniques, tips and information and the quilters' grapevine which makes this possible.

To my husband, Peter, and daughters Kate and Emma, for help and encouragement.

Little Hills Press Pty Ltd,
Regent House,
37-43 Alexander Street,
Crows Nest, NSW 2065
Australia

Tavistock House,
34 Bromham Road,
Bedford MK40 2QD
United Kingdom

ISBN 1 86315 010 2

Designed by Christie & Eckermann, Art and Design Studio, Sydney.
Edited by Jo Rudd.
Photography by Suzanne Grundy, Imagetrend Ltd.

National Library of Australia
Cataloguing-in-Publication data

Adams, Pauline, 1931-
Quiltmaking made easy.

Bibliography.
Includes index.
ISBN 1 86315 010 2.

1. Quilting. 2. Quilting - Patterns.
I. Title.

746.46

CONTENTS

INTRODUCTION

Patchwork, appliqué and quilting all have a long and fascinating history. Quiltmaking as a craft has survived lean times and is now becoming more and more popular as a relaxation and means of artistic expression. Once, all little girls were made to learn sewing as a necessary skill 'at Mother's knee', often by making simple patchwork. Now, many have never been taught to sew and may be scared off from starting by the apparent difficulty of making even a small article in patchwork or quilting. Others are convinced that they cannot 'design', or are unwilling to try new things because of a fear of failure.

As a traditional thrift craft making quick much-needed bedcovers for use in bitterly cold winters, patchworkers' tools and materials were restricted to what was available in the sewing box, rag-bag and around the home. Patchwork was hand sewn from linens, cottons or woollens, the earlier fabrics often handspun, handwoven and home-dyed, and very often from the better parts of cast-off clothing. Quilt fillings were mostly carded cotton or sheepswool. Sometimes the recycling extended to fillings made from old blankets, worn clothing, worn-out quilts and even corn husks or paper. When funds and the availability of supplies allowed, fabrics for patchwork (and especially appliqué) would be bought specially. In wealthier homes and in more affluent times the craft became also a leisure activity rather than a necessary chore; extra care would be lavished on special quilts, for weddings or presentations. These would be of more complex design and a higher standard of stitching (especially quilting). Naturally, because they were cherished and would have received less use, proportionately more of these special quilts have survived than the workaday ones.

Yesterday's quilters took advantage of any way of lightening their quilting workload. In America, the quilting bee was a favourite way of combining socialising with work, as it still is among quilting groups today. Old-time quilters were as anxious to save time as we are, and made early use of the sewing machine when they could afford it. It was used particularly for piecing the long seams in quilt backs and in joining blocks together.

In the last ten to fifteen years, there has been a huge worldwide revival of interest in patchwork and quilting, and a consequent upsurge in the development of new techniques, new tools and new approaches to design. Now a whole quilt can be made using a sewing machine in a fraction of the time that it would have taken if all done by hand. Aesthetics come into the balance of personal choices too, because the appearance of machine quilting is not at all the same as hand quilting, and it is *your* choice what you spend your precious time on.

Many books have been written which explain one or another method of easy patchwork, but I think this is the first where most of the methods have been drawn together in one book. Often the new ideas have been developed simultaneously in different places around the world.

When I first started patchwork, I was overcome by the rules and complexity of the processes and didn't know where to start. On top of that, I was overwhelmed by the enormous design choices available. So I have tried to write this book in a way which, while showing how to do things in simpler or quicker ways, also explains why things are done in this or that way. Disasters *can* happen — I have had a few myself, as well as some near misses – so I will give methods which should lead you past the pitfalls.

As a quiltmaker, I am stimulated by fabrics and pattern, enjoy puzzling out how to make what looks un-makeable, and get my relaxation from hand quilting. I find hand piecing is too slow for me, although English piecing over papers (Chapter 10) can be relaxing occasionally. My patchwork is made almost entirely on the sewing machine, which is very fast, but only if you are accurate enough to avoid having to unpick faulty piecing. Because my eyesight is now poor, making it more difficult to be accurate, and because I hate to waste time unpicking [ripping out], I have been glad to find new methods and tools which almost guarantee accuracy. I have even managed to develop some of the methods myself!

The two fundamentals to accuracy are cutting and sewing. If you are planning to make patchwork, particularly large quilts, do invest in the ROTARY CUTTING EQUIPMENT; and whatever you plan to make with machine piecing, save unpicking time later by working through the SEAM ALLOWANCE TEST in Chapter 5. The accuracy of all your subsequent work will depend on your using the correct seam allowance and this test is the key to that accuracy. It is the quilter's equivalent to a knitter's tension square.

The new techniques include: methods of quick machine piecing without the need to make templates or cut out little individual pieces of fabric before sewing them together again; faster methods of sewing and assembly; different ways of doing hand and machine appliqué; and quilting with the sewing machine. The old methods of hand piecing, appliqué and quilting are included here too, as all have their place in the quilter's repertoire of techniques.

Finally, there is a special section in which I discuss the problems of working in groups, or assembling different blocks or techniques into a coherent whole.

CHAPTER ONE

HOW TO USE THIS BOOK

The next three chapters give background information on design, colour, fabric, tools and equipment.

After that, each chapter covers a different aspect of patchwork, quilting or appliqué, with techniques explained in the first part of the chapter, followed by projects made using those techniques.

Americans, and older British and Australian quilters, use imperial (feet-and-inches) measurements, but metric measurements are used by younger quilters and in Europe, so I have given the instructions for all projects in both metric and imperial. As when following cookery recipes, do not mix two sets of measurements, but stick to one or the other.

Every project will call on several different techniques, described in other chapters, so instead of saying "see page so-and-so" I have put the technique in capital letters, e.g. "PREPARE fabric" or "LAYER quilt". All you need to do is look in the index for the right page number.

Different countries have differing availability of supplies and use different words to describe things. In America, plastic-coated 'freezer paper' is much used in patchwork and appliqué techniques. It is not available in England except as an import, although I have found the heat-sealing paper wrapped round packets of photocopy paper to be a good substitute. In England, I use 'greaseproof paper' for an appliqué technique and for tracing, but it seems to be unknown in America, where they would have to substitute thin tracing paper. Because the recent upsurge of quilting started in America and their market is very much larger, specialist quilting equipment has naturally been designed for the American market. This is causing problems for quilters who work in metric measurements and want to use rotary cutting techniques, as the special rulers have up to now been marked in inches — but see Chapter 4 for ways around the difficulty.

Language can cause problems too, and words have to be translated from time to time. This book is writtten in 'English' English, and the first time in a chapter a word is used that has an alternative in 'American' English, I give it in square brackets, e.g. wadding [batting]. The translations are also in the GLOSSARY, in case you forget. Try reading the glossary anyway, it might surprise you! There is also a bibliography of helpful books, a short list of suppliers and a section called reminders where useful information is collected.

Here and there in the text, especially at the end of sections, you will see a • symbol. This is to mark a specially helpful tip or watchpoint.

CHAPTER TWO

IDEAS AND DESIGN

If you have never done any patchwork before, it can be difficult to decide how to start. I began my first quilt because I was bored waiting for my first child to arrive. I planned to use up my dressmaking scraps on a hexagon quilt — nothing like starting big! At that time, in 1957, I had never heard of any other type of patchwork. To me, hexagons *were* patchwork and I didn't realise the limitations of having only five fabrics plus white in the rag bag and of not working out what I was doing before I started. Consequently, the quilt didn't get finished for eighteen years and was a rather peculiar and unsatisfactory design, but I love it dearly, as it contains so many memories.

Then in the early 1960s I bought Marguerite Ickis's *The Standard Book of Quilt Making and Collecting*. I couldn't believe the richness of the history and all the patchwork patterns. There were so many that I could never decide which one to make, but I kept reading and re-reading it and, later, other authors like Ruby Short McKim and Averil Colby. All the books then advocated hand sewing as the only true method. In the end, after one or two cushions [pillows] in hexagon adaptations, I did make my very first proper quilt (the hexagon quilt still wasn't finished!) to a block of my own design. It was all done by hand and even quilted, but I still have difficulty choosing which block to use, and tend to finish up using my own designs.

TRADITIONAL QUILTS

Most historic patchwork comes from North America, and some authors appear to think it originated there. However, there is strong evidence that quilts were made in Britain before North America was settled, and that some patterns originated in Britain and were carried by emigrants to North America and Australia. Because of necessity and their harsher winters, patchwork was then developed to a much greater extent in America. In Britain, the traditional quilts of northern England (Northumberland and Durham) and Wales are the best known, but many other fine examples have been documented from Scotland, Ireland, the West Country and the Isle of Man.

A quilt is a sandwich. The 'bread' layers are fabric, which enclose and protect a fragile warm filling, generally some form of WADDING [batting]. The three layers are held together to prevent shifting and clumping of the wadding by TYING or QUILTING. If the top layer of fabric is made of PATCHWORK, the whole thing is called a PATCHWORK QUILT. A piece of patchwork which is LINED or BACKED but not wadded is called a COVERLET. A quilt can also be decorated by APPLIQUÉ, or it can rely for its design on its quilting patterns alone, when it is called a WHOLECLOTH QUILT.

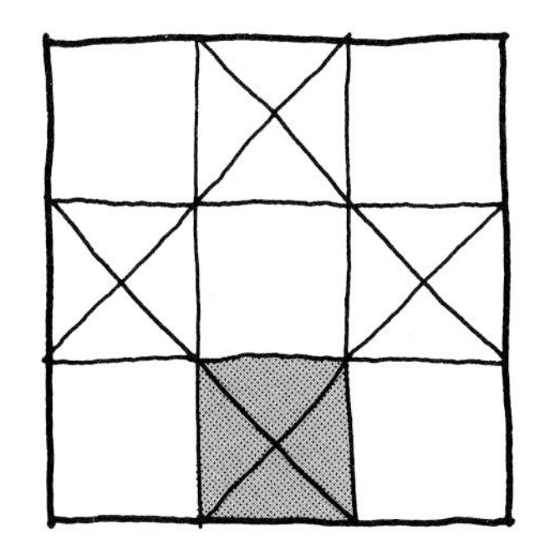

2-1 UNIT SQUARE

The easiest way to make a patchwork quilt is in sections, called BLOCKS. These are usually square, and may be from 6in (15cm) to 24in (60cm). A useful and manageable size is 12in (30cm) square. A patchwork block is made from a pattern of triangles, squares or strips of fabric (PATCHES), sewn (PIECED) together, and is mostly able to be divided into smaller squares (UNIT SQUARES) (2-1). Blocks are categorised by how many unit squares (or patches) make up one block (4-patch, 9-patch, etc) or sometimes by how many squares there are on each side (5-patch). Block patterns also have names, such as Ohio Star, Brown Goose, etc (2-2).

If a plain [solid] fabric block is decorated with a cut-out piece or pieces of contrasting fabric sewn on, then it is an APPLIQUÉ block.

When enough blocks have been made, they are joined together (SET) to make the QUILT TOP. Pieced blocks can be set SOLID, one next to the other (like FLOTILLA) or they can be set alternately with plain blocks, like a chequerboard (SINGLE IRISH CHAIN). This gives a fine opportunity for special quilting in the plain blocks. Instead of alternate plain blocks, they can be set with a differently patterned block to create intricate patterns (FIREWORKS).

Blocks can be separated by SASHING (narrow strips of fabric) and they can be surrounded by one or more plain or pieced BORDERS. Some very effective quilts turn the blocks diagonally, others make a feature of a larger central block (MEDALLION) and surround it with related blocks and/or borders.

Some patterns are linear like FLYING GEESE and lend themselves to STRIP quilts where the patchwork patterns run lengthwise down the quilt. When a quilt top is made from a single pattern shape — square, hexagon, triangle, etc — the pattern is called an ALLOVER one and relies for effect on colour placement, e.g. the small squares of TRIP AROUND THE WORLD.

Once the whole of the top has been made it should at least be BACKED or LINED to prevent wear on the seams, and the outside edges FINISHED. To give added warmth a layer of wadding can be incorporated, then the top decorated and held with QUILTING, or TIED through the layers.

DESIGNING

Although you can decide to learn 'how to' by following the instructions for the projects, your result is bound to be different from mine because your fabric supply will be different, and very likely so will your taste in colour. This means that from the beginning you will be making design choices about colour and fabrics, even if you copy all the instructions exactly. This is a good thing. Everyone's colour preferences are different, and if you want to make a project up in purple and green, where I have used pale colours, go right ahead.

Some people get inspiration for a project from the fabrics themselves — the accidental placing of two or three colours together can be all they need to get going. Others like to play around with pencil and paper. Whenever I go on holiday, I take a large pad of detail paper, some 1in (2.5cm) graph paper and felt pens and just play around with shapes and colours by tracing the graph paper grid. But at the same time I miss my fabrics! Names can also be very inspirational and sometimes the name of a quilt will spark off a design.

Or try playing with a child's box of coloured wooden mosaic shapes, or the TANGRAM. Both will give you an awareness of the relationships of geometrical shapes. Later, you can cut out lots of similar shapes from coloured paper or card and practise block-designing with the shapes. Or you can focus on the tonal values rather than colours, and cut out the pieces in black, white and two shades of grey.

The Bibliography gives a number of excellent books on designing quilts, and traditional quilt patterns.

I have included (2-2) a variety of block patterns to experiment with — there are 9-patches, 4-patches and 5-patches. There are also one or two which make good alternating blocks for more complex patterns.

It is best to start simply and then, when you are more confident, try more advanced things like altering the proportions of a block. I haven't included any quilt blocks with curved seams, although there are some very attractive ones, nor any that can't be made without TEMPLATES.

Ninepatch

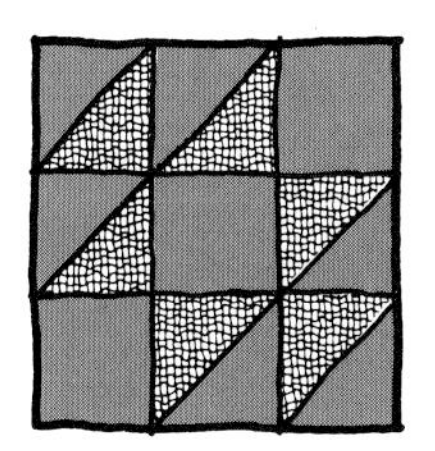
Double X

Snowball

Friendship Star

Churn Dash

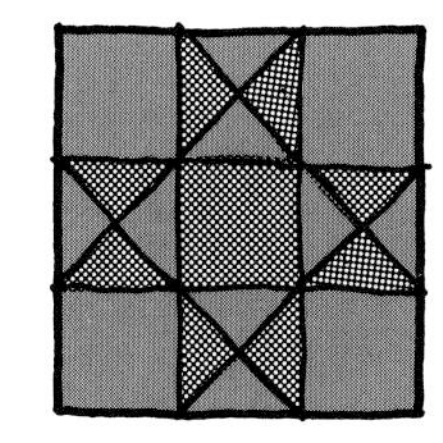
Ohio Star

Maple Leaf

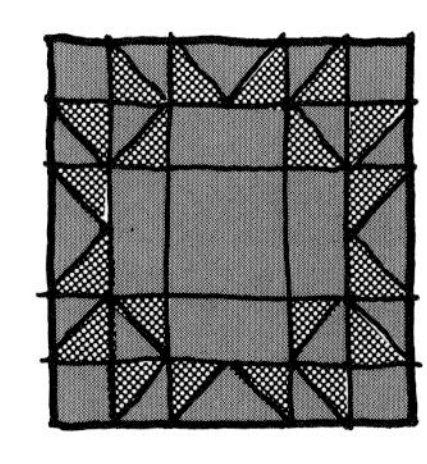
Robbing Peter to Pay Paul

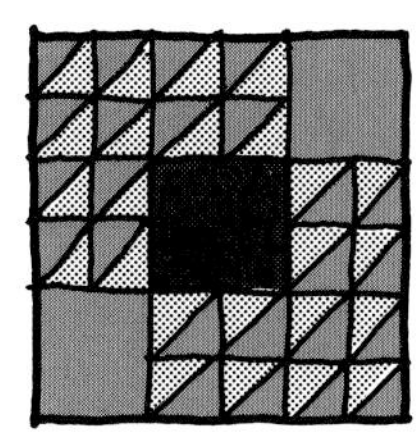
Winged Square

Road to California

Corn & Beans

Rambler

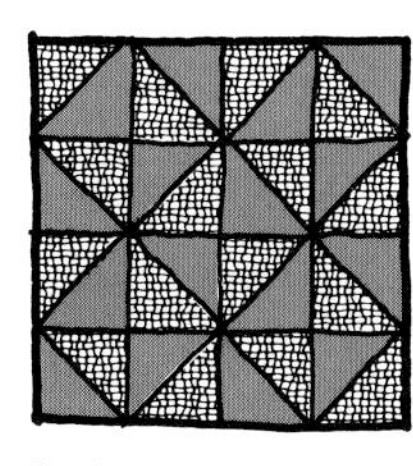
Broken Dishes

Dutchman's Puzzle

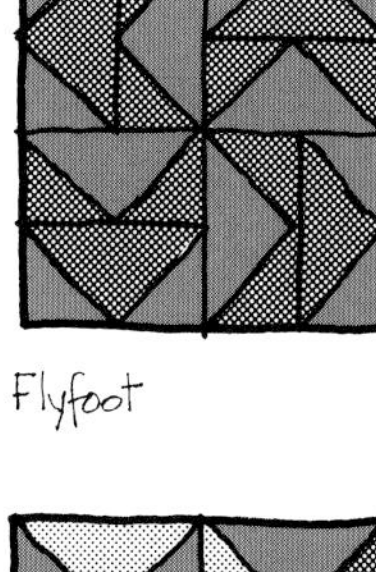
Flyfoot

Pieced Star

Brown Goose

Evening Star

Windblown Square

Birds in the Air

2-2 A FEW SIMPLE PATCHWORK BLOCKS

COLOUR CHOICE

This is the most difficult of all to teach. It is tempting to play safe and make a quilt in co-ordinating colours, and all quilting suppliers have delectable ranges of small prints. But beware of blandness. Try to get contrast in tone [value] and in the scales of different prints, use some plain fabrics as well for contrast, and add the jolt of a slightly 'off' colour to give excitement. If you are really stuck, find a piece of printed fabric you like, and look at the colours that have been used in it. Translate these colours, in the right proportions, to your patchwork (I did this in the BARGELLO CUSHIONS). You will almost certainly find an 'off' colour in the selection, but will finish with a harmonious arrangement.

AGE FABRICS
117
1989
S.O.S

CHAPTER THREE

BEFORE STARTING — MATERIALS AND PREPARATION

CHOICE OF FABRICS

The most satisfactory fabric to use for patchwork is dressweight cotton. It is easy to sew, press and wash, and has stood the test of time. Pure cotton prints [calicoes] are probably most easily obtained in specialist quilting shops, rather than fabric stores catering for the home dressmaker where dressweight cottons are generally blends containing synthetics. It is not impossible to work with blends, but it becomes more difficult as the proportion of synthetic to cotton increases. This is partly because blends are more stretchy, but also because they don't press so sharply.

If you are going to hand quilt your work, then choose a fabric which is not too closely woven. Poplin, glazed chintz and percale sheeting (very often chosen for a quilt backing because of its conveniently large size) are all tougher to sew by hand, and therefore difficult and frustrating to quilt. Mixing fine fabrics and heavy ones is also likely to cause problems as the heavier cloth puts undue strain on the lighter, so it is best to choose fabrics of similar weight. Beware also of very cheap fabrics — they may have a great deal of filler disguising an open weave. Mixing synthetics and cottons in the same quilt can cause difficulties in sewing, from differential stretching, and in ironing, when you should always set the iron to suit the synthetics.

Be cautious in using fabrics from cast-off clothing. Jumble sales are a good cheap source of patchwork fabrics, especially for filling gaps in the colour range of your fabric larder, but used fabric will inevitably have a shorter life in your quilt then new fabric. If you do plan to use thrift fabrics, always wash the garments first, cut away all seams, zippers and noticeably worn areas, and then check again for wear while ironing the pieces, and again while cutting out.

For the BACKING of your quilt choose a not-too-heavy fabric. A print will disguise uneven stitching. Calico [muslin] is a good, cheaper choice, but it must be washed (not just dunked) first in very hot water to be rid of shrinkage and dressings.

FABRIC PREPARATION

If you plan ever to wash your quilt, then the fabrics *must* be pre-washed before being cut, in water as hot as will ever be used. This will prevent later shrinkage or colour running [bleeding]. Of course, both have happened to me, but don't be tempted to skip these important steps, or they might happen to you too, and spoil your masterpiece.

1 Dunk each piece of fabric in hot water, separately. This will ensure that any colour-run will not transfer itself, and also you will know which fabrics run. This is why it is better to wash by hand rather than dumping a whole load of differently coloured fabrics into the washer. Start with the lightest colour and work through to the darkest. If any fabric runs, remove it for further treatment, and change the washing water.

2 For the non-fast colours, add a handful of cooking salt to the repeat wash. Somehow, this tends to set dyes and prevent them transferring to other fabrics.

3 Do not pre-wash glazed chintzes or the finish will be lost — plan to dry clean the quilt, as you would any other fabric not suitable for washing. A quilt for a child must be washable.

4 Dry and press the washed fabrics, trying to keep grainlines straight and square. Store folded, away from light, and not in plastic bags, which can't breathe. Cut off the selvages before use, as they are thick, liable to shrink, and often flawed.

HOW MUCH TO BUY

If you need to buy fabric for a special project, work out how much you need before going shopping. Fabric comes in different widths. Cotton is commonly 36in (90cm) or 44in (110cm). Calculate for both widths. Upholstery and curtain fabrics come in other widths again — 48in (120cm) and 60in (150cm) — and sheetings wider still. Later in this chapter there is a section on how to estimate. If in doubt, buy too much, and always add on a little for insurance against shrinkage and mistakes.

If you are buying fabric without a special project in mind, do not get less than ¼ yard (22cm), and more if it is a particularly useful colour or a specially tempting fabric. I tend to snap up quite large lengths of plain colours [solids], as fashion colours change every season and what is fashionable this year will be unobtainable soon. Think of your fabric store as a painter's palette; it needs variety to choose from, so if you see a fabric you like, get it if you can.

WADDING [BATTING]

Here there seems to be a lot of confusion. Some early synthetic waddings caused problems because of 'bearding' — a fuzz of fibres which comes up through the fabric and won't go back down again. I think the problem is now largely overcome. For hand quilting, a 2 to 2½oz (56-70g) weight polyester wadding is comfortable to sew. Thicker 4oz (112g) and 8oz (224g) waddings should be reserved for tied quilts or clothing. If possible, seek advice in a quilter's supply store, which may also carry extra wide waddings that save joining, or bed-sized pieces. In general, if the wadding is very soft, easily pulled apart and has no stiffened surface, you may have problems with bearding. Wadding comes in several different widths, which is why I have given no quantities in the projects.

Also available in some places are needle punched wadding (a denser more felt-like polyester wadding), cotton wadding, 80%/20% cotton/synthetic wadding, domette (a fine light fluffy wool knit) and, exceptionally, carded wool or prepared silk.

SEWING THREAD

If you are sewing pure cottons, then use cotton sewing thread for hand or machine sewing. If some of the fabrics have synthetic in them, you will need to use a synthetic thread, because without its built-in stretch the fabric will pucker when machine sewn. For sewing silks, use silk thread.

QUILTING THREADS

For hand quilting I prefer a pure cotton thread. It seems to tangle less, but is not so easy to find as the cotton-wrapped polyester quilting thread. If quilting on silk, use a silk thread. Quilting thread needs to be stronger than hand or machine sewing thread, because it is under more strain.

For machine quilting use synthetic thread on spool and bobbin, or nylon on spool and synthetic on bobbin.

PRESSING

You will need a steam iron (or non-steam iron and water mister) and ironing board or pad. Have it set up near your sewing machine. Press all fabric before cutting it out. Press machine-pieced patchwork after seams have been sewn, and before further assembly. Try to avoid distorting the patches when pressing.

Generally, strips should be pressed from the front, to avoid creases, and both seam allowances should be pressed in the same direction. For pressing pieced triangles etc, it is customary to press in the direction of the darker fabric.

Special pressing instructions are given in the projects if required, but one general aim is to have crossing seam allowances facing in different directions. This helps to get accurate seam crossings.

For hand-pieced patchwork, it is usual to press after a block is completed, turning the seam allowances in the direction most convenient and least bulky.

Do not press after a quilt has been LAYERED for quilting, or you will flatten the wadding.

QUILT CARE

After all your hard work, your quilt will need the right storage environment. Do not keep in a plastic bag or in the airing cupboard.

The best place for a quilt is on a bed, but keep pets and children away from special quilts. If the quilt is not in use, cover it with an old sheet to exclude light or turn upside down. If the quilt has to be stored folded, try to refold on different lines every month or so, or roll up right side out with a white tissue paper sausage inside, and wrap in a clean old sheet or pillowcase.

Dry cleaning is quite a tough process for a quilt and out of your control. It seems to make a quilt lose body, and may result in lingering cleaning fluid residues. But if a quilt has to be dry cleaned because it contains non-washable fabrics, instruct "no pressing" at the dry cleaners, and hang out to air until all fumes have gone.

If you have a quilt which runs badly (why ever did you use that fabric?) the choice is between dry cleaning and its risks, and washing and the possibility of further colour loss.

When washing, do it in the bathtub, with a mild liquid detergent. If in doubt about colour fastness, add a couple of handfuls of salt to the water before immersing the quilt. Leave to soak briefly, then agitate the sudsy water through the fabric without lifting the heavy, wet quilt. Drain the water away, pressing it out of the quilt, before refilling the tub for rinsing. If colour ran in washing, add more salt for the rinsing. Continue rinsing until the water is clear of suds. Press excess water out of the quilt. Do not spin as creases can be set into the fabric. Instead, use lots of bath towels to soak up water. Dry spread out flat with towels under, and covered with a sheet, or over two parallel and freshly wiped washing lines, in a shady place. A large quilt is very heavy when wet, so enlist help. Squeeze the dripping edges of a line-hung quilt, and shake gently from time to time.

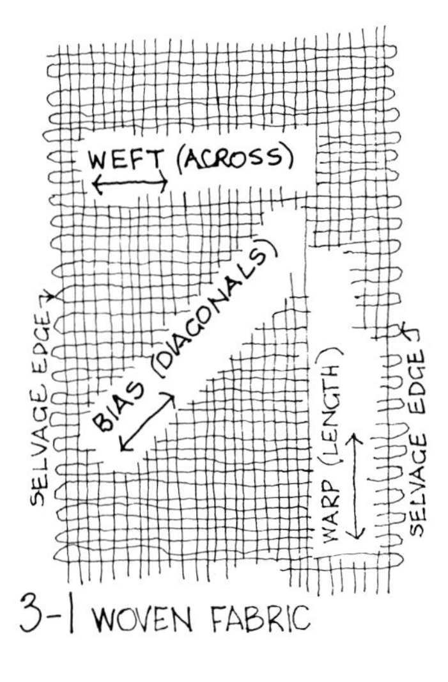

3-1 WOVEN FABRIC

GRAINLINE

Woven fabrics are made up of lengthwise threads (warp) and widthwise threads (weft). The long, thicker edges are the SELVAGES. Any cuts made parallel to the warp or weft are on the STRAIGHT GRAIN. Any cuts made on the diagonal are said to be on the BIAS (3-1). The peculiarities of the weaving process mean that fabrics tend shrink in their length when washed or pressed, and stretch in their width. The bias is very stretchy. Strips are best cut along the warp, but this is not always practical because short lengths of fabric dictate cutting across the width.

It is easier if grainlines of patchwork pieces are in line with block edges, but not essential — your higher priority may be the placement of a stripe or pattern.

ESTIMATING FABRIC QUANTITIES

If you are making any of the projects in this book, then fabric requirements are given. Otherwise, you will need to start with a sketch of what you are going to make, so that you can count the number of pieces of each shape you need to cut from each fabric. It helps to use a pocket calculator, and to remember that the selvages of the fabric (woven edges) will have to be cut off and thrown away. You must reckon to lose 2in (5cm) across the width from this trimming.

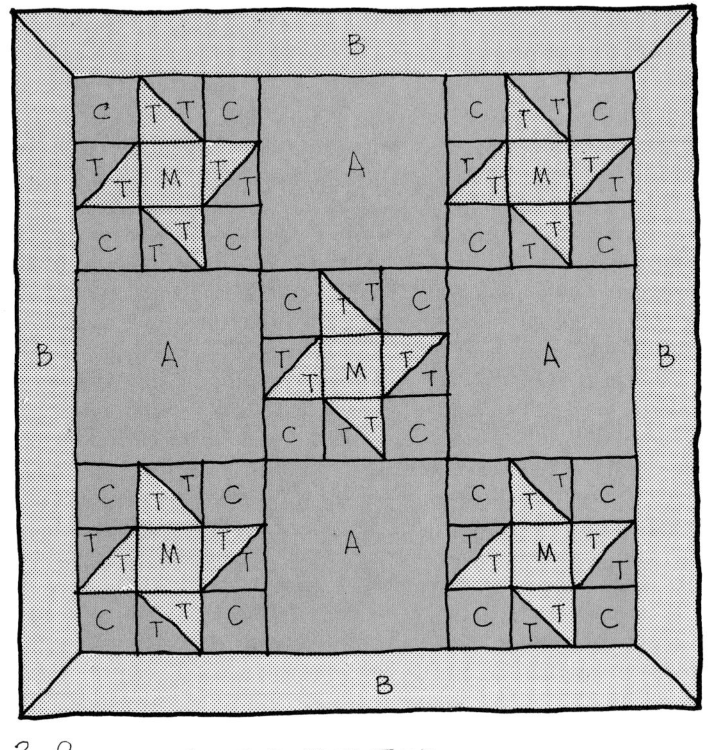

3-2 LAYOUT OF QUILT TOP

EXAMPLE

You plan to make a small quilt (3-2). It has five 12in (30cm) blocks of FRIENDSHIP STAR with 4 alternate plain blocks, and a 4in (10cm) mitred border in the same fabric as the stars. The background to the stars is the same fabric as the plain blocks. The front will turn over to the back (no binding). The fabric is 44in (110cm) wide, reduced to 42in (105cm) when the selvages come off. The finished size of the quilt is 44in x 44in (110cm x 110cm).

1 Allow for borders (B) cut lengthwise: 4 x 5in (12.5cm) wide equals 20in (50cm) in total width. Border lengths should always be overestimated, so length is 48in (120cm).

Add 6in (15cm) strip (L) to supplement backing. This lays out on the fabric as (3-3) and leaves 16in (40cm) of width for the patchwork pieces, which is plenty.

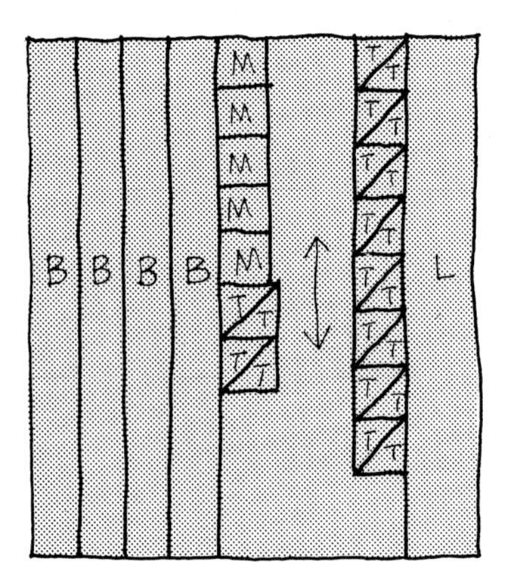

3-3 CUTTING LAYOUT-DARK

For the patchwork pieces you will need:
5 squares (M) of 4 ½in (11.2cm)
2 squares (T) (to cut diagonally into triangles) in 5 blocks
= 10 squares 4 ⅞in (12.2cm)

2 The background fabric:
4 squares (A) of 12½in (31.2cm)
4 squares (C) in 5 blocks = 20 squares 4 ½in (11.2cm)
2 squares (T) (to cut diagonally into triangles) in 5 blocks
= 10 squares 4 ⅞in (12.2cm)

This lays out as (3-4). If there were no errors, no wastage and no trimming, you might just get it out of 1yd (90cm) of fabric, but don't chance your luck. Buy 1¼yd (1.20m).

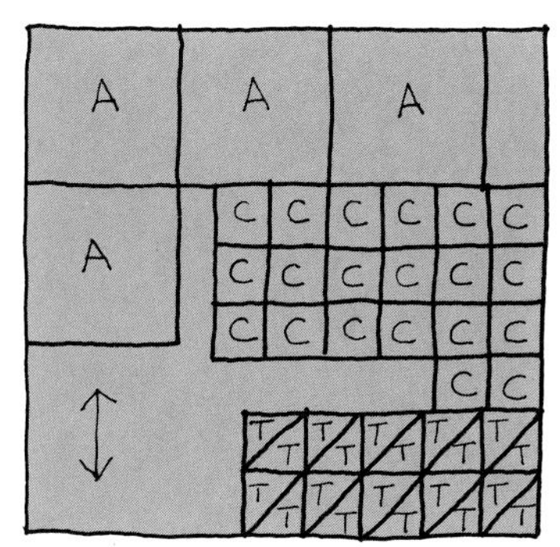

3-4 CUTTING LAYOUT-LIGHT

3 Backing must be allowed larger, say 48in (120cm) square. This is an uneconomical width. Why not put a strip of border fabric down the centre back — allow a 6in (15cm) strip cut at the same time as the border strips. Backing can then comfortably come out of 1½yd (1.40m) length.

CHAPTER FOUR

TOOLS AND EQUIPMENT

SEWING MACHINE

Some of the projects in this book are hand-pieced, and many more of them can be. A quilt can even be completely handmade, but most people will wish to use the sewing machine for some of the chore sewing of a quilt, such as joining backing fabrics, blocks, sashings and borders. For this, there is no need to have more then a basic sewing machine that will sew a good straight even stitch, with adjustable stitch length.

For more elaborate work, such as machine appliqué or machine quilting, you will need a swing-needle machine for the zig-zag and satin stitch. I have a Bernina electronic with free-arm, and mostly use an even-feed foot attachment for strip piecing and straight machine quilting. This is not a cheap accessory, but the difference it makes is fantastic. It ensures that strips do not curve when sewn together, and helps prevent slippage of the layers in machine quilting. One of my MACHINE APPLIQUÉ techniques uses the blind hemming stitch, which cannot be done on the earlier generations of swing-needle machines.

Whatever sewing machine you use, it should be regularly oiled and de-fluffed in accordance with the manufacturer's instruction book. For every new project your machine deserves a new needle, which should be the right size and type for the sort of fabric and thickness of thread being used. Seek advice from your local sewing machine shop if you have difficulty achieving a satisfactory stitch.

- When you are sewing, be sure to sit exactly in line with the needle. It helps to keep seams accurate.

NEEDLES FOR HAND SEWING

The quilter's needle is the 'between', a shorter needle than the 'sharp'. Use a size 9 or 10 'between' for all sewing and quilting, a long 'straw' needle for TACKING and a 'chenille' or sharp yarn needle for TYING. Use a thimble on the middle finger of your sewing hand. If you hand quilt, you may want the protection of another on one of the fingers of the other hand too.

PINS

You will need ordinary dressmaking pins, and sometimes longer glass-headed pins. For quilting, I strongly recommend safety pinning instead of tacking. You will need 300-400 1in (2.5cm) pins for a full-size quilt (see SUPPLIERS). You will also need a pincushion.

MEASURING

A tape measure is necessary. A yard (metre) stick is helpful, and so is a 10ft (3m) steel tape for extra large quilts! Cheap measuring equipment is inclined to be inaccurately marked, so check one against the other.

MARKING

You will need to mark your fabric with cutting out, sewing or quilting lines. It can be difficult on some fabrics to get a mark which shows up. For temporary marks, like cutting lines, try a fine soap sliver. Otherwise a fine (0.5mm) propelling pencil or a silver or white Berol

'Verithin'® should do. The widely sold turquoise washout and purple fading pens are suspect for causing fabric to rot prematurely, and not now recommended. **Never use a ballpoint pen for marking.**

For quilting marking, Conté pastel pencils, well sharpened, are also good. Choose a colour a shade darker than the fabric, or on a darker fabric a brighter colour. Always check that your markers wash out before use — you don't want the marks permanently on display!

CUTTING

You will need fabric scissors, as good a brand as possible, and kept for fabric only. Hide them if necessary! You will also need a pair of paper scissors and some small sharp-pointed general purpose scissors. I do not recommend seam-rippers, as there have been too many accidents where fabric has been slit. Unpick any machining mistakes more slowly and surely by lifting, pulling and snipping off the thread on one side of the fabric and then the other. This has the extra advantage of not distorting bias edges.

You may like to have a craft knife and steel ruler for cutting card or template plastic. When using them, protect your table with a layer of very thick card.

ROTARY CUTTING EQUIPMENT

The revolutionary cutting tool is the rotary cutter. It is the best investment I ever made for ensuring accuracy and saving time. Most of the projects in this book were cut out with one. The cutter is hand-held and shaped rather like a pastry cutter, with a circular steel blade on a handle. The blade is razor-sharp and capable of cutting through eight layers of fabric at a time. Fortunately, it has a protective shield, which you should get into the habit of using at the end of each cutting stroke. Get the 45mm diameter size, and keep it under lock and key, especially from children. Instructions for ROTARY CUTTING come later in this chapter.

The rotary cutter should be used with a special mat, which protects the sharpness of the blade and the surface of your table. (Cardboard and hardboard are not suitable, as they will blunt the blade.) Mats come in various sizes, and can be obtained marked in metric or imperial grids. The imperial mats also have extra quarter-inch markings round the edges, and a 45° angle line. The metric ones have a 5cm or 1cm grid. Shop around for the right sort of mat for you and, if you can, buy one about 18in x 24in (45cm x 60cm). This will enable you to cut folded 44in (110cm) fabric. Keep your mat flat and away from heat.

Also needed in the rotary cutting kit is a wide thick plastic see-through quilter's ruler. There are various different makes, in different sizes. If you start with a small one, you will probably end up wishing you had bought one 6in x 24in (15cm x 60cm). All are marked with vertical and horizontal ⅛in grids and a 45° line. Some have 30° and 60° lines as well. Coming on the market, in response to demand from metric workers, is a similar ruler marked in metric. Also available are some special shapes — squares, triangles, etc for special-shape cutting.

DRAWING EQUIPMENT

At some point you will need pencils, ruler, set square(s) [triangle(s)], and maybe protractor and compasses. You will also need a pencil sharpener and inevitably a rubber [eraser]. For sketching and colouring block patterns, coloured pencils or felt pens and a pad of detail paper, squared paper or graph paper are useful.

Some projects require greaseproof paper, freezer paper (substitute the paper wrapped round packets of photocopy paper) or thin card.

QUILTING EQUIPMENT

All the projects were made using a 14in (35cm) quilting HOOP except FIREWORKS which was quilted on a frame. Other sorts of QUILTING FRAMES are discussed in Chapter 12, and so are marking methods.

MAKING AND USING TEMPLATES

Many of the projects in this book are suitable for making without templates. The strips or pieces of fabric are cut directly with the ROTARY CUTTER, and incorporate a standard ¼in (6mm) seam allowance, unless otherwise stated.

Most of the projects can also be made, more slowly, by the traditional cut-each-piece-out-and-sew-it technique, whether by hand or machine. They will need templates for each shape, to mark the stitching line. Some templates, such as the hexagon and clamshell, should be bought. Others can be made of card, graph-paper-on-sandpaper or template plastic. The plastic wears longest and is specially good for QUILTING TEMPLATES, as it can be seen through. Graph paper is useful because of the accuracy of its square grid. Card and graph paper come from artists' suppliers, template plastic from quilting suppliers.

Make the templates required to the exact sizes stated. Mostly, I have not drawn full-size template patterns, because printing processes are not sufficiently accurate. It is easiest to draw the exact template shapes directly onto graph paper, and glue them to the smooth side of sandpaper before cutting them out on the drawn line. Use card templates for large 'specials' as in the OAKLANDS WALLHANGING. Remember that you will be drawing round your templates on the back of the fabric, giving a reverse effect, so be sure to draw them taking that into account. Mark each template with the preferred GRAINLINES and some form of identification.

CUTTING WITH TEMPLATES

Two or sometimes more layers can be cut if your scissors are good. But the more layers you try to cut, the more distortion of some of the patches there is likely to be. Make sure all the fabrics are laid wrong side up. Place template on top of the fabric. Be economical with the fabric, but make sure that there is at least ¼in (6mm) on each side of the template to cater for the SEAM ALLOWANCES. Hold the template down firmly, and MARK round it. Cut by estimating the seam allowance round the template, or draw ¼in (6mm) away from the marked lines (4-1). If you cut more than one layer at a time, the stitching line (the line drawn round the template) will need to be put onto the backs of all the layers except the top one, which will already be marked.

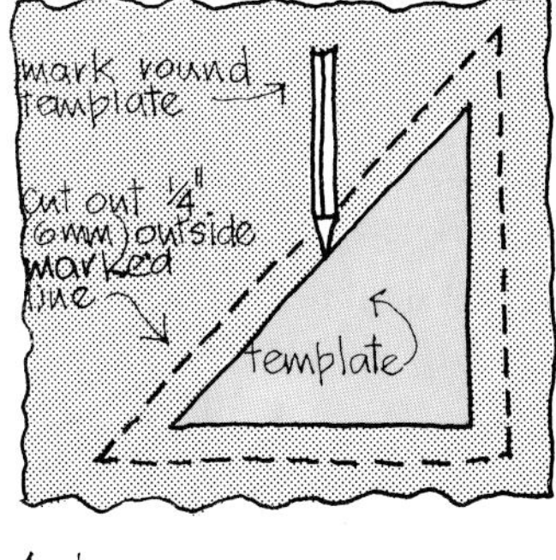

4-1 USING TEMPLATES

- If you are using templates and scissors for cutting out, the fabric requirements for the projects will need to be increased. They were estimated for rotary cutting, which uses less fabric than cutting out with scissors.

MACHINE PIECING

In all piecing, the aim is to sew straight seams. Look at your block pattern and decide the order of sewing for each block. In the projects this is done for you. This usually involves sewing smaller patches

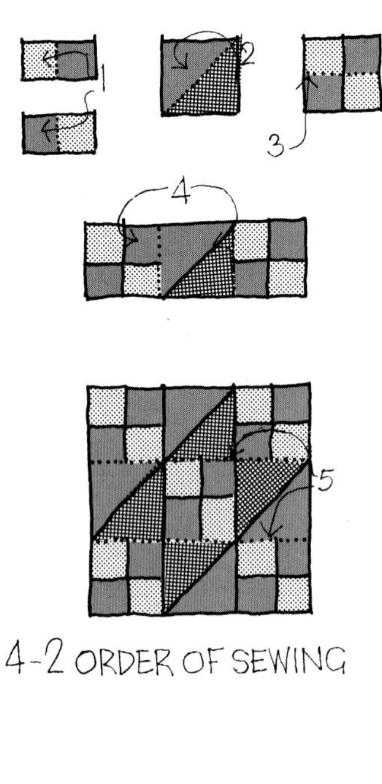

4-2 ORDER OF SEWING

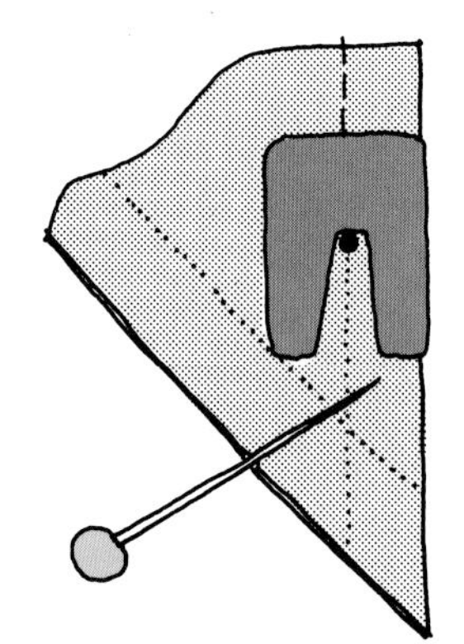

4-3 GUIDING SEWING

together before they are joined to other patches to make sections of the block (4-2). Pin if you need to, checking that the marked sewing lines are one above the other, and machine on the marked line. Watch out at the beginning and end of triangle pieces that the narrow points are fed straight into the machine — there is a tendency for them to drift off line. Use a long pin to guide them on the right path (4-3).

Save time and sewing thread by CHAIN SEWING. Sew two patches together, do not cut thread, but feed in a second pair of patches and sew them, and so on (4-4). Afterwards, cut the threads between patches.

When sewing pairs of patches together, it is a good idea to match cross-seams and hold with a pin (4-5). Always take pins out just before you sew over them. Apart from maybe breaking a needle, the ensuing jarring can damage the internal workings of your machine.

PRESSING MACHINE PATCHWORK

Press all patches after they have been joined to other patches, but be careful not to distort the shapes. It is customary to press both seam allowances towards the darker fabric, to prevent the shadow of the dark fabric showing through the lighter one. Sometimes, especially if you will be machine quilting IN THE DITCH, seams will need to be pressed open. The aim is always to reduce the bulk of seamlines on the back of the patchwork, so try to have some turn one way and some the other. When sewing strips of squares together, it helps to have the cross-seams of one facing in the opposite direction to the cross-seams of the other, so that the seam allowances nestle together and the crossing is accurate.

Georgia Bonesteel, the American quilter and television quilting personality, showed me a tip called the Billings Bonus for reducing bulk when dealing with cross-seams. Sew the last seam across with previous seams staggered. Pick out the machine stitches of all the intersecting seams (but only on the outside of the last row of stitching). Fan the seam allowances and press (4-6).

HOW TO USE THE ROTARY CUTTER

These practice instructions are for a right-handed person and ignore the markings on the mat.

1 Place mat at the corner of a steady table, in good light. Press ¼yd (23cm) fabric and fold selvage to selvage. Fold first fold to meet

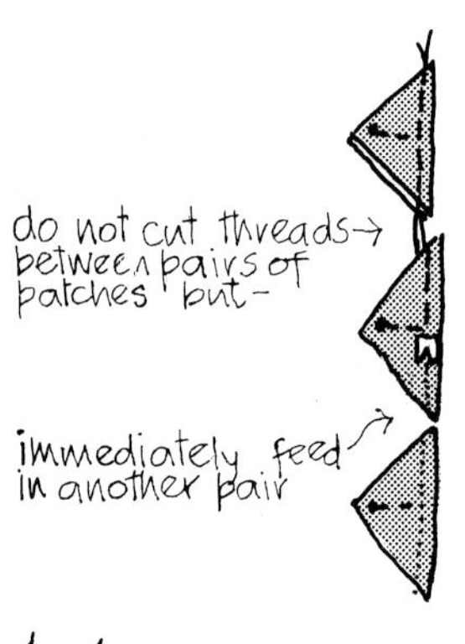

4-4 CHAIN SEWING

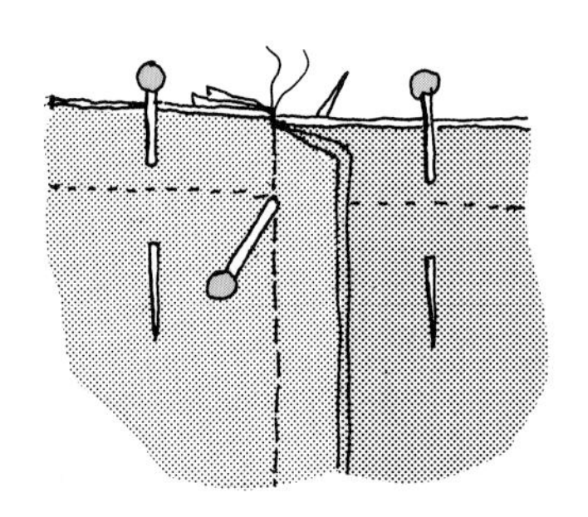

4-5 STAGGER SEAMS

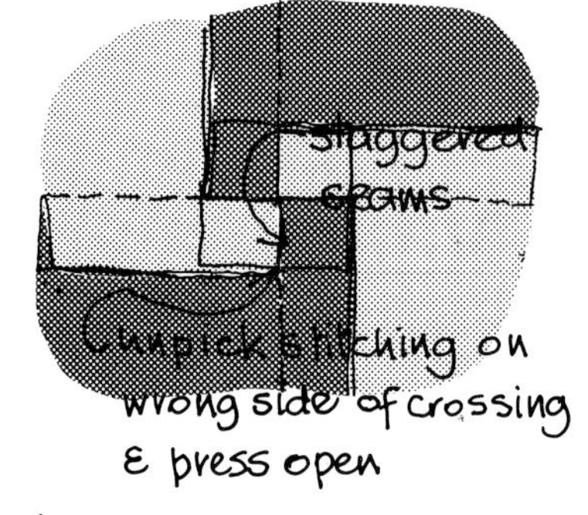

4-6 ELIMINATING BULK

selvages. Lay fabric on mat with second fold away from you and raw edges to right and left. Line up ruler so that one of its crossways lines is exactly on far fold, and its right long edge is near right-hand side of fabric, but with all rough fabric edges free (4-7).

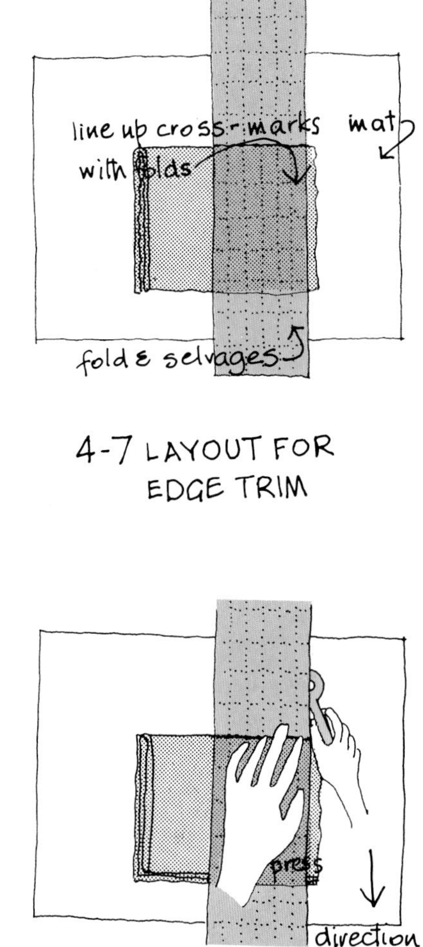

4-7 LAYOUT FOR EDGE TRIM

4-8 ROTARY-TRIMMING EDGE

2 Lay left hand firmly on ruler, fingers away from its edge. Unshield cutter and hold in right hand, with all fingers kept around handle. Place cutter just beyond folded edge of fabric, with blade vertical and against ruler. Make a firm ruling motion with cutter, keeping ruler steady and finishing beyond selvages (4-8). Lift raw edge strips away. If they are still attached anywhere, repeat the cut. Shield blade again. For safety, you should cut away from yourself, but I find this makes the fabric ruckle, so I don't. I make sure to stand to one side of the line of cut, in case of accidents. Do not try to cut from side to side — you can't control blade and pressure properly. For a long cut, you will need to move the 'ruler-leaning' hand once or twice. Pause with the cutting while doing this, or creep the leaning hand like a caterpillar [inchworm], while continuing the cut.

3 Turn mat right round, with fabric still on it, so the edge you have just cut is to your left. Decide how wide a strip you want, and line up that ruler marking exactly along the cut edge. Hold down ruler and cut. Repeat several times, to gain confidence (4-9).

4 Clear mat. Take one cut strip of fabric and lay on mat, doubled and with edges matching, fold to left and selvages to right. Trim off selvages as in step 2. Turn mat and cut squares from strip in the same way that you cut strips before (4-10).

- Cutting strips on the bias (45°) and other angles is explained in Chapter 7.

ROTARY CUTTING EQUIPMENT ADAPTATIONS TO METRIC/IMPERIAL

It is difficult for workers in inches to work with metrically marked mats, and for metric workers to have to use imperial rulers. These adaptations are for large mats (45cm x 60cm/18in x 24in) and give you a graph paper border to the mat, divided and marked to suit you. You will need a sheet of graph paper, either metric or imperial, and masking tape. When buying the graph paper, have it rolled to avoid creases.

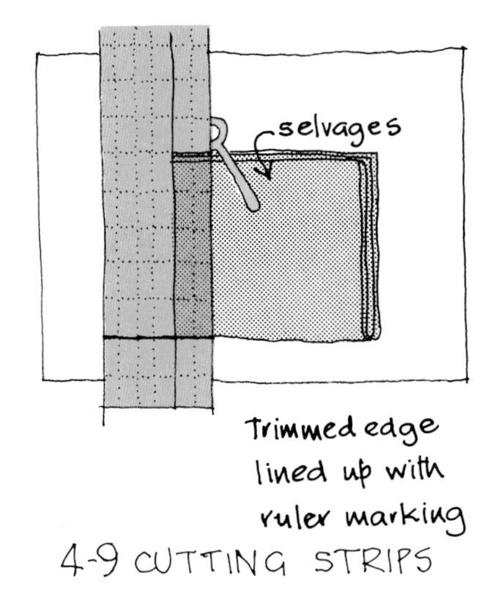

4-9 CUTTING STRIPS

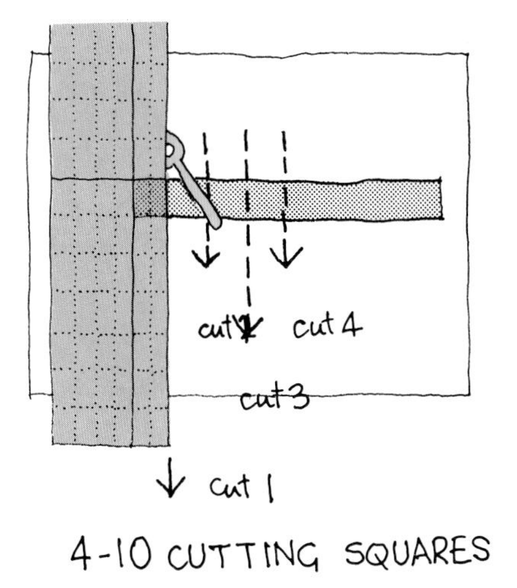

4-10 CUTTING SQUARES

1 For **metric,** cut out a rectangle 45cm x 60cm, and cut out the inside of the rectangle, leaving a 3cm wide border. For **imperial,** the rectangle should be 17in x 23in and the border 1in wide.
2 Lay graph paper 'frame' on mat, lining up divisions on mat with those on paper. If paper and mat markings are not compatible, use plain back of mat. Tape paper temporarily to mat, smoothing out any wrinkles before securing with a strip of masking tape all round the outside edges. Mark paper at desired intervals.

- If your board is smaller, aim to cut a frame 1in wide, and 1in smaller than your board size, or 3cm wide and 2cm smaller for a metric frame.

USING 'FRAMED' OR EDGE-MARKED MAT

1 Lay ruler from one side of mat to the other, lined up with marks on sides. Butt folded edge of fabric to it (4-11). Lift and turn ruler, replace on fabric, but now lined up with marks on top and bottom edges, and with rough fabric edge to its right. Cut off raw edge and remove trimming (4-12). Move ruler left to cut strips, lining it with edge markings.

- Do not roll mat. Keep it flat and away from heat and sun.
- **Do not use quilter's ruler and mat with a scalpel or craft knife.** They will notch the ruler edge and mark the mat surface, making rotary cutting difficult.
- When using an unmarked and unframed mat, trim from the right and cut from the left (if right-handed).
- When using an edge-marked or framed mat, trim *and* cut from the right (if right-handed).
- Tape a 60° set square (or strip of tape) on top of your ruler if it has no 60° line. Make sure the side of the set square lines up *exactly* with the ruler edge.
- You will be more accurate if you use edge markings rather than ruler markings, as cumulative errors cannot occur.
- To help prevent fabrics shifting when several different kinds are being cut at the same time, press one, lay the next evenly on top and press it, and so on, before laying the stack on the cutting mat.
- When cutting fabric which is already pieced, do not stack, but cut one layer at a time only.

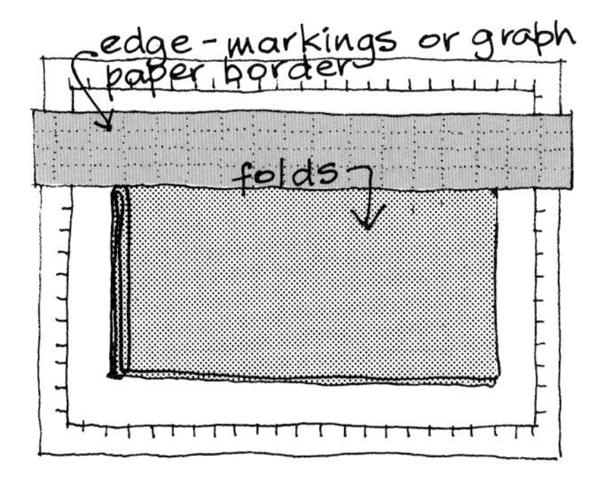

4-11 SQUARING-UP FABRIC ON EDGE-MARKED MAT BOARD

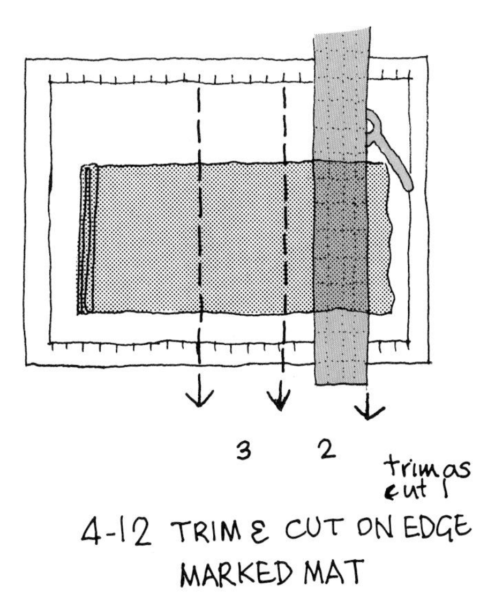

4-12 TRIM & CUT ON EDGE MARKED MAT

N
ERLE STANLEY GARDNER
ERLE STANLEY GARDNER

CHAPTER FIVE

PATCHWORK FROM STRIPS

All patchwork looks better if it is accurate and corners and points meet in the right place. But this is not easy without practice, and is certainly not fast if you hand sew or have to do lots of unpicking to correct machining errors. If you can rely on your piecing being accurate, then there is much less difficulty when it comes to putting a complex quilt together. Anyone who has struggled with assembling a group quilt will know that supposedly similar 12in (30cm) blocks can vary wildly in size.

It is quite difficult to cut out *really* accurately with scissors, especially on the bias, even when you have a marked line to guide you. Also, it is quite difficult marking some printed fabrics with a line that is visible enough to follow.

It is tempting to tear your fabric into strips. Don't do it. There will be no exact edge to guide you (where is it in all that fuzzy fringe?) and the pulling and tearing weaken and disort the fabric. Instead use the ROTARY CUTTER. Once you can cut out accurately half the battle for accurate patchwork has been won.

SEAM ALLOWANCES

The other half of the battle is to use a consistent, accurate seam allowance. This is just as important as accurate cutting. The traditional quilter's seam allowance is ¼in (6mm), and this is what has been allowed on all patches in the projects in this book. This is enough on most fabrics to ensure that a seam won't fray [ravel] while working on the quilt, but is not so large that it is extravagant in fabric. All the many quilt books I have read recommend machine sewing an accurate ¼in (6mm) from the edge of the fabric. They say this is to be done either by using the edge of the presser foot as a guide or by marking a line on the base of the sewing machine exactly ¼in to the right of the needle, and using it as a guide for the edge of the fabric. Both are wrong. Presser feet come in different widths, which may or may not be exactly ¼in (6mm). Anyway, for some strange reason, to ensure that your patchwork pieces finish up the right size, and particularly that several small patchwork pieces fit properly against one larger one, it is necessary to sew a *scant* ¼in (6mm) seam. I know this is impossible to believe, so please do the following test of sewing a traditional full ¼in (6mm) seam, and prove it for yourself.

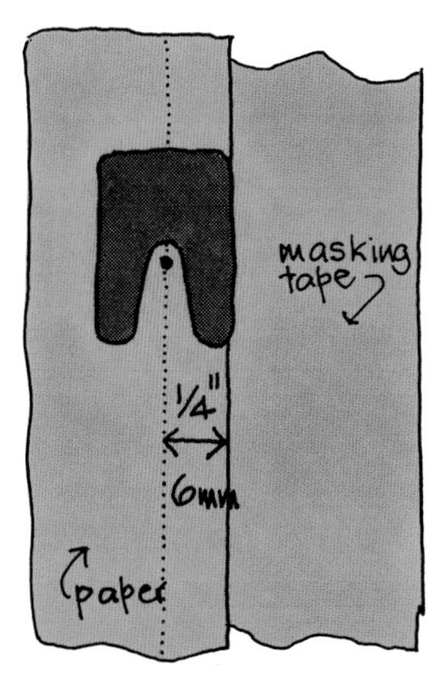

5-1 SEAM ALLOWANCE TEST

SEAM ALLOWANCE TEST

1 Rule a line exactly ¼in (6mm) from the edge of a piece of paper, and insert it under your sewing machine needle, so that the paper edge is to the right and, when you test it, the needle goes through the marked line (which of course runs from front to back) (5-1). Lay a piece of masking tape on the base of the sewing machine, exactly butting up to the edge of the paper. You may find this slightly overlaps the machine dogs (teeth); if it does, cut out the tape that covers them. Take away the piece of paper.

2 Cut three strips of cotton fabric, each 2in (5cm) wide and 12in (30cm) long. Using the left-hand edge of the masking tape as a guide for the edge of the fabric, stitch the three pieces together to make a SERIES of three. PRESS. (5-2).

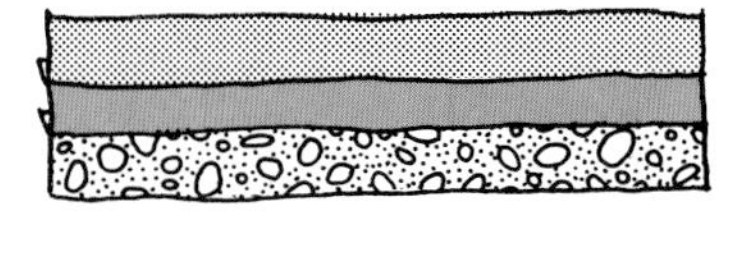

5-2 SERIES OF 3 STRIPS FOR SEAM ALLOWANCE TEST

3 Trim off the end of the strip series, at right angles to the edge (5-3). Make two further cuts, at 5in (12.5cm) spacings. Lay out the two cut SLICES, right sides together, with the seams of one at right angles to the seams of the other. You will see that the width across the ends of the three strips of one slice is smaller than the long side of the other slice, although in theory they should be the same. The full ¼in (6mm) seam allowance is just a fraction too big. I think this is because of a take-up of fabric by the thread thickness, and by the bend of the fabric in pressing out from the seam line into the flat.

Do not worry. The trick is to sew your seam a tiny fraction smaller. This can be helped either by moving the masking tape that fraction to the left, or sewing with a glimmer (only a thread thickness or so) of space between the edges of the fabric and the masking tape. I find it is about 1/32in (1mm). The ⅛in (4mm) that this would add up to from four seam allowances may even be less than the error you found in doing the test. Think how much this would add up to over a whole quilt of small patches!

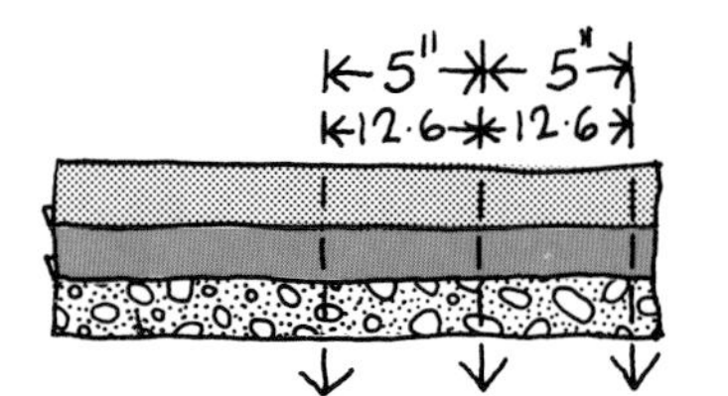

5-3 CUTTING SLICES FOR SEAM ALLOWANCE TEST

- On some swing-needle sewing machines, the masking tape will partly cover the machine's feed dogs. Try the whole SEAM ALLOWANCE TEST again, but with the needle positioned to the right.
- Try to accustom yourself to where the fabric edge should be in relation to your machine presser foot, as there are some quick techniques (TRIANGLES) later in this book where the masking tape will be invisible.

5-4 STRIP

TERMINOLOGY

In the rest of this chapter and the next four chapters, there will be a lot of projects made of varieties of STRIP PIECING. Here are the ways I will describe certain standard things.

1 STRIP — this of course you know. It is a long, thin piece of fabric. Seam allowances of ¼in (6mm) will always be included when sizes are given, and width will be given before length (5-4).

2 SERIES — the result of sewing several STRIPS together. A series of three would be like a sandwich, a series of 5 more like a layer cake (5-5).

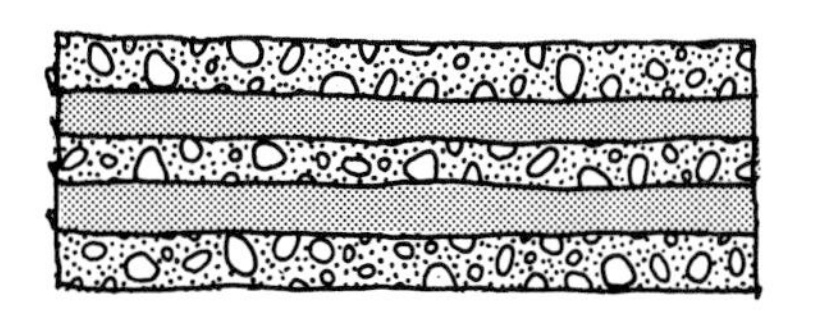

5-5 SERIES OF 5 STRIPS

3 SLICE — a SERIES cut across from side to side. Slices can be the same width as the original strips, or narrower or wider (especially in SEMINOLE PIECING). A series can be cut into diagonal slices (STAR OF BETHLEHEM or SEMINOLE) (5-6).

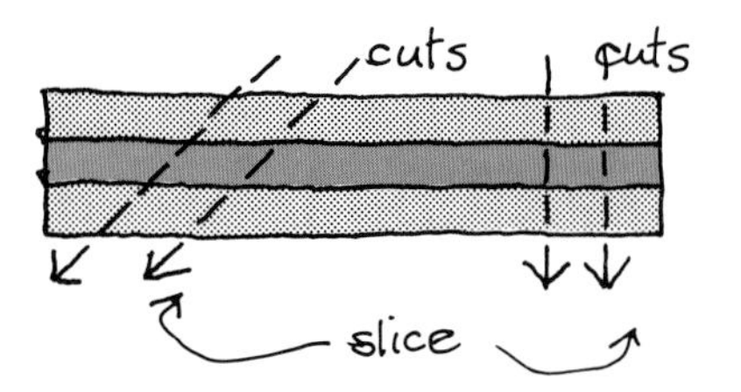

5-6 DIAGONAL & STRAIGHT SLICES

4 RE-CUT — after a STRIP has been cut, it may be RE-CUT into squares or rectangles. Squares can be RE-CUT DIAGONALLY into two or four triangles (5-7).

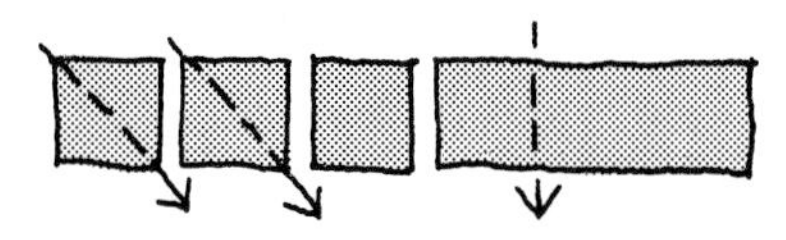

5-7 RE-CUT STRIP

5 RE-PIECE — after one or more series have been SLICED, the SLICES can be re-arranged and RE-PIECED. (NINE-PATCH, STAR OF BETHLEHEM, SEMINOLE) (5-8).

6 STRINGS — these are either strips of varying or random widths (almost always narrow), or tapered strips (HEARTSTRINGS COT QUILT), which are sewn into a SERIES.

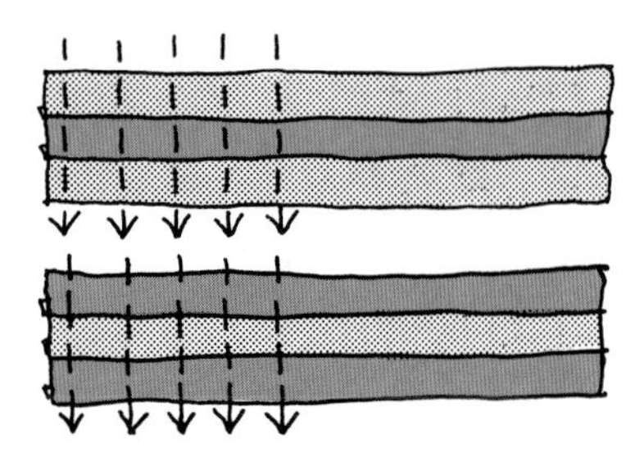

5-8 SLICES RE-PIECED

RAIL FENCE POTHOLDER

One block of Rail Fence is easy as a practice piece — you could even use up the strips made for your seam allowance test.

MATERIALS: for potholder 9 ½in (24cm) square
⅛yd (10cm) of each of 3 cotton fabrics.
Backing — 10in (25cm) square cotton fabric.
Wadding — 10in (25cm) square towelling (two thicknesses if using old thin towelling).
Binding and hanging tab — cotton strips 1½in x 40in (4cm x 100cm) and 1½in x 5in (4cm x 12.5cm).

PREPARATION
PREPARE fabrics.
Cut 3 strips from cotton fabric, each 2in x 24in (5cm x 60cm)
Cut backing, wadding and binding strips to sizes given above.

MAKING
1 Sew STRIPS into SERIES of 3, with scant ¼in (6mm) seam. TRIM one end of series and cut to make four 5in (12.5cm) wide SLICES. RE-PIECE into pairs. Join pairs (5-9).
2 LAYER backing, towelling and patchwork. MACHINE QUILT in the ditch of all seams. Stitch all round, scant ¼in (6mm) in from patchwork edge. Trim wadding and backing even with patchwork.
3 Fold small fabric strip lengthwise, wrong sides together, folding in and slipstitching raw edges. Make into a loop and tack in one corner on the back (5-10). BIND with SINGLE BINDING with MITRED CORNERS.

- Towelling is more heatproof than synthetic wadding.

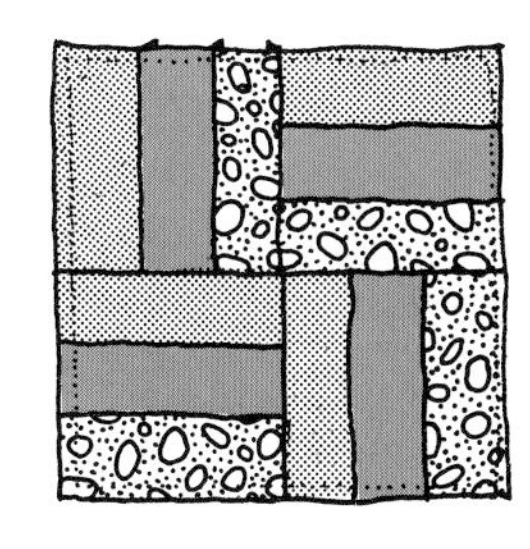

5-9 RAIL FENCE POTHOLDER

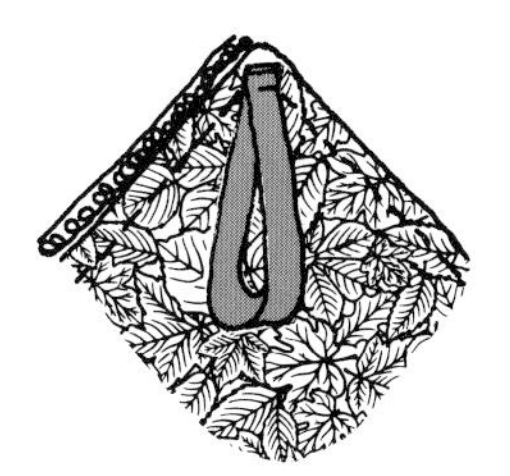

5-10 HANGING LOOP

SINGLE IRISH CHAIN NAP QUILT

These pieced 9-patch blocks are set alternately with plain blocks to make this very old pattern. It is made to look more complex than it really is by the random joining of different printed fabrics, which may even come within some of the small squares. This is intentional — it gives a more random effect and is quicker.

MATERIALS: for quilt 54 ½in x 66 ½in (136cm x 166cm)
All fabrics 44in (112cm) wide.
Background fabric — 2 ¾ yd (2.5m) plain cotton.
Patterned fabric — variety of remnants totalling about 1yd (90cm) of cotton prints.
Backing — 3 ½yd (3.2m) cotton.
2oz wadding — 56in (142cm) by 70in (178cm).
Binding — 2in by 7 yd (5cm by 6.4m) bias strip.
Heavy yarn for ties.

PREPARATION
PREPARE all fabrics.
From background fabric: cut 4 borders lengthwise, all 6 ½in (16cm) wide, two 54 ½in (136cm) long and two 42 ½in (106cm) long.
From remaining background fabric cut 6 ½in (16cm) strips, and RE-CUT to make 31 squares. Cut 2 ½in (6cm) strips totalling approximately 360in (900cm) in length.
From patterned fabrics, cut 2 ½in (6cm) wide strips, totalling about 450in (1143cm) in length.

MAKING
1 Join strips of background fabric together to make longer lengths, and strips of patterned fabric together to make longer lengths. PRESS seams open. Sew strips together in series of 3 (5-11), making twice as much type A as type B.
2 TRIM series square. Cut 2 ½in (6cm) SLICES — 72 slices of type A and 31 slices of type B. Arrange colour placement by laying out plain blocks alternately with A-B-A slices. RE-PIECE the slices, two A slices outside a B slice (5-12), to make 36 9-patch blocks.
3 Assemble pieced blocks alternately with plain ones into rows, then join rows (5-13).
4 Sew top and bottom borders to patchwork. Sew remaining 4 blocks to ends of long borders, and sew borders to quilt.
5 Piece backing as necessary to make it the same size or larger than the wadding. Press seam open.
6 LAYER quilt and TIE in centres of plain blocks and corner squares of pieced blocks, and evenly along border. BIND with DOUBLE BIAS BINDING and PLAIN CORNERS.

- Each pieced block may be made of a different patterned fabric, in which case it is not really worth strip-piecing — cut 5 patterned and 4 background 2 ½in (6cm) squares, stitch together in rows, press seams towards patterned fabric, and sew rows together.
- QUILT instead of tying. This could be as simple as diagonal lines through the centres of the squares, or combined with a motif in each larger square, and a border pattern.
- Single Irish Chain is a very effective pattern when SET diagonally.

2½" 2½" 6·2cm 6·2cm
type A type B

5-11 SERIES FOR 9-PATCH

5-12 9-PATCH BLOCK

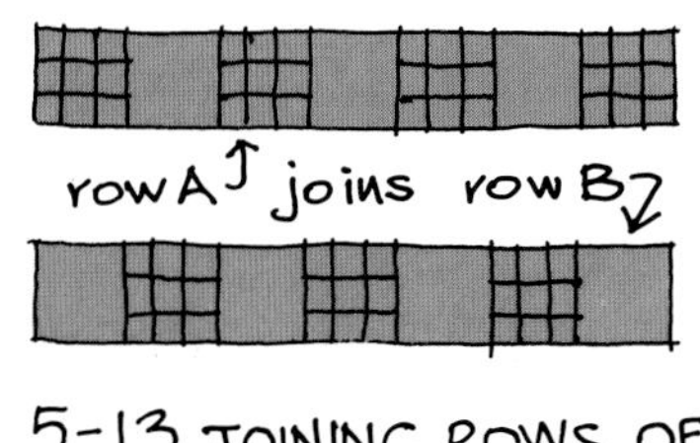

5-13 JOINING ROWS OF BLOCKS

BARGELLO CUSHIONS

The design was inspired by the Bargello (or Florentine) embroidery technique, and I worked it out on squared paper before I started. The cushions [pillows] were made for a favourite old cane chair, with colours chosen to reflect those in a wallpaper which we plan to use in the room. The fabrics include glazed chintzes, so they were not pre-washed, as otherwise the glaze would have been lost.

The first two projects in this chapter have covered strips SERIES, SLICED and RE-PIECED (Rail Fence Potholder) and two STRIP-SERIES sliced and RE-PIECED with plain blocks in between (Single Irish Chain). This project gives practice in SLICING, 'LOOPING' and SLIDING before RE-PIECING.

MATERIALS: to make 2 cushions, each 22in x 22in (55cm x 55cm).
44in (112cm) wide fabric for strips, 11 different, each ¼yd (20cm).
2 oz wadding — 2 pieces each 24in (60cm) square.
Nylon thread for quilting.
48in (120cm) wide fabric for cushion backs — ¾yd (70cm).
2 zip fasteners, 20in (50cm) long.
2 cushion pads [pillow forms] each 22in (55cm) square.

PREPARATION
PREPARE fabrics.
Cut one fabric strip from each of 11 fabrics, 4 ½in (11.2cm).
Cut backing fabric into 4 rectangles, 2 of 22 ½in x 4in (56.2cm x 10cm) and two of 22 ½in x 19 ¾in (56.2cm x 48.4cm).

MAKING
1 Stitch strips into SERIES of 11 with scant ¼in (6mm) seam allowance. Press seams open.
2 TRIM series edge square. Cut SLICES across series, 11 slices 1 ½in (3.7cm) wide, 4 slices 2 ½in (6.2cm) wide, and 1 slice 3 ½in (8.7cm) wide. There will be some waste at the end, to allow for miscuts or errors.
3 Stitch ends of each slice together in scant ¼in (6mm) seam to make a LOOP.
4 Starting from left-hand side of diagram (5-14), take 2 of the narrowest loops, and SLIDE the seam lines by 1in (2.5cm). Pin and sew loops together, right round and back to the beginning.
5 Take the third loop, and sew to the second, SLIDING as in the diagram. Continue sewing on loops but note that some will be slid the other way, and some are slid by 2in (5cm) or 3in (7.5cm). Press all seams open.
6 MARK a line right across the loops, midway between seamlines. Cut through the top layer only (with scissors) on the marked line. Your bargello piecing is now opened up instead of looped. Mark another line across the centre of the piece and cut again.
7 MARK quilting lines at 1in (2.5) spacings down the wider strips. LAYER with wadding only (no backing required). MACHINE QUILT, IN THE DITCH and on the marked lines.
8 INSERT ZIP FASTENERS, noting that each cushion has one larger and one smaller backing piece. Join cushion back to front, making sure the zip fastener is partly open before starting. Open zip fastener fully. Turn cover right side out. Insert cushion pad.

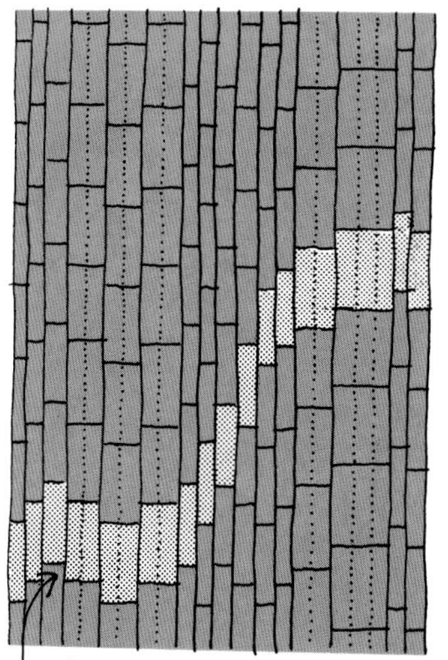

5-14 BARGELLO PATTERN

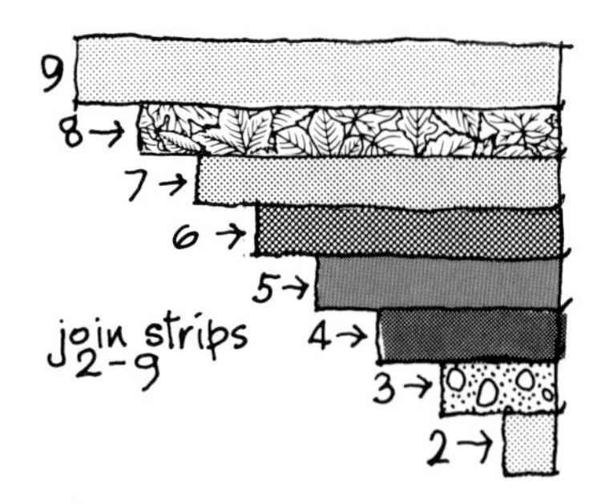

5-15 STEPPED SERIES

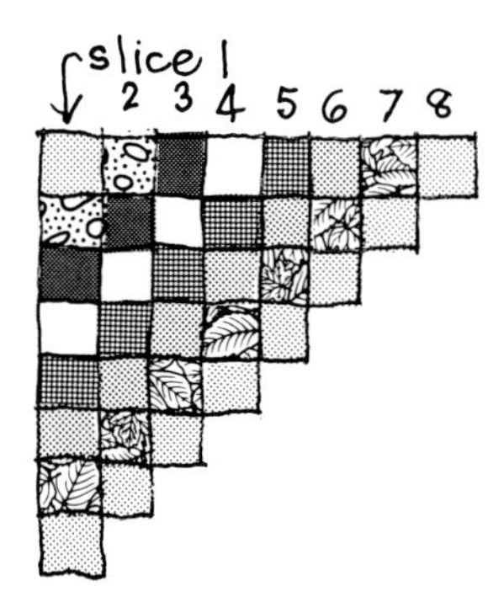

5-16 SLID & RE-PIECED SLICES

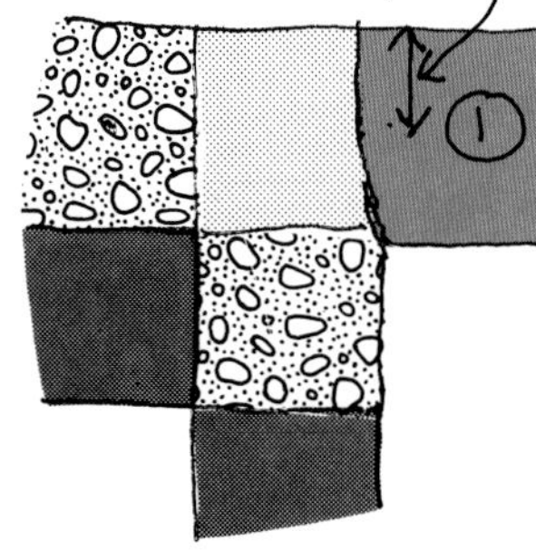

5-17 JOINING FIRST QUARTER TO CENTRE SQUARE

TRIP AROUND THE WORLD WALLHANGING

This wallhanging is a variation on the traditional pattern, Trip Around the World. The colours and quilting symbolise the furrowed green earth surrounded by wave-swirled sky and sea. I quilted compass points in the empty corners, and then hung it diagonally on a wooden framework. Because it is a wallhanging and will not need laundering, I was able to choose from fabrics which suffer from washing — several pretty colours of cotton sateen curtain linings, and glazed chintz. Each quarter is made of a stepped SERIES which is SLICED and slid before RE-PIECING and then in turn stitched to the single centre square. This is a good exercise in matching corners.

MATERIALS: to make wallhanging 31in (76cm) square
Cotton prints or plains 44in (112cm) wide:
Colours 1-4, ⅛yd (10cm).
Colours 5-8, ¼yd (20cm).
Colour 9, ¾yd (70cm).
Wadding, 36in (90cm) square.
Backing, 1 ½yd (1.20m).
Sewing and quilting threads.
3 ½yd (3m) 1in sew-on Velcro®, or 4in x 31in (10cm x 80cm) fabric for hanging sleeve.

PREPARATION
PREPARE fabrics.
ROTARY CUTTING is recommended for the strips.
Fabric 1, cut one 2 ½in (6.2cm) square.
Fabric 2, cut four 2 ½in (6.2cm) squares.
Fabric 3, cut 4 strips 2 ½in x 5in (6.2cm x 12.4cm)
Fabric 4, cut 4 strips 2 ½in x 7 ½in (6.2cm x 18.6cm)
Fabric 4, cut 4 strips 2 ½in x 10in (6.2cm x 24.8cm)
Fabric 5, Cut 4 strips 2 ½in x 12 ½in (6.2cm x 31cm)
Fabric 6, cut 4 strips 2 ½in x 15in (6.2cm x 37.2cm)
Fabric 8, cut 4 strips 2 ½in x 17 ½in (6.2cm x 43.4cm)
Fabric 9, cut 4 strips 2 ½in x 20in (6.2cm x 49.6cm) and 4 border strips 5in x 36in (12.5cm x 90cm).

5-18 JOINING SECOND QUARTER TO CENTRE SQUARE

MAKING

1 Put square of fabric 1 aside. Allocate one strip of each of fabrics 2-9 to 4 piles. Working with each pile in turn, pin and then stitch with scant ¼in (6mm) seam into a stepped-edge SERIES (5-15). Make sure that the starting edge is even, and strips finish exactly 2 ½in (6.2cm) before end of next longer strip. PRESS (on two series, press towards the longest strip, and on the other two series press towards the single square).

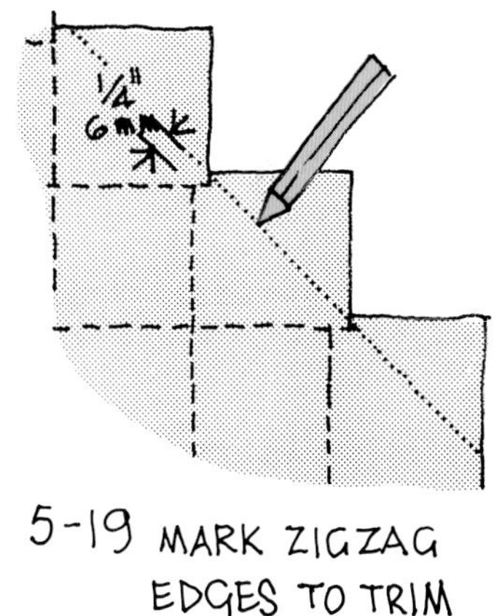

5-19 MARK ZIGZAG EDGES TO TRIM

5-20 WAVE QUILTING PATTERN – ONE REPEAT

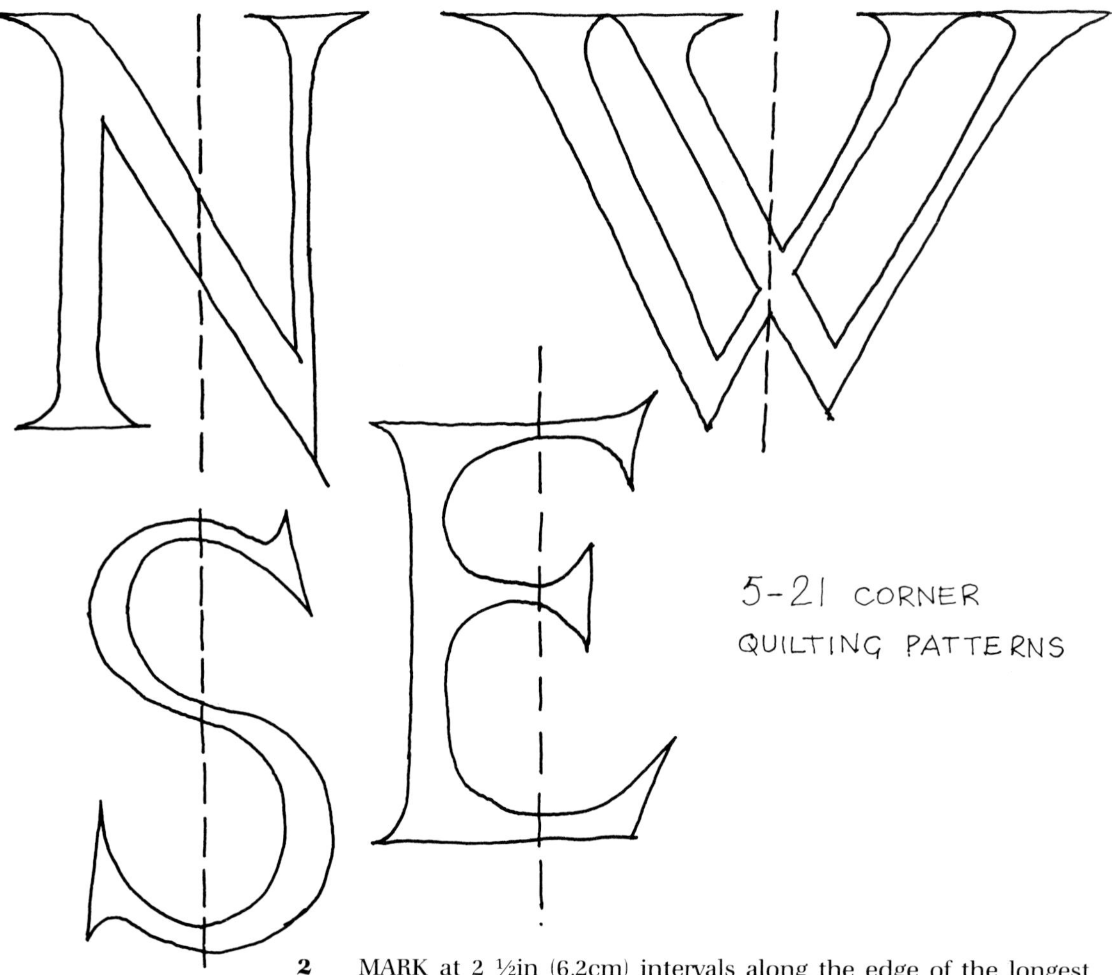

5-21 CORNER QUILTING PATTERNS

2 MARK at 2 ½in (6.2cm) intervals along the edge of the longest strip. Rotary cut straight across from these marks to the corresponding stepped corner, or draw lines and cut.

3 Take SLICES from alternate series (so that the seam pressings go in alternate directions) and slide and RE-PIECE (5-16). Take care to match seam crossings.

4 Take one pieced section, sew its corner single square to centre square 1, but only along half the length of the centre square (5-17). Take next section and sew to centre square and right along first section (5-18). Do the same with remaining sections.

5 Trim zigzag edge; draw line on reverse, ¼in (6mm) out from seam crossings (5-19), and cut on line.

6 Attach BORDERS with MITRED CORNERS. To give an easy turn and straight edge, stitch all round ⅝in (1.5cm) from outside edge.

7 Mark quilting lines on diagonals, at 1in (2.5cm) spacings from a centre 2in (5cm) diagonal square. Make quilting template from diagram, or trace quilting motif onto border, reversing at centres and corners (5-20). Trace compass points (5-21) onto corners, if desired.

8 LAYER and QUILT.

9 Trim backing to match front. Trim wadding level with front staystitching. Turn front to back over wadding, rolling on staystitching line, but having it invisible from the front. Turn backing in a fraction more. Pin and hem. Do another line of quilting ⅛in (3mm) from edge.

10 If hanging diagonally, hand stitch soft Velcro® strip to back of hanging 1in (2.5cm) from edge, and staple or nail hooked Velcro® strip to hanging frame. If hanging straight, stitch 3in (7.5cm) hanging sleeve to back of top edge. Make sure stitching does not show through to front.

LUCY'S QUILT

Three things came together for Lucy's wedding quilt — pastel colours, a varying grid size and mock weaving. Lucy's bed is king-size and very high, so the quilt needed to be simple or it would have taken forever to make. She requested 'sugared almond' colours, which meant no darks or medium tones. I do not usually work in pastel colours, preferring a more brilliant colour range, and knew that without the contrast of lights and darks it would be impossible to make effective patchwork blocks. Because of this, I found it very difficult to get any design ideas until I re-read Valerie Campbell-Harding's *Strip Patchwork,* and two sections started me thinking. The first was a mention of the Fibonacci Series (a progression of numbers which relate to each other), and the second was some woven strip patterns, like those that children make in kindergarten from coloured papers.

Fibonacci was a 13th century Italian mathematician, and his series works out like this:
0 + 1 = 1; 1 + 1 = 2; 1 + 2 = 3; 2 + 3 = 5; 3 + 5 = 8; 5 + 8 = 13; 8 + 13 = 21 etc, always adding the last two numbers to make the next one. The numbers can be converted into measurements, and any unit of measurement (whether imperial or metric) can be used to represent the figure 1. Because each step in the series has a direct proportional relationship to all the other steps, it is very harmonious as a basis for designs. It appears a lot in nature in the organic growth spirals of things like shells and the seed heads of sunflowers.

I decided to use a 2in (5cm) measurement to represent the number 1, so the strip widths are 2in, 4in, 6in and 10in. Anything larger than 10in became unmanageable, so the sizes reverse down again to 2in. The 'sugared almond' colours ended up as white, pink, mauve, pale blue, pale green and pale yellow polycotton. I very carefully drew out and coloured a diagram to follow, imitating a woven strip pattern with squares and rectangles of colour. Careful piecing was needed to continue the illusion of weaving, which would have been lost if the corners had not met properly.

Because the top was too big and bulky to machine quilt in one piece, I made it in three sections and joined them after quilting. The quilting (on the diagonals of pieces and IN THE DITCH) threw up a totally unexpected and very interesting subsidiary mock curve pattern across the top. The wide borders were also each made and quilted separately, before assembling with little wadded 'flaps' which emphasise the woven effect by pretending to be the ends of the strips. They also help to disguise the lumpy corner transition between the top and sides of a quilt which is used over a duvet.

MATERIALS: to fit bed 80in (200cm) long, 60in (150cm) wide and 25in (63.5cm) high
All fabrics 44in (112cm).
Blue — 11yd (10m) (includes for border and binding)
Pink, mauve, white, pale yellow, pale green — 1 ¼yd (1.60m) of each.
2oz polyester wadding — If 62in wadding is used, its width fits width of quilt top and top and bottom borders, and is halved for side borders. The quilt will require 8 ½ yards (7.70m). Recalculate for different widths, allowing extra on all sides of all sections.

PREPARATION

PREPARE all fabrics.

Cut borders first, running the length of the fabric, two each 25 ¼in x 60 ½in (64cm x 151.2cm) and two each 25 ¼in x 130in (64cm x 327cm).

The diagram of the quilt top (5-22) gives the finished measurements of the strips, and the reference letters of the rows. Don't forget to add the standard seam allowances on all sides of all pieces (e.g. a 4in (10cm) square will be cut 4 ½in (11.2cm)).

For the top, ROTARY CUT strips of the fabric lengthwise. The PATCHES can then be RE-CUT from these strips. For example, row B (white) finishes 4in (10cm) wide, so a lengthwise strip 4 ½in (11.2cm) wide is RE-CUT at 4 ½in, 4 ½in, 10 ½in, 4 ½in, 4 ½in, 10 ½in, 4 ½in, 4 ½in, 5in and 5in spacings (11.2cm, 11.2cm, 26.5cm, 11.2cm, 11.2cm, 26.5cm, 11.2cm, 11.2cm, 12.5cm and 12.5cm spacings). The last two pieces are for the flaps at each end.

Some time can be saved by STACKING the strips for rows B, F and H, which are all the same width and with the same sequence of cuts, and cutting them together. Similarly with rows A and G; C, E, I and K; and D and J on the vertically 'woven' strips, and rows L, N, R, T, X and Z; M, S and Y; O, Q, U, W and ZZ; and P and V on the horizontally 'woven' strips. To ensure that all the correct pieces have been cut, lay them out in horizontal rows, and keep the pieces of each row separate. At this stage also keep separate the end flap pieces, which look better if they are of different lengths.

MAKING

1 Sew pieces together into rows, with scant ¼in (6mm) seam. PRESS seams open. Start at top left hand corner (Row L) and, to avoid muddle, label the last piece in each row with the row letter.

2 Sew rows together into three sections: L to Q inclusive, R to W inclusive and X to ZZ inclusive, matching corners of pieces. PRESS seams open.

3 MARK quilting lines on pieced sections on the diagonals of each patch. Around the edges of a section mark a spot on the seamline, ¼in (6mm) in from the raw edge, and mark the diagonals to those spots.

4 Cut out and seam lengths of backing fabric together. The pieces should be 2in (5cm) larger on each side than the corresponding top or border. Press seams open. LAYER the three pieced sections. MACHINE QUILT on marked lines and in all DITCHES of seamlines but no nearer than 2in (5cm) to edges of rows Q, R, W and X, to allow for later assembly.

5 Join sections of top as for QUILT-AS-YOU-GO. Complete machine quilting of top. Trim excess wadding and backing.

6 MARK quilting lines on border strips at 2in (5cm) spacing, with chevron lines at corner positions on the long strips. LAYER and MACHINE QUILT each border in turn. The long side borders will be easier to handle if the left-hand half is layered and quilted first, and the remaining wadding joined on and layered and quilted afterwards. Trim off excess wadding only on upper edges of border pieces.

7 Make flaps by folding each piece of fabric in half, wrong side out, and pinning the doubled fabric on top of a piece of wadding. Stitch the two sides. Trim off excess wadding and turn right side out. Tack [baste] around edges.

8 Pin flaps to quilt top, with flap colours and widths matching the relevant strips, and raw edges matching. Pin quilt top to top border, right sides together, and matching raw edges to raw edge of border main fabric and wadding. Align border quilting lines with seamlines

A	B	C	D	E	F	G	H	I	J	K	
2" (4cm)	4" 10cm	6" (15cm)	10" (25cm)	6" (15cm)	4" (10cm)	2" (5cm)	4" (10cm)	6" (15cm)	10" (25cm)	6" (15cm)	
pk	wh	blue	pink	yellow	wh.	pk	gr.	mauve	blue	yellow	
pk	wh.	pink	pink	pink	wh.	pk	gr.	pink	blue	pink	← ROW L 4"(10cm) pink
m.	wh.	blue	white	yellow	wh.	pk	wh.	mauve	white	yellow	← ROW M 2"(5cm) white
gr.	wh.	green	pink	green	wh	gr	gr	green	blue	green	← ROW N 4"(10cm) green
m.	yel.	blue	yellow	yellow	yel.	pk	yel.	mauve	yellow	yellow	← ROW O 6"(15cm) yellow
m	wh.	mauve	pink	mauve	wh	m.	gr	mauve	blue	mauve	← ROW P 10"(25cm) mauve
m	gr.	blue	green	yellow	gr.	pk	gr.	mauve	green	yellow	← ROW Q 6"(15cm) green
b	wh.	blue	pink	blue	wh	b.	gr	blue	blue	bluc	← ROW R 4"(10cm) blue
m	wh.	blue	white	yellow	wh	pk	wh	mauve	white	yellow	← ROW S 2"(5cm) white
pk	wh.	pink	pink	pink	wh	pk	gr	pink	blue	pink	← ROW T 4"(10cm) pink
m	yel.	blue	yellow	yellow	yel.	pk	yel.	mauve	yellow	yellow	← ROW U 6"(15cm) yellow
bl	wh.	blue	pink	blue	wh	b	gr	blue	blue	blue	← ROW V 10"(25cm) blue
m	mauve	blue	mauve	yellow	m	pk	m	mauve	mauve	yellow	← ROW W 6"(15cm) mauve
wh	wh	white	pink	white	wh	w	gr	white	blue	white	← ROW X 4"(10cm) white
m	green	blue	green	yellow	gr	pk	gr	mauve	green	yellow	← ROW Y 2"(5cm) green
pk	wh	pink	pink	pink	wh	pk	gr	pink	blue	pink	← ROW Z 4"(10cm) pink
m.	yel.	blue	yellow	yellow	yel.	pk	yel.	mauve	yellow	yellow	← ROW ZZ 6"(15cm) yellow

5-22 LAYOUT OF QUILT TOP.

of piecing. Tack and stitch through all layers. Trim backing fabric to ⅝in (1.5cm), turn under to enclose raw edges and hem down. Attach lower border similarly, and then the two side borders. Trim lower edge of border, and make CURVED CORNERS if desired. BIND lower edge with DOUBLE BIAS BINDING cut from pale blue fabric.

- A smaller quilt can be made by omitting one or more strips in length or width, and/or reducing width of border. Recalculate fabric requirements.
- Hand quilting can be used in place of machine quilting.
- The colour scheme or arrangement of widths can be changed. Make a coloured chart of design and recalculate fabric requirements.

CHAPTER SIX

LOG CABIN PATCHWORK

The Log Cabin pattern is a very old one, but still very popular and versatile, with a number of variations such as Pineapple. It was probably started in Scotland, as there is evidence of patterns being handed down from the time of the 1745 Jacobite rising. Another variation (they maintain it's the true Log Cabin, called Roof Pattern) was developed in the Isle of Man and other early examples come from Ireland and Canada, probably carried over the Atlantic by immigrants.

Each Log Cabin block is composed of narrow strips of fabric, sewn together around a centre square of fabric, with dark fabrics kept to one side of the block and light fabrics to the other. Further variations in the assembly of the blocks make some most effective graphic designs. Tradition has it that the centre square should always be red (to represent the hearth). Because of the small size and variety of pieces needed, Log Cabin patchwork is ideally suited to using rag-bag fabrics, but they should be sorted into lights and darks. It is also a good idea to choose colours from one area of the spectrum.

Traditionally, a larger centre square is used, and each pair of adjacent 'logs' is made of the same fabric. This is what I have done in the CHRISTMAS PLACEMATS. However, I prefer the extra graphical effect of having the centre square the same width as the strips, and all the strips in one square of different fabrics, and this is what I did in the large LOG CABIN QUILT, even though it makes a bit more work. If your strips are more than about 1 ½in (4cm) finished width, then the blurring and melding of fabric colours which is necessary to make a proper illusion will be lost, as the wider strips will begin to read as individual fabrics. I know the quilt will be much quicker to make if the pieces are bigger, but expect a different effect.

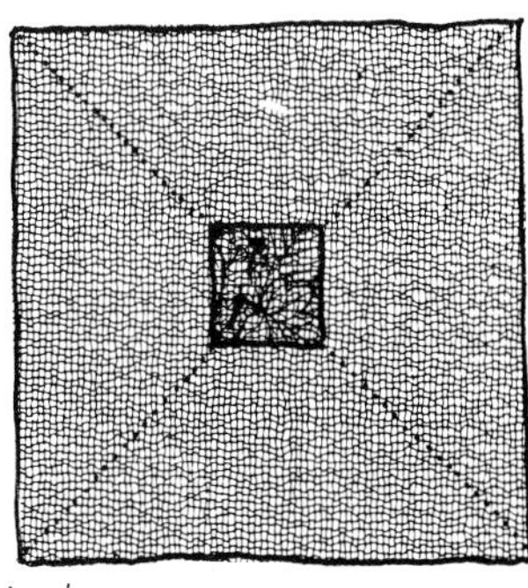

6-1 PINNING CENTRE SQUARE

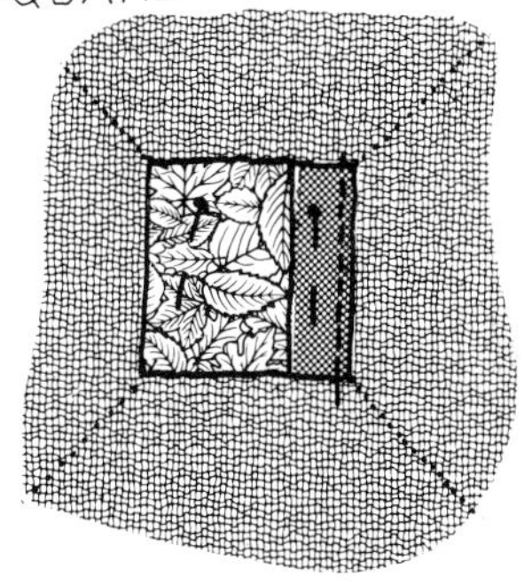

6-2 SEWING FIRST STRIP

LOG CABIN TECHNIQUE 1

In this technique, a square of backing fabric is used as a base on which to sew the strips. To make one 12in (30cm) block, with 1in (2.5cm) finished-width strips you will need a selection of dark and light toned fabrics, cut in 1 ½in (3.7cm) wide strips, and a central 2 ½in (6.2cm) square, which should be a contrast fabric. The backing square should be 12 ½in (31.2cm). This may be sewn by hand or machine.

1 PREPARE all fabrics. Fold backing fabric diagonally and press the fold. Open up and fold the other diagonal and press. Open again. Pin the centre square in the centre, face up, with its corners touching the diagonal creases (6-1). Cut a length of dark strip to the width of the centre square, and pin it right side down on the centre square, matching ends and one side of the square. Stitch in a scant ¼in (6mm) seam (6-2). Press strip away from square.

2 Take a strip of a second dark fabric, the length of the square plus the attached strip. Pin in place and stitch (6-3).

3 Continue thus, in the same direction round the central square, making the next two strips of light fabric, followed by two dark strips and so on, always pressing each strip away from the central square before sewing on another strip. Figure 6-4 shows the order of piecing and the placement of lights and darks.

- The diagonal creases on the backing fabric may be omitted, and the diagonals pencilled in instead. Or for extra accuracy, a stitching line grid (spaced out every 1in (2.5cm) from the centre point) may be pencilled on the front of the backing fabric.

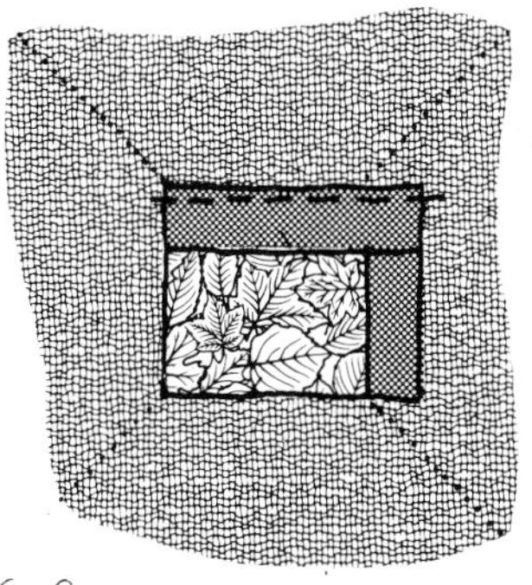

6-3 SEWING SECOND STRIP

6-4 LOG CABIN BLOCK

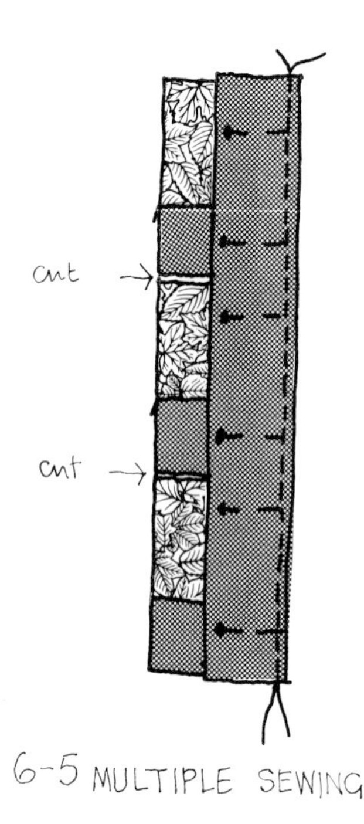

6-5 MULTIPLE SEWING

- If the backing fabric is a thinnish Vilene®, then diagonals or grid lines may be traced through from a master drawing.
- When assembling into a quilt, wadding may be omitted, as the extra layers of fabric provide some warmth. Whether wadding is used or not, this sort of Log Cabin is usually TIED because of the difficulty of quilting through the extra layers of fabric.

LOG CABIN 2

Here the arrangement and order of piecing is exactly the same, but no backing fabric is used. The strips are sewn in turn around the centre to make a square block. Strip widths and seam allowances are the same as in Log Cabin 1, and the resulting Log Cabin blocks may be quilted.

- Save time by pinning several part blocks onto one long strip, and cutting the strip after sewing (6-5).
- Either technique can also be used to make COURT HOUSE STEPS, where the lights and darks are kept to opposite quarters of the block (6-6), but note that the order of sewing is different.

6-6 COURTHOUSE STEPS BLOCK

ARRANGEMENT OF BLOCKS

Standard Log Cabin blocks have one diagonal half looking dark, and the other diagonal half looking light. They can be arranged in all the ways that HALF SQUARE TRIANGLES (Chapter 9) can be arranged. They also have their own traditional SETS. The commonest are probably Barn Raising and Straight Furrow. To come out correctly, Barn Raising needs an even number of blocks both across and down the quilt, but Straight Furrow does not (6-7 and 6-8).

VARIATIONS

The simplest variations in Log Cabin are in block size, strip width and size of central square.

Log Cabin blocks may also be made in rectangles, triangles, diamonds, hexagons etc, without too much difficulty. The centre will always be a triangle in a triangle block, a diamond in a diamond block, etc. It is probably easier to make them in LOG CABIN TECHNIQUE 1, using Vilene® as the backing, with traced guide lines.

Within any Log Cabin block, the centre piece can be put off centre. But because there must always be the same number of logs on each side, the logs on two sides will need to be narrower and those on the other two sides wider. It is recommended that a drawn backing be used for this variation. This technique has been used for some very exciting and innovative quilts and, because apparent curves can be formed within the blocks, it lends itself to pictorial quilts.

6-7 LOG CABIN– BARN RAISING SET

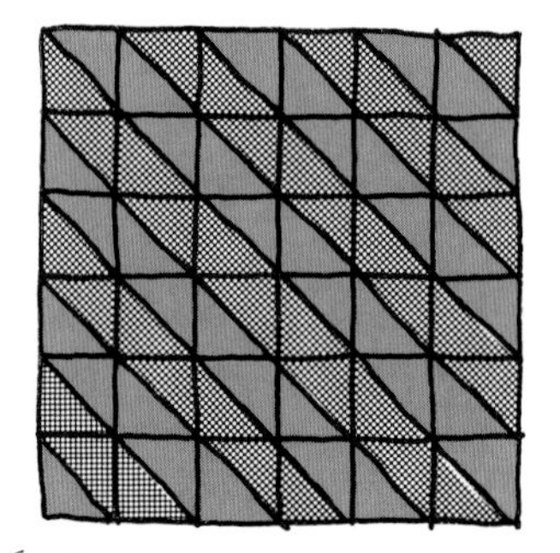

6-8 LOG CABIN– STRAIGHT FURROW SET

CHRISTMAS PLACEMATS

These mats are made from the traditional red, white and green Christmas-print patchwork fabrics [calicoes], keeping the reds to one side and greens to the other. LOG CABIN TECHNIQUE 1 is used, on a backing of pelmet Vilene®, which makes a nice firm base with sufficient insulation to protect the table from hot plates. The instructions are for a set of 4 mats. A table centre can be made by setting 4 blocks together.

MATERIALS: for four 10in (25cm) mats
All fabrics 44in (112cm) wide.
⅜yd (30cm) backing fabric.
⅛yd (10cm) red cotton for centres.
⅛yd (10cm) of Christmas fabrics, minimum assortment of prints 4 each of green/white and 4 red.
1 ¼in (4cm) wide green bias strip, 170in (435cm) long.
¾yd (60cm) pelmet Vilene®.
Sewing thread.

PREPARATION
PREPARE fabrics. PRESS Vilene®.
Cut four 10in (25cm) squares pelmet Vilene®, and MARK with 1in (2.5cm) stitching grid.
Cut 11in strip across backing fabric and SLICE across into 4 equal pieces.
Cut four 2 ½in (5.6cm) squares red fabric for centres.
Cut 2 ½in (5.6cm) wide strips of green and red fabrics.

MAKING
1 Lay Vilene® square centrally on wrong side of backing fabric, with grid upwards. Pin at corners.
2 Pin red square centrally on grid. Start with red print as first and second logs, and stitch following TECHNIQUE 1, but stitch from one edge of Vilene® to the other. This acts as a form of quilting. PRESS each log after stitching.
3 Stitch through all thicknesses, close to edge of Vilene®, and trim fabrics back to Vilene® edge. BIND with SINGLE BIAS, MITRED CORNERS.

LOG CABIN QUILT

This quilt started out as a pair of curtains, which were abandoned before completion and recycled as the basis of a wedding present quilt for my son.

The Log Cabin method that I used then advocated tearing fabric into strips. It was both slow and inaccurate, hence my loss of interest. When the quilt was resurrected, I cut the fabrics instead of tearing them. It was all still very slow, because the rotary cutter was not then available.

The fabrics were from my rag-bag, and many were jumble sale purchases or from used clothes. The darks I chose were browns through maroons and tans with some dark green, and the lights were pinks, pale yellows and beiges. By the time all the blocks had been sewn together, the quilt needed washing. I knew that many of the fabrics had not been pre washed, so for the first time I used the added-salt tip, and it worked. I watched the washing water turn brown and maroon, but none of the loose dye stained the light fabrics.

I wasn't going to use unwashed fabrics again, so I took special care to machine wash the maroon brushed cotton backing fabric. After the quilt had been in use for some time, I offered to wash it, and because of the previous problems with colour running from the Log Cabin fabrics, I again used salt in the washing water. This time the colour rolled out of the backing! I realised I had not checked what colour the rinse waters were when machine washing it. But again, thanks to the salt, no dye re-deposited on the patchwork.

This was the first large piece of quilting I ever did. The whole quilt was laid out on my living room floor, and pinned. Because I had no HOOP, I sat on the floor with my legs out under the quilt and just quilted. My feet were warm, but I became very stiff and was well pricked by the pins! Unfortunately, I knew no better than to use ordinary sewing cotton for quilting, so some of the quilting has since given up under the strain. Now I can see that the quilting is too sparse and very uneven. One lives and learns, and making this quilt was certainly an effective learning experience for me.

Moral 1 — Pre-wash fabrics and, for extra insurance, use salt in the wash water of those fabrics that bleed colour.

Moral 2 — Do not tear fabrics.

Moral 3 — Use proper quilting thread and a hoop or frame, and quilt more closely.

Moral 4 — Don't be discouraged.

MATERIALS: for 104in (260cm) square quilt
Fabrics 44in (112cm) wide.
Borders — 3yd (2.80m)
Backing — 9yd (8.30m)
Assorted light prints and plains totalling 5yd (4.60m) minimum.
Assorted dark prints and plains totalling 5yd (4.60m) mimimum.
(You will need 9 different darks and 8 different lights in each block, so the number of different fabrics should be at least three times those numbers — say 30 lights and 30 darks).
Wadding.
Sewing and quilting threads.

PREPARATION
PREPARE fabrics.
Cut 9in (23cm) wide borders, two 88in (225cm) long, and two 108in (275cm) long.
ROTARY CUT quantities of strips 1.7in (4.2cm) wide. Cut more later as needed.
Cut 64 centre squares from one dark strip.

MAKING

1 Following instructions for LOG CABIN 2, make 64 blocks, having 4 logs on each side of the central square (6-10), and not repeating any one fabric within any one block. Seam allowance the usual scant ¼ in (6mm).

2 Arrange blocks to make an agreeable balance of colour and tone. The original is a Barn Raising pattern. It helps to lay all the blocks out on the floor then, when satisfied, pin them in order onto a large sheet. Join blocks together to make rows. Join rows. Attach PLAIN CORNER borders.

3 LAYER for quilting. TIE or MARK diagonal lines for quilting. QUILT with dark thread on dark areas, and light thread on light areas. Make TURNED IN EDGES, and quilt one or two more rows around outside edge.

- Vary size of block or numbers of blocks, or omit borders and substitute a bound edge.

CHAPTER SEVEN

STRIPS AND DIAGONAL SLICES

In Chapter 4 I explained how to use the ROTARY CUTTER, and in Chapter 5 how to sew accurate STRAIGHT STRIPS. Now you can try several very simple ways of making things where made-up fabric from strip cutting and piecing (a SERIES) is SLICED at an angle and RE-PIECED. Your quilter's ruler should have 45°, 60° and 30° lines marked on it. If it hasn't, you can use it in conjunction with a 45° or 60°/30° set square [triangle], following the instructions below.

7-1 TRIMMING CORNER

PRACTISING DIAGONAL CUTTING (Ruler marked with 45° angle, right-handed)

1 Lay a piece of pressed cotton fabric on your cutting mat. Using ROTARY CUTTER (re-read [review] Chapter 4 if necessary), TRIM one edge, and turn the mat so that the cut edge is away from you.
2 Line up the 45° angle on the ruler with the cut edge, and cut off the top right-hand corner of fabric (7-1).
3 Turn board so the last edge you cut is to your left. Keeping 45° line on lower edge of fabric, move ruler along so that its 2in (5cm) line is on the cut diagonal edge. Cut (7-2).
4 Cut further strips in the same way, checking always that 45° angle is maintained.

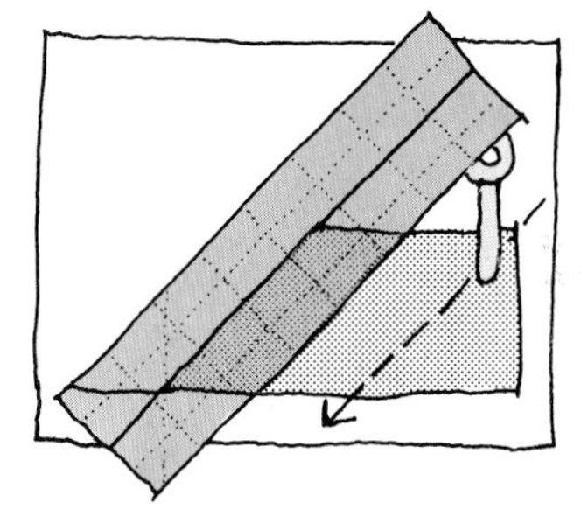

7-2 CUTTING DIAGONAL STRIPS

PRACTISING DIAGONAL CUTTING (Using ruler and 45° set square [right triangle]

1 Follow step 1 above.
2 Lay 45° set square in top right-hand corner, lined up with top edge, and hold it there while butting ruler up against it. Remove set square and make diagonal cut (7-3).
3 Make further cuts at 2in (5cm) spacings (7-4). It is more difficult with this method to be sure subsequent cuts don't go off the angle. You could try laying a piece of narrow masking tape across the ruler at 45°.

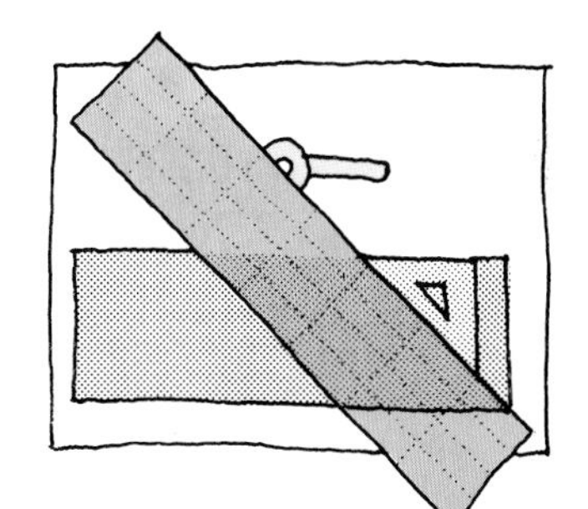
7-3 TRIMMING CORNER USING SET-SQUARE

USING DIAGONAL CUTTING

The most obvious use is for cutting bias strips for appliqué work or for binding your quilt. Here it is possible to cut through several layers of fabric by folding it (make sure the 45° bias edges are all in line) once the first 45° cut has been made.

- Do not STACK several SERIES for SLICING: the seam allowances tend to make them shift, and your cuts will be inaccurate. Cut one SERIES at a time.

ROMAN STRIPE

This is an attractive example of a block which is traditionally set 'solid', without alternate plain blocks or sashing. One block consists of a plain triangle pieced to a triangle made of several coloured strips (7-5). Most often, the plain triangle is black. Roman Stripe blocks are very quick and easy to make using ROTARY CUTTING and STRIP PIECING. The following instructions will make four 9in (23cm) blocks. The formula for calculating requirements for different sized blocks comes afterwards.

1 Cut strips from 5 plain [solid] fabrics, each 1 ¾in (4.5cm) wide, and about 36in (90cm) long. Sew with ACCURATE PIECING and scant ¼in (6mm) seams to make a SERIES of 5 strips. PRESS.
2 Check measurement across series. It should be 6 ¾in (17cm).

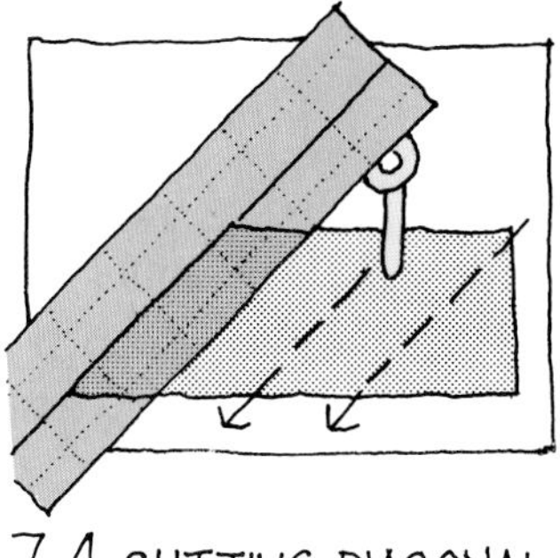
7-4 CUTTING DIAGONAL STRIPS

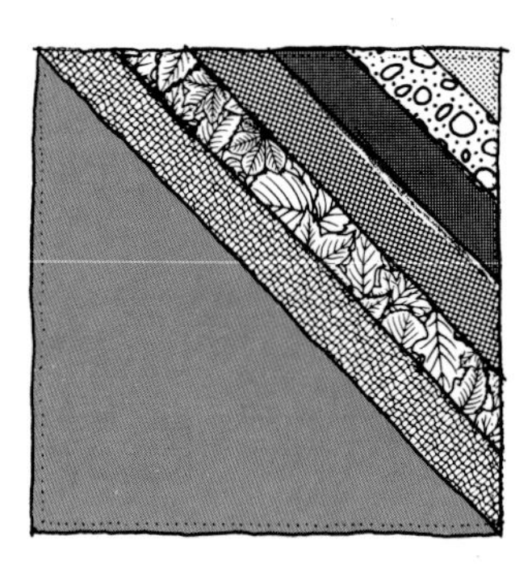

7-5 ROMAN STRIPE BLOCK

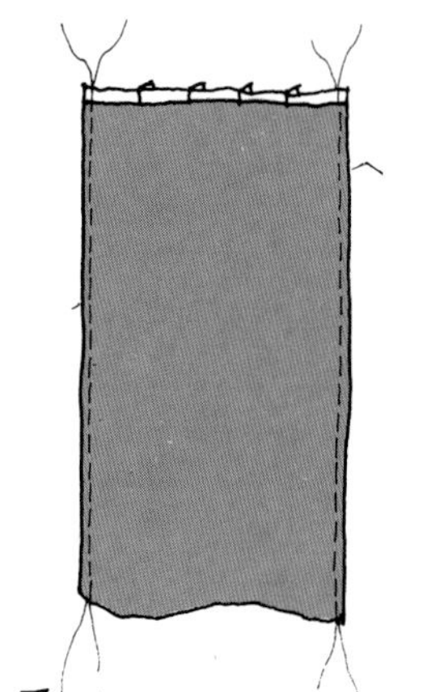

7-6 SEWING PLAIN STRIP TO SERIES

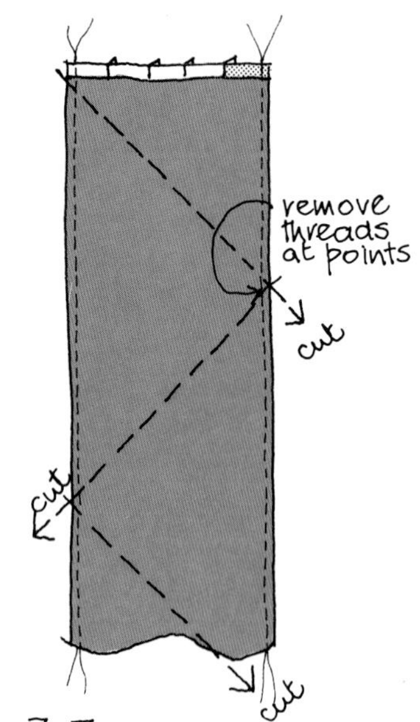

7-7 CUTTING ON DIAGONALS TO MAKE COMPLETE PIECED BLOCKS

Cut a strip of contrast fabric to that width and 36in (90cm) long. Stitch to series, right sides together, down both long edges (7-6). Press. You will then have a long flat tube.

3 Lay SERIES on cutting board with single wide strip upwards. Cut diagonally across from one end, alternating direction of cuts (7-7). Remove the one or two stitches at points of triangles. Press triangles open to give four squares. You will notice that two squares have one colour across the tip of the corner, and the other two have the same colour across the centre.

ROMAN STRIPE VARIATIONS

- Vary the number of stripes in the series.
- Vary placement of stripe colours and/or background colour.
- Vary the width of stripes within a series.
- Use blocks in a Log Cabin layout.

ROMAN STRIPE CALCULATIONS

1 Imperial calculation: Decide on finished block size, and number of stripes. Say 12in block and 6 stripes. Series width must be the same as half the diagonal of the square, plus seam allowances. It's a great help to use a calculator.

2 Magically, if you multiply the side measurement of a square by 1.414 you will get the diagonal measurement of that square. So the diagonal of the 12in square is 12in x 1.414 = 16.968in. The striped half is 8.484in across. There are 6 stripes, with 5 internal seam allowances of ½in each, one edge seam allowance of ¼in and one seam allowance at the point of ⅜in. These seam allowances total 3 ⅛in or 3.125in. Adding them to the half diagonal (8.484in plus 3.125in) gives 11.609in. If you divide this by 6 (for the 6 strips) each strip will need to be just over 1.9in. Here I think I might 'round up' to 2in strips, and settle for a slightly larger block.

3 Metric calculation: Read steps 1 and 2 above for the easy explanation. The block size is 30cm with 6 stripes. SERIES width must be half the diagonal of the square i.e. 30cm × 0.707 = 21.21cm, and then seam allowances must be added. The 5 intermediate seams take 12mm each, the edge seam takes 6mm and the point takes 9mm total seam allowance of 7.5cm. Total width of strips before piecing is 21.21 + 7.5 = 28.71cm. Divided into 6 strips, this gives almost exactly 4.8cm cut width per strip.

EIGHT-POINTED STAR

This is a very attractive pattern, but it puts a lot of quilters off because they think it is difficult to piece, or should be done over PAPERS. Because the diamonds that make it have all their sides the same length and opposite sides parallel (imagine them as squares that have been leaned on), they can be cut from strips very easily. Even quicker is to cut diagonal SLICES from strips which have already been joined into SERIES. You will need to practise diagonal (45°) cutting before starting.

Figure 7-8 shows a small star. You will see that it is made up of eight identical large diamonds each of which is made of concentric coloured rows of smaller diamonds. Trace the diagram and colour it with felt pens or coloured pencils.

1 Isolate one large diamond by hiding the rest of the star with scraps of paper. Count how many times each colour appears in one of the large diamonds. You will find that the colour at the points only comes once, the next rows in have two diamonds in each colour and

7-8 EIGHT-POINTED STAR

7-9 CUTTING UP COLOURED DIAGRAM

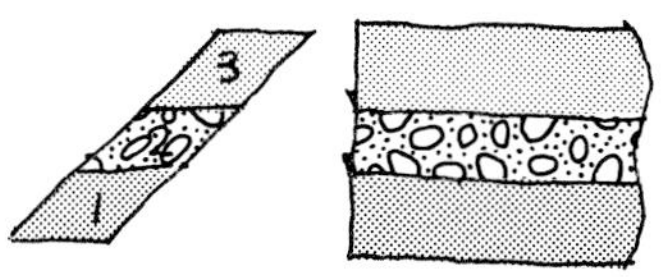

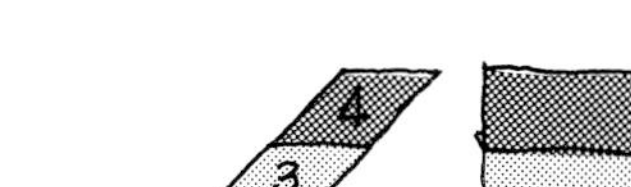

7-10 MAKING 3 SERIES

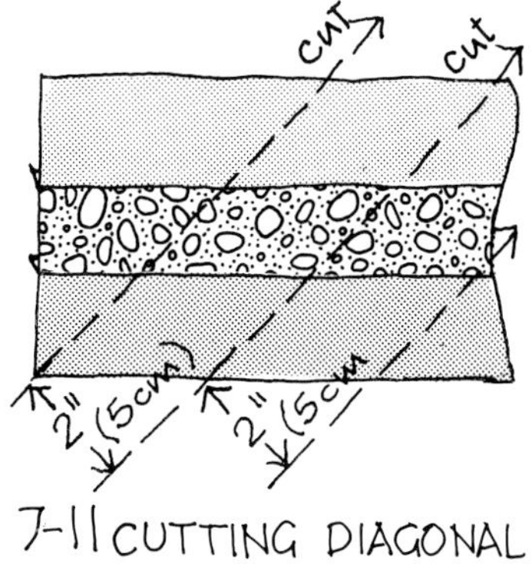

7-11 CUTTING DIAGONAL SLICES FROM SERIES

the middle row has three. Choose 5 fabrics, one for each row of diamonds.

2 Cut one 2in (5cm) wide strip of fabric for each time the colour appears in the large diamond. Each strip should be 28-30in (about 75cm) long.

3 Cut the isolated diamond from your coloured diagram. Slice it up into 3 sections (7-9).

4 Arrange your fabric strips in the same way, and sew with scant ¼in (6mm) seam into three SERIES of 3 strips each (7-10). PRESS.

5 Lay each SERIES on the cutting board in turn, right side up, and cut 8 diagonal (45°) SLICES from it, each 2in (5cm) wide (7-11). Allocate one slice to each of eight piles.

6 Following your coloured diagram, lay out the three SLICES from one pile, right sides up, in the right order for one large diamond. Pin, matching cross seams, and stitch together. Press. Stitch the other seven diamonds in the same way. One trick to get the seam allowances crossing accurately is to make sure the V at the beginning of the seam is exactly the scant ¼in (6mm) from the raw right-hand side of the fabric, and to have your machine needle lined up exactly in the centre of the V (7-12).

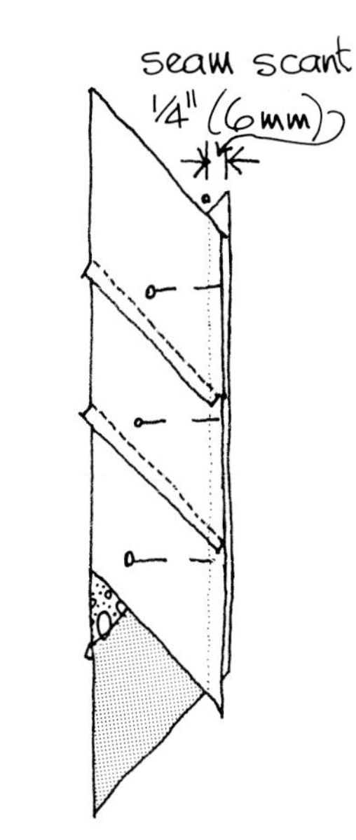

7-12 JOINING SLICES

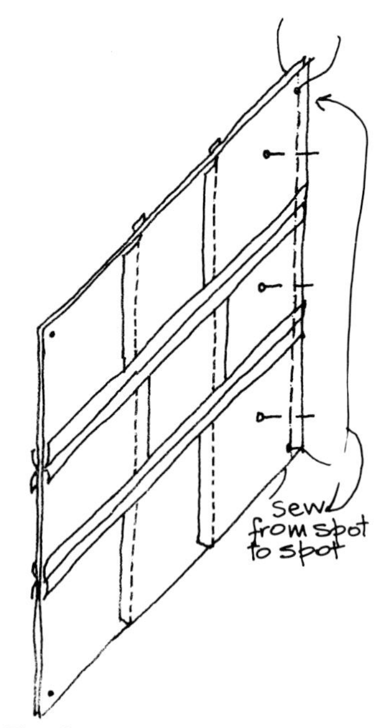

7-13 JOINING SECTIONS OF STAR

7 Following the coloured diagram for assembly, pin and stitch pairs of pieced diamonds together, starting and finishing the seam one seam allowance short of both the corner and the point (7-13). This will help in assembling the star and finishing it. PRESS seam to left. Join the other three pairs of diamonds together in the same way, then join pairs to make half-stars, and finally join half-stars in the same way — still not sewing across the centre, but only right up to it. You will note that pressing always in the same direction results in the centre seam allowances fanning round in a circle. This reduces bulk and makes the tricky joins at the centre more accurate (7-14).

8 Finishing off depends on what you are making, but will involve setting in the corners of triangles or squares. I suggest cutting squares and triangles oversize and trimming down after they are set in. So for the corners, measure the projecting point of a large diamond and cut four squares 1in (2.5cm) larger. For the side triangles, measure across the points, cut one square 2in (5cm) larger, and cut it into 4 triangles diagonally. Stitch in squares, starting from the inside corner, and only sewing from the CORNER POINT. Then stitch in triangles, again only sewing from the corner point but finishing by sewing across excess of previously sewn-in squares (7-15).

9 MARK a line on the wrong side, joining CORNER POINTS of diamonds. Trim ¼in (6mm) outside it, if necessary, to square up the patchwork.

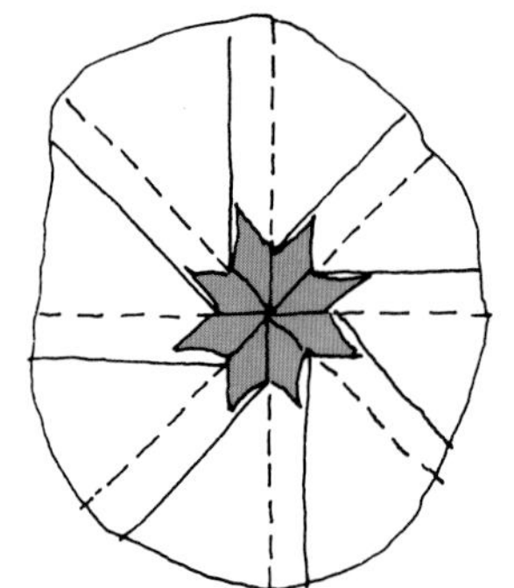

7-14 SEAM ALLOWANCES AT STAR CENTRE

LARGER EIGHT-POINTED STARS

Larger stars can either be made from wider strips (remember to cut the slices the same width as the original strips) or they can have more rows of diamonds in each section, and will therefore need that many more strips cut. When they have more rows of diamonds, the basic principle is the same — cut one strip for every small diamond, and join more strips into each SERIES, making more SERIES as well, but only cutting eight diagonal SLICES from each SERIES (one for each large diamond). It is more economical of fabric to stagger strips when sewing into series for larger diamonds (7-16).

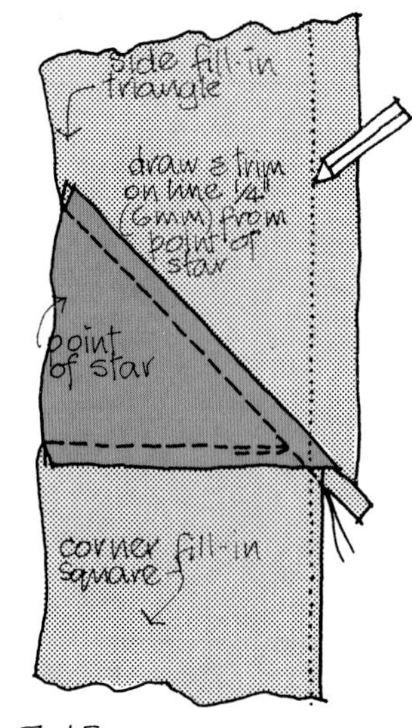

7-15 SEWING-IN & TRIMMING EDGE PIECES

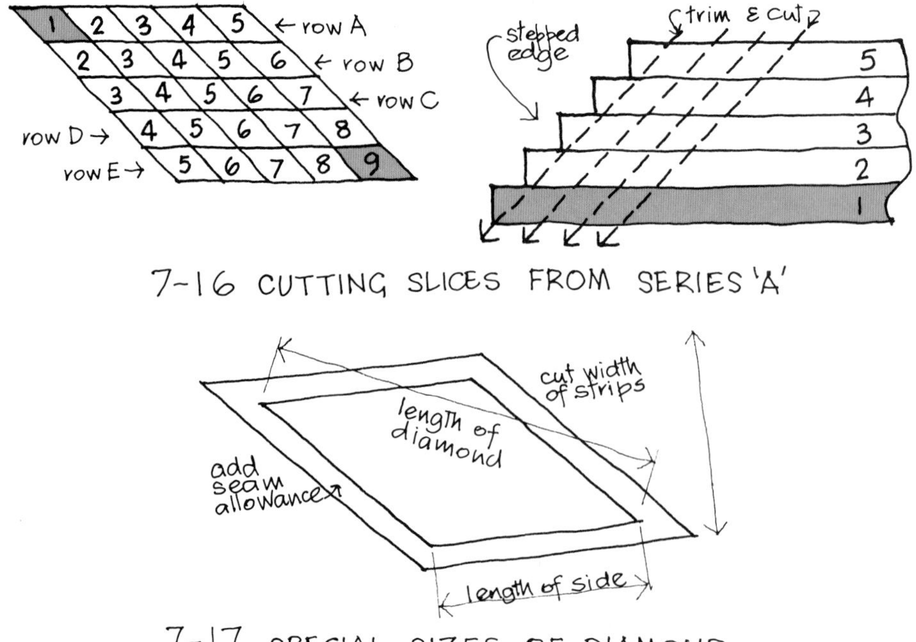

7-16 CUTTING SLICES FROM SERIES 'A'

7-17 SPECIAL SIZES OF DIAMOND

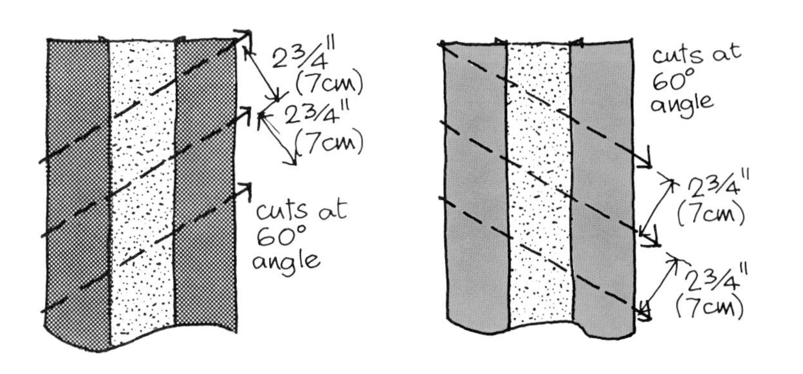

7-18 CUTTING SLICES

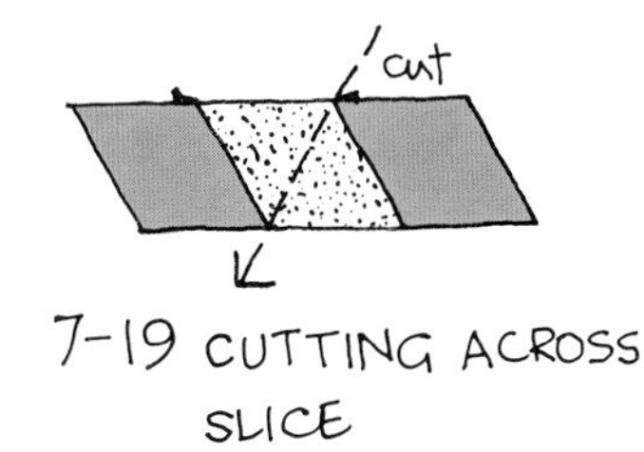

7-19 CUTTING ACROSS SLICE

If you want a diamond of a particular size for a special project, draw it out on graph paper, with seam allowances, and measure across (7-17) to get the correct strip width. The length of strip must be enough to cut 8 slices after piecing and allow also for the wasted triangle at each end.

The eight-pointed star can be arranged into many exciting patterns and lends itself to subtle colour arrangements (see BIBLIOGRAPHY).

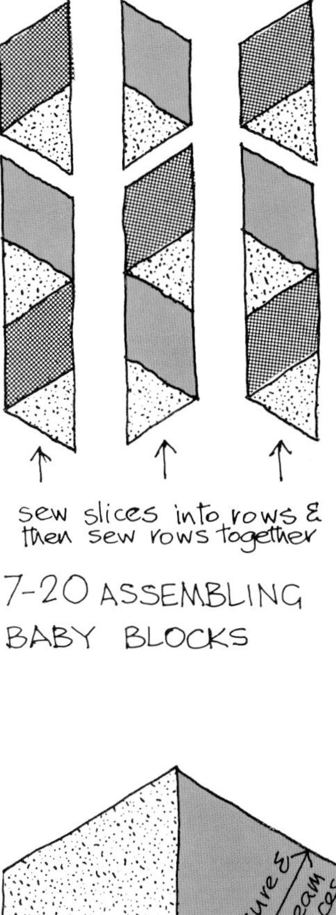

7-20 ASSEMBLING BABY BLOCKS

BABY'S BLOCKS

This design is also called Tumbling Blocks. It is made from 60° diamonds (three diamonds this shape fit together into a hexagon) and is one of those ancient mosaic patterns where the use of tone deceives the eye into thinking that the pattern is three-dimensional. It is considered a difficult pattern to piece, because it has set-in corners, unless done by the method of ENGLISH PIECING over papers (Chapter 8). I have worked out a way of piecing it from strips, which makes it very easy and very accurate. You will need three fabrics, one light, one dark and one medium-toned. It helps to disguise the seam across the medium-toned fabric if you choose a fabric with a small pattern.

1 Cut 2 strips of light and 2 strips of dark, each 2 ¾in (7cm) wide and 36in (90cm) long and 2 strips of medium each 3 3/16in (8.2cm) wide and 36in (90cm) long.

2 Stitch into two SERIES, one of light/medium/light and the other of dark/medium/dark, with scant ¼in (6mm) seam. PRESS seam away from medium fabric.

3 Using rotary cutter, trim end at 60° and cut one SERIES at 60° into SLICES 2 ¾in (7cm) wide (7-18). Cut the other SERIES into SLICES likewise, but make sure that the 60° angle is reversed, otherwise the pattern won't work.

4 ROTARY CUT each slice diagonally across the centre strip (7-19).

5 Lay out cut-up SLICES to form pattern and stitch together (as always a scant ¼in (6mm) seam) into rows (7-20), being careful to match seam intersections (pin if necessary). PRESS. Stitch rows together, again matching crossing seams. PRESS.

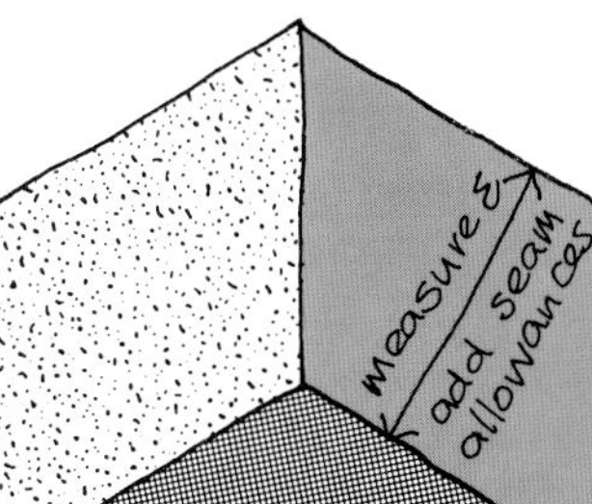

7-21 MEASURING FOR SPECIAL SIZES OF BABY BLOCKS

- These instructions make diamonds which are 2 ¼ (5.8cm) across from side to side. If you want to make diamonds of a different size, first draw out the finished size you want, measure across (7-21), and add ½in (1.2cm) to the measurement to get the width of dark and light strips and 15/16in (2.4cm) for the medium strip width.

STRIPED CUSHIONS

These cushions [pillows] always intrigue people, until their very simple construction method has been explained: the patchwork part is made from a square of strips, which is cut diagonally into four triangles. Each cushion is made of two of the striped triangles, with borders and backs added. Use printed fabrics ranging from light to dark, and a border colour that highlights the patchwork.

MATERIALS: for 2 cushions 14in (35cm) square
Fabrics 44in (112cm) wide.
⅛yd (10cm) of 9 fabrics for strips.
2 oz wadding (batting), 2 pieces 15in (40cm) square.
¾yd (70cm) fabric for borders and backs.
2 x 12in zip fasteners.
2 x 14in (35cm) square cushion pads [pillow forms].
Sewing thread, nylon quilting thread.

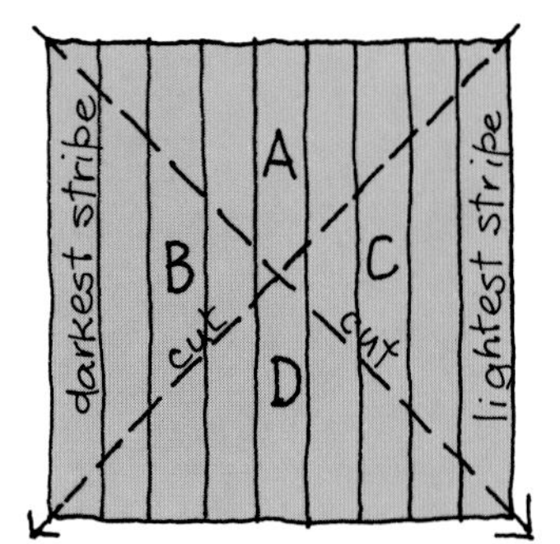

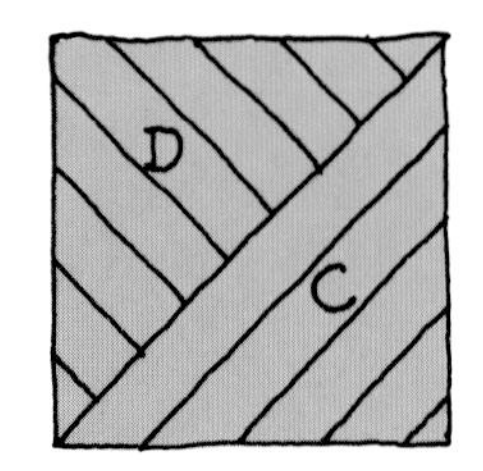

7-22 CUTTING PIECED SQUARE & RE-JOINING

PREPARATION
PREPARE fabrics.
CUT strips, one from each of the 9 fabrics, 2 ½in x 20in (6.5cm x 50cm).
Cut eight border strips, each 1 ½in x 16in (3.8 x 37cm).
Cut 2 backing pieces each 14in x 15 ¼in (35.5cm x 38.6cm).

MAKING
1 With scant ¼in (6mm) seams, join strips into a square, grading tones from light on one side to dark on the other. PRESS. Trim square to 18 ½in (47cm).
2 Cut square into 4 along both diagonals. Arrange and join pairs of triangles to make 2 new smaller squares (7-22).
3 LAYER each square with wadding only. QUILT IN THE DITCH. Attach BORDERS with MITRED CORNERS.
4 Cut 3in (8cm) off the length of each backing piece. INSERT ZIP FASTENERS between large and small pieces. Sew backs to fronts, right sides together and with zip fastener partly open. Fully open zips, and turn cushion covers right side out. Insert pads.

ROMAN STRIPE VARIATION QUILT

This quilt was made as a wedding present for my nephew, Christopher. I asked him to tell me the size of the bed (length, width and height to the top of the mattress) and the colour scheme of the bedroom. The Roman Stripe pattern is very quick to make; the variation comes in using the blocks to make a non-traditional pattern. The usual Roman Stripe has all the blocks set facing the same way. Lay out all the blocks on the floor and move them around, trying different permutations of layouts until you have one that pleases you (it needn't be symmetrical). In this quilt, the patchwork area is six blocks wide and eight blocks long, and covers the top of the bed. The inner border of three stripes helps to define the edge of the bed, and also stabilises the bias edges of the blocks. Fabrics are all polycottons and the quilt is tied.

MATERIALS: Finished quilt is about 93 ½in x 113in (235cm x 280cm)
All fabrics 44in (112cm) wide.
Border and triangles — 6yd (5.30m).
Lightest stripe (1) — ½yd (50cm).
Stripe (2) — ⅞yd (80cm).
Stripe (3) and binding — 3yd (2.70m).
Stripe (4) — ⅞yd (80cm).
Darkest stripe (5) — ⅝yd (60cm).
Backing 6 — ¼yd (5.60m).
2oz wadding [batting] 2in (5cm) larger on each side than finished size (joined if necessary).
Sewing thread.
Heavy cotton yarn for ties.

7-23 ROMAN STRIPE QUILT BLOCK LAYOUT

PREPARATION

PREPARE fabrics.

Cut border fabric to give a length of 137in (338cm). Divide this in 3 to give 3 lengthwise strips. Cut one strip in half for top and bottom border; the other 2 long strips are side borders.

From remaining border fabric ROTARY CUT 9 crossways strips, 7 ¼in (18.4cm) wide.

From stripe fabric 1 (lightest) cut 9 crossways strips, each 1 ¾in (4.4cm) wide.

From stripe fabrics 2, 3 and 4 cut 16 crossways strips from each fabric, each strip 1 ¾in (4.4cm) wide.

From stripe fabric 5 (darkest) cut 9 crossways strips, each 1 ¾in (4.4cm) wide and four 4 ¼in (10.8cm) squares

Divide backing fabric into three.

From remaining stripe fabric 3, cut 2in (5cm) bias strips, about 410in (10m) in length.

MAKING

1 Join 9 strips of each stripe fabric into long lengths. Join the 9 strips of border fabric into a long length. Press seams open. Make SERIES of five of stripe fabrics, scant ¼in (6mm) seam allowance. Lay SERIES and border fabric right sides together, and sew together along both long edges.

2 Cut 48 triangles from this double thickness, cutting at 45° from alternate edges (7-7). Open and PRESS. Lay out into pattern (7-23) or as desired, but keeping to 6 blocks wide and 8 blocks long. Join into rows. Join rows.

3 Join 7 strips of each of stripe fabrics 2, 3 and 4 into long lengths. Press seams open. Make SERIES of 3.

4 Check dimensions of pieced top. Cut 2 lengths from 3-strip SERIES to width of top, and sew onto top and bottom edges of top. Cut 2 lengths from SERIES to length of top (before top and bottom borders were attached), sew squares of fabric 5 to each end of the lengths. Attach lengths to sides of top.

5 Attach top and bottom borders. Attach side borders. MARK top for tying (make card template size of block and pierce holes [7-24]).

6 Join 3 lengths of backing (seams will go crosswise). LAYER quilt. Make CURVED corners. TIE. BIND with DOUBLE BIAS BINDING.

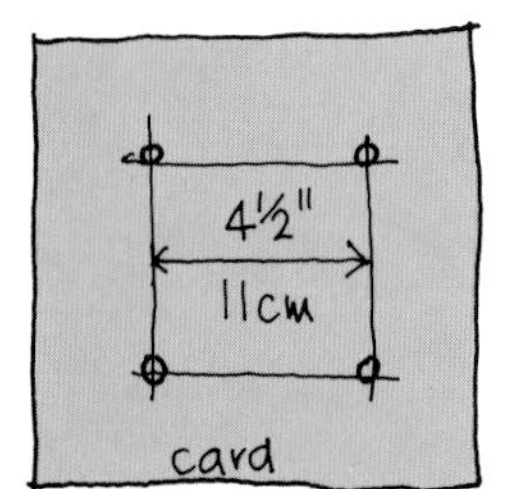

7-24 TYING TEMPLATE

STAR FLOOR CUSHION

Choose firm, closely woven cottons and you will not need to quilt unless you want to. Notice in the picture that the colour of the centre diamonds seems paler than the fill in pieces around the edge. It isn't, but it's a good example of the way one colour can seem to change because of the colour next to it. The star is made exactly to the instructions for the EIGHT-POINTED STAR earlier in this chapter.

MATERIALS: for cushion (pillow) 23in (60cm) square
Fabrics 44in (112cm) wide.
Centre and outside diamonds fabrics — ⅛yd (10cm) each.
Next row diamonds — ⅛ yd (20cm) each.
Middle row diamonds — ¼yd (20cm).
Corners and backing — 1yd (90cm) of 48in (120cm) heavy fabric
22in (55cm) zip fastener.
Cushion pad [pillow form] 23in (60cm) square.

PREPARATION
Trace star diagram 7-8 and colour for reference.
PREPARE fabrics.
ROTARY CUT straight strips across width of fabric, 2in (5cm) wide, one strip of each colour for diamonds 1 and 5; 2 strips of each colour for diamonds in rows 2 and 4; and 3 strips for diamonds in row 3.
Cut backing pieces 23 ½in x 20in (61.2cm x 55cm) and 23 ½in x 4 ¾in (61.2cm x 9.2cm).

MAKING
1 MACHINE PIECE strips into SERIES. Then follow instructions for EIGHT-POINTED STAR earlier in this chapter.
2 When the star is made and pressed, measure its points and cut corner squares and larger square for the side triangle fill-in pieces. Cut larger square into quarters diagonally. Insert fill-in corners, then triangles, still following earlier instructions. Press.
3 Check size of finished patchwork: the star should be square, although the edges will not be even. Trim off edges, to make a square of 23 ½in (60cm). There will probably be a small rim of background around the star, making its points seem to float on the background.
4 INSERT ZIP FASTENER into backing. Sew front to back, with ¼in (6mm) seam. Turn right side out and insert cushion pad.

Baby Blocks Pram Quilt

This little quilt was made for my first grandchild, Ben, and the colours were chosen to tone with his pram. I used small remnants of Liberty Tana® lawns, with a printed wool and cotton mixture Liberty fabric as backing. The optical effect is not as startling as it might be, as the medium-toned fabric is not quite dark enough. The quilt finishes with a zigzag top and bottom, following the edges of the blocks.

A good tip when trying to judge the tones [values] of different fabrics is to scrunch up your eyes into slits and look at the fabrics in a blurry sort of way. Or you can stick small samples of likely fabrics onto paper and photocopy them. The copier doesn't see colour, only tone.

MATERIALS: for quilt finishing 22 ¾in x 28in (58cm x 71cm)

½yd (40cm) of light, medium and dark fabrics, all 36in (90cm) wide.

Backing fabric and 2oz polyester wadding [batting] both 25in x 30in (65cm x 75cm).

Matching sewing and quilting threads.

PREPARATION
PREPARE fabrics.
ROTARY CUT 4 light strips and 4 dark strips, 2 ¾in (7cm) wide, across the width of the fabrics, and 4 medium strips, 3 3/16in (8.2cm) wide, also across the width of the fabric.

MAKING
1 Follow instructions for making BABY BLOCKS, to the end of step 4.
2 Lay out pieces (7-25). RE-PIECE the SLICES, and continue following BABY BLOCKS instructions.
3 The quilt may be machine or hand quilted. If you choose to hand quilt, MARK a line ¼in (6mm) inside each block, and ½in (12mm) all round inside raw edge. ALL-IN-ONE LAYER the quilt, trimming off points and snipping into corners of zigzags.
4 Machine quilt ¼in (6mm) in from outside edge and ¼in (6mm) inside all blocks, or hand quilt on marked lines.

7-25 LAYOUT OF BABY BLOCKS QUILT

- You need not restrict yourself to three fabrics only but, in sewing the SERIES, ensure that the same medium fabric is in both light *and* dark series. For a small quilt of this size, it means that you could have 4 different lights, 4 darks, but only 2 medium-toned fabrics. In arranging the pattern (7-25), make sure that the medium triangles will be sewn to others of the same print.
- This pattern can be made with straight top and bottom by trimming across.
- If you want to make the quilt in the traditional way, over papers, use a 60° diamond template with 2 ⅝in (7cm) sides. The quilt will then finish very slightly larger. Follow English hand-piecing instructions in Chapter 9.
- An alternative quilting pattern may be used inside each block, but beware having to quilt in the centre of the block where 6 seams meet.
- If you make the diamonds a lot larger, a small motif could be quilted in the centre of each one, as if it was the decoration on toy building blocks.

CHAPTER EIGHT

SEMINOLE PATCHWORK

Seminole patchwork is a much more modern technique than most patchwork. It is a form of small-scale, intricate and often brightly coloured machine strip piecing developed by the Seminole Indians of Florida. It was first made in the early 1900s and used for decorative bands on their clothing, but now it is often made for the tourist and souvenir trade as well. There are many different patterns, formed with varying combinations of: same strip widths; different strip widths; reversing slices; sliding slices; combining slices from two or more different series; cutting slices at right angles; and cutting slices at angles.

In Chapter 4 I explained how to cut extremely accurately and quickly with the ROTARY CUTTER, and in Chapter 5 we looked at STRIP-PIECING and how to sew accurately by practising the SEAM ALLOWANCE TEST. In that chapter all the examples used SLICES cut at right angles to the STRIP SERIES. Then in Chapter 7 we progressed to DIAGONAL cutting of strip series. All the examples in those two chapters were for patchwork on a much larger scale than the Seminole work. Often, we cut strips 2in (5cm) or more wide. Here, quite usual widths are ¾in, 1in, or 1 ¼in (1.8, 2.5 or 3.1cm), including seam allowances. The narrower the strip width, the more important it becomes to cut and sew as accurately as possible. With the small size of the Seminole strips, there is no scope for any 'easing' into place of off-size elements.

It is very difficult to estimate how long strips need to be cut, to finish up with the required length of patchwork. A lot depends on the complexity of the pattern and the size of the pieces. Small-scale intricate Seminole patchwork made from narrow strips uses proportionately more fabric for seam allowances than bolder work, because of its more frequent seams.

Do not waste fabric in working out complex patterns. Instead, draw out and colour your pattern on squared paper (use the paper diagonally if you are drawing a diagonal pattern). Cut out the FINISHED strip widths from coloured paper, and make a paste-up of the pattern. This can be cut up, and the assembly process reversed to get back to the original piecing of strips. After you have worked out a satisfactory design, and are calculating what strips need to be cut, don't forget to add seam allowances onto these mock-up patterns.

8-1 TRIMMING BAND EDGES

EDGING

All bands of Seminole patchwork should be completed with edging strips on both sides. On bands where the slices finish up on the diagonal, you will need to mark a seamline on the wrong side, running through all the outside crossing points. Then cut off the wasted points ¼in (6mm) outside this line (8-1).

BAND ENDS

Bands with diagonal designs will naturally have both ends on the skew. Once you are sure you have made your band long enough, LOOP it, and cut vertically through the band at some point (8-2).

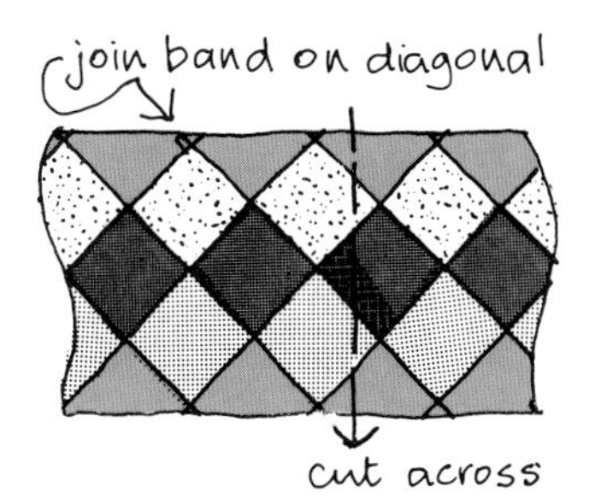

8-2 JOINING BAND ENDS

CHEQUERED STRIP

This is the simplest pattern and very similar to the 9-patch of Chapter 5. Two colours of strips are needed, and the same number of strips of each colour. The strips are sewn alternately into a SERIES,

PRESSED, SLICED at right angles to the same width as the original strips, and alternate slices turned top to bottom before RE-PIECING (8-3).

DIAGONAL CHEQUERED STRIP

If a number of different coloured but equal-width strips are pieced into a SERIES and SLICED, the slices can be SLID to the next seam allowance, to make a DIAGONAL CHEQUER. Variations possible are in the numbers of strips, and the numbers and arrangement of colours. The pattern illustrated (8-4) has 7 strips with a symmetrical repeat. This is a very easy pattern and useful for fitting onto clothing as it is slightly stretchy. In order to get the seam allowances going in different ways, it is necessary either to REVERSE strips (as in the illustration) or, if the colour arrangement is not a repeating one, to PRESS the seam allowances on half the SERIES length in one direction, and on the other half in the other direction.

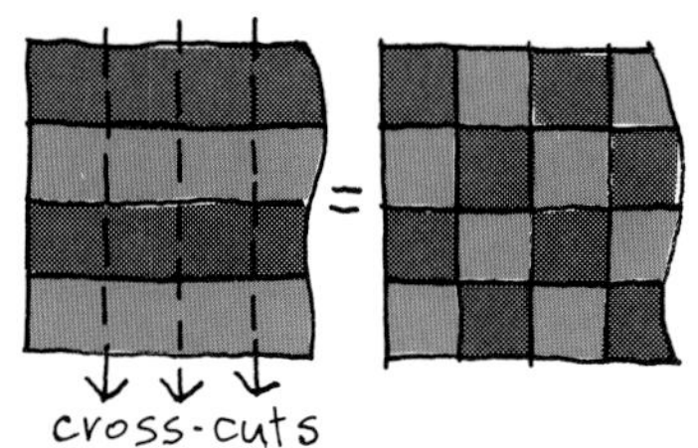

8-3 CHEQUERED STRIP

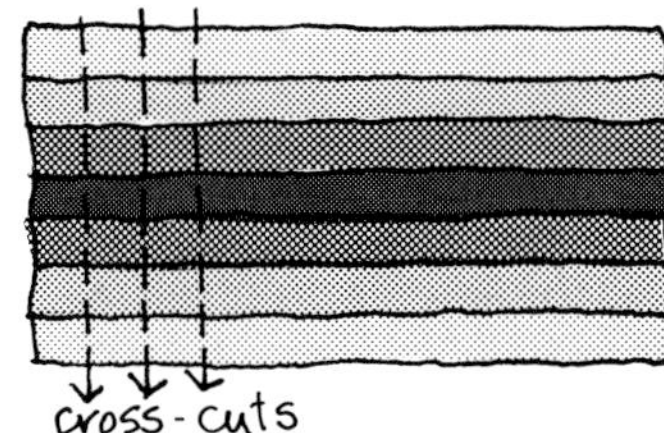

8-4 DIAGONAL CHEQUERED STRIP

INCORPORATING OTHER PATTERNS

This pattern uses an initial SERIES of two strips, one wide and the other narrow. After SLICING they are REVERSED but a third strip introduced between them. This can be the same colour or a different one (8-5), or another pattern.

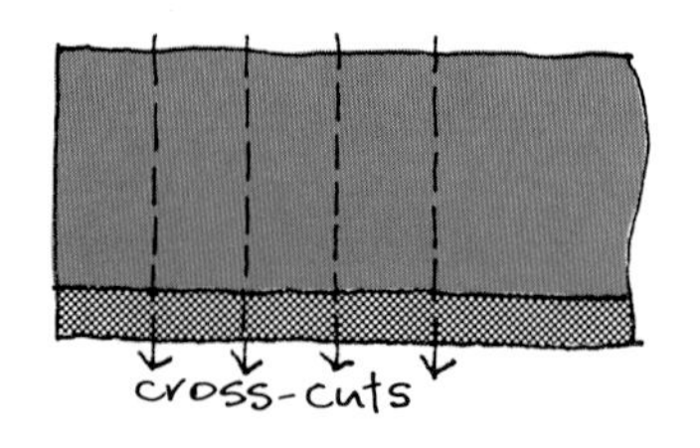

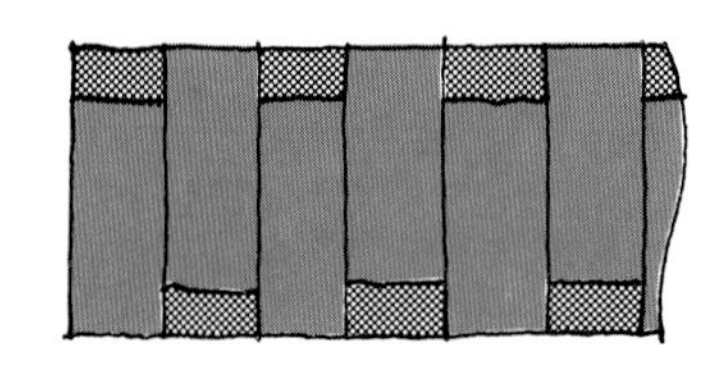

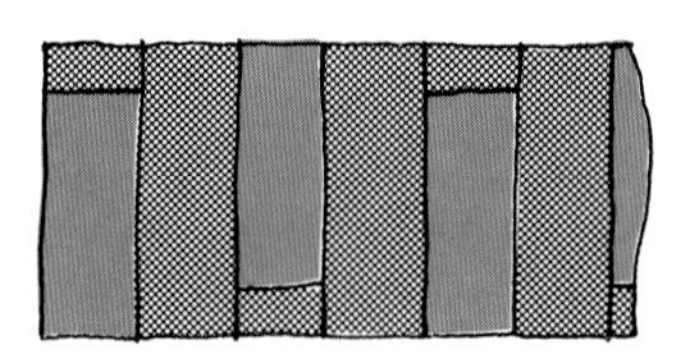

8-5 REVERSING SLICES/ INSERTING SLICE

SLICES AT ANGLES

Many patterns SLICE a SERIES at an angle, like the next pattern (8-6). This can vary from just off vertical (say 80°) to less than a diagonal (say 30°). Only 45° and maybe 30° and 60° lines will be marked on your ROTARY RULER. Never mind. Cut a strip of card, the width of your SERIES. Mark the distance A onto it, and cut out the triangle (8-6A). Use as a GUIDE to the first cut, and CHECK every 4 or 5 cuts to make sure the cutter is still on the correct angle.

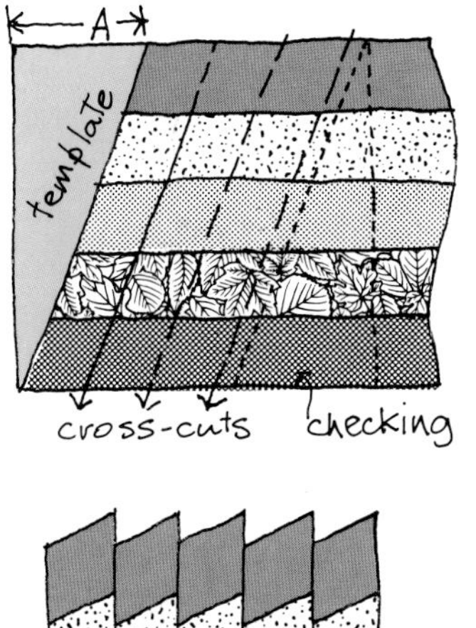

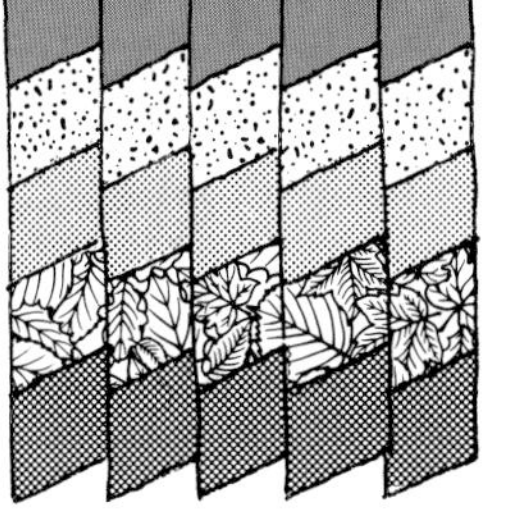

8-6 ANGLED SLICES

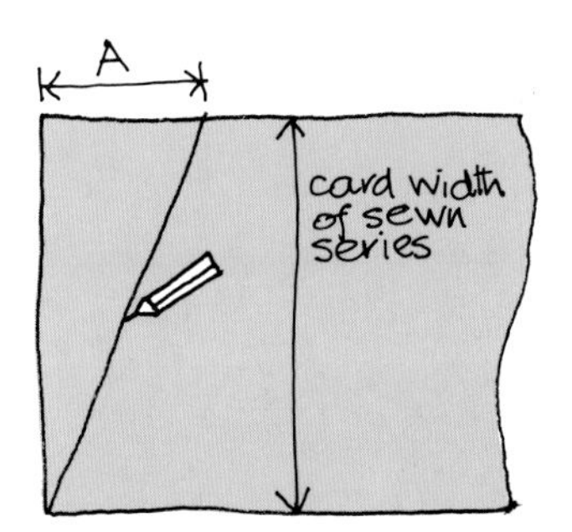

8-6A MAKING ANGLE TEMPLATE

USING SEMINOLE PATCHWORK

The small scale and apparent intricacy of the patterns makes them ideal for incorporating into personal treasures, like jewellery rolls, spectacle cases, sewing kits or box tops. On clothing, they can be used on cuffs, pockets or yokes, or, as in the project, to make a wide band to decorate the bottom of a skirt. On a larger scale, they have been successfully used to decorate cushions [pillows] and quilts. I feel that the technique is essentially one that uses plain [solid] colours, and loses a great deal of its graphic clarity if prints [calicoes] are used. Of course, this may be exactly what you would like to happen!

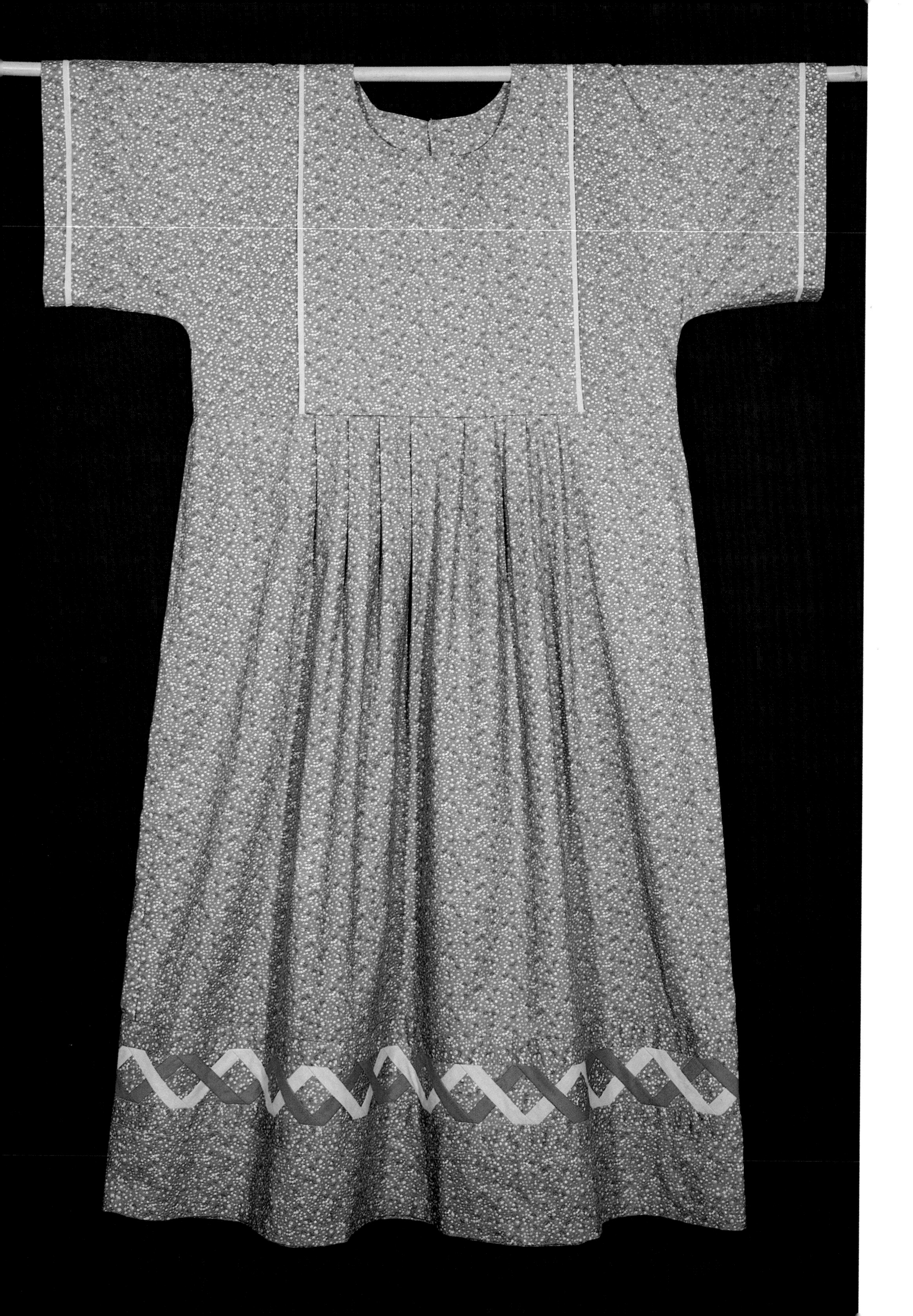

DRESS WITH SEMINOLE BORDER

I don't usually like small patchwork patterns [calicoes] but fell for this pretty lavender print. The contrasting pink and purple in the Seminole band bring out the colours of the print, and look like interlacing folded ribbons. The dress pattern is an attractive and versatile American one (fits all shapes and sizes) called the Ultimate T-Dress, and is specially designed for patchwork or appliqué embellishments. In choosing a dress pattern, you must remember that a band of Seminole patchwork will not fit round a circular shape, although there is a certain amount of give in this and other Seminole patterns where the fabric is on the full bias, and it can be stretched or coaxed into a slight curve. It is better to choose a pattern where you can decorate a straight part. In the instructions, I have given the design, the method of calculating requirements to fit the design, and how to apply it — not the pattern for the dress itself which is, of course, copyright.

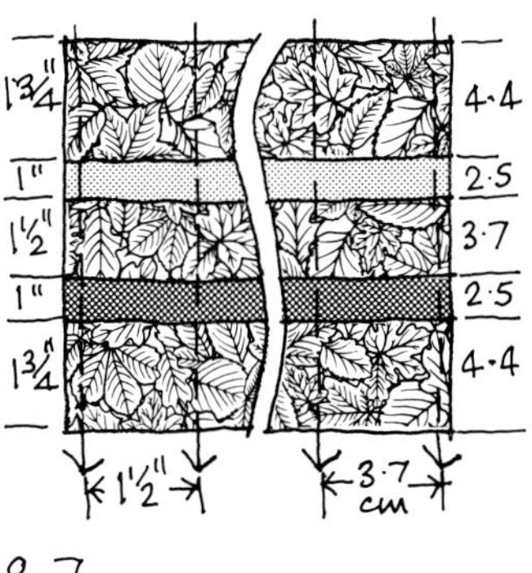

8-7 SERIES FOR DRESS

MATERIALS: for the Seminole band itself only, sufficient for a band finishing 4 ¾in x 72in (12cm x 1.8m) — 44in (112cm) fabric
½yd (40cm) print.
¼yd (30cm) of 2 plains (solids).

PREPARATION
PREPARE fabrics.
ROTARY CUT strips across width of fabric:
From print, cut 4 strips 3in (7.5cm) wide for strip edges; 4 strips 1 ¾in (4.4cm) wide and 2 strips 1 ½in (3.7cm) wide.
From each plain, cut one strip 4 ½in (22.8cm) wide and 2 strips 1in (2.5cm) wide.

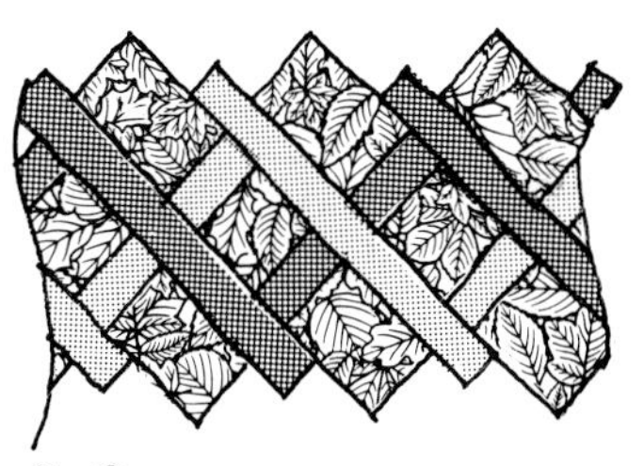

8-8 RE-PIECED SLICES

MAKING
1 MACHINE PIECE strips into 2 SERIES of five (8-7) with scant ¼in (6mm) seam. PRESS. ROTARY CUT into 1 ½in (3.7cm) SLICES.
2 Cut wide plain strips into 1in (2.5cm) slices.
3 Arrange as Figure 8-8, having alternately one and then the other plain thin slice between the pieced slices, with the pieced slices turned alternately up and down. To get the correct stagger, line up seamlines of plains and pin before stitching. PRESS.
4 Join the two pieces of Seminole patchwork to make one long band, making sure pattern runs through correctly. Measure length over the maximum number of complete repeats. This measurement is the total available for the full finished width of the skirt yet to be made, so adjust skirt pattern or plan to reduce length of strip. Note that one repeat should measure about 4 ¼in (10.8cm).
5 Join remaining print strips into 2 long strips. PRESS seams open. Sew one to top of Seminole band, and one to bottom (8-9). Trim seam at back and press seam allowances towards edge strips. Stitch ends of whole band together, matching pattern. Press. Turn in and press ¼in (6mm) on each edge; position, pin and top stitch to skirt.

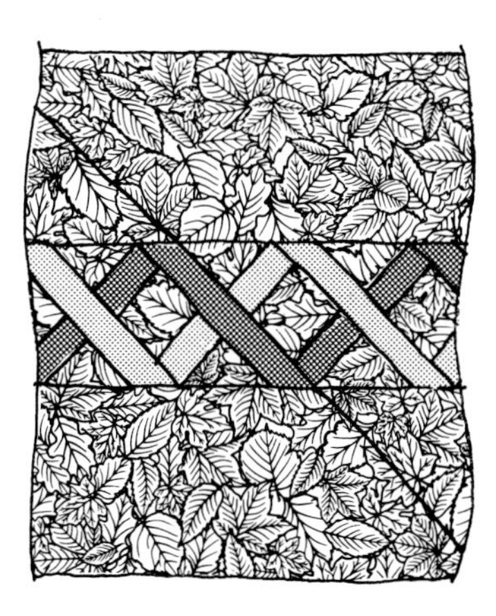

8-9 EDGING & JOINING BAND

CHAPTER NINE

QUICK PIECED TRIANGLES

Triangles play a big part in many quilt blocks and add visual movement to block designs. They are not easy to piece accurately on the sewing machine, because it is difficult to control the fabric at triangle points, where you are also sewing on the bias. Often, at the beginning of a seam, the sewing machine tries to gobble the point of the triangle down into the hole in the throat-plate or, at the end of the seam, the fabric will slew in the machine, making a wiggle in the line of stitching and an inaccurate seam width at the corner point. I am glad to say that there are some quick and easy methods which overcome these difficulties and are extremely accurate into the bargain.

When I was first taught how to sew quick pieced triangles several years ago at a workshop, we had to draw out each triangle and all its seam allowances. In one exercise, with four triangles nestled together, that meant drawing twelve seam allowances outside the four triangles. Even though I was used to drawing, and trying to be very careful, it was still all too easy to make mistakes, so I was very glad to realise, soon after, that there is a STANDARD SEAM ALLOWANCE ADDITION for each sort of shape. Later, I bought Barbara Johannah's *The Quick Quiltmaking Handbook* and found she had thought of it too. Later still, Trudie Hughes adapted the system for her book *Template-Free Quiltmaking*. It seems that quilters worldwide are working on the same ideas simultaneously.

Before I give instructions for how to make these quick triangles, I will explain more fully about STANDARD SEAM ALLOWANCE ADDITIONS. Throughout this book, you are working with a seam allowance of ¼in (6mm). This is what you add on to the desired patch shape in order to get the right sized patch to cut out. If you add it onto both sides of a 2in (5cm) square, you will have a square of 2½in (6.2cm). The STANDARD SEAM ALLOWANCE ADDITION for a SQUARE is ½in (12mm), whatever size square is inside it. How about a 10in square? It adds up to 10 ½in with seams. Or a 50in square — it adds up to 50½in with seams. The ½in seam allowance (¼in on each side) is always the same; it's the size of the square inside that changes (9-1). The same goes for metric, of course.

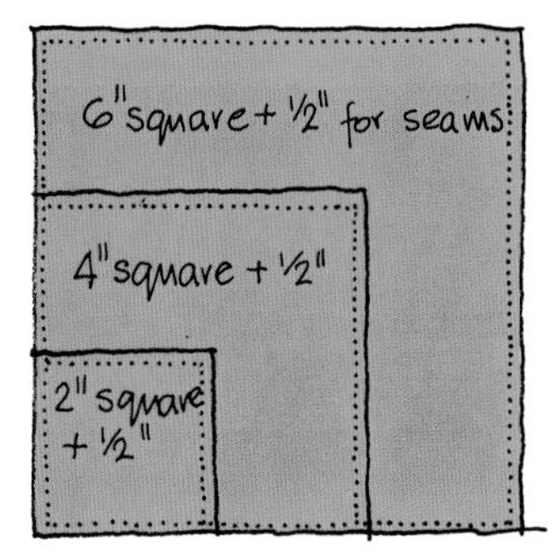

9-1 SQUARES & SEAM ALLOWANCES

The same is true for all other standard shapes, whether rectangle, triangle, hexagon or whatever: when you wish to add seam allowances for cutting the shapes **there is a standard seam allowance addition for each particular shape, whether you are cutting out a small or a large version of that shape.**

The variation in seam addition between different shapes is directly related to the angles at the corners of those shapes — a square corner (right angle) seam addition is ¼in (6mm), and a 45° corner addition is ⅝in (1.5cm). So a right-angled triangle plus seam allowance measured from the square corner to the 45° corner would be cut out the length of the side plus ¼in plus ⅝in (length of the side plus 6mm plus 1.5cm). A triangle measured from one 45° corner to another 45° corner would be cut out the length of the side plus ⅝in plus ⅝in (length of the side plus 1.5cm plus 1.5cm).

It is difficult to believe this unless you try it out for yourself. Draw a careful right-angled triangle on graph paper. From a corner where two heavy lines cross draw a line upwards on one line for 2in (5cm) and a line sideways along the other line, also for 2in (5cm). Now draw a line to join the ends of the two lines (9-2). Draw another triangle outside the first one, as if you were adding the seam

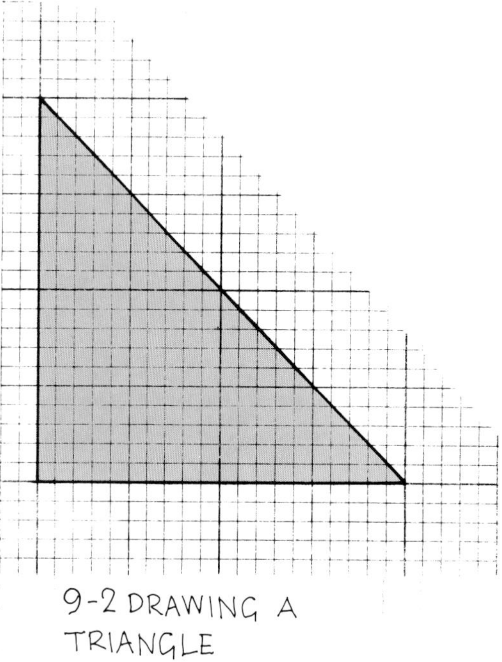
9-2 DRAWING A TRIANGLE

allowances, by measuring and marking ¼in (6mm) out all round, and drawing through the measure marks. Measure the length of the shorter side of the outside triangle. It should be ⅞in (2.1cm) larger than the short side of the original triangle. Next, test with a much larger triangle the same way. This time, make the first two lines 5in (12cm) long, and draw the ¼in (6mm) line all round it. You will find once again the seam allowance side is ⅞in (2.1cm) larger than the triangle side (9-3). Now draw lines up and across from the corners of the triangle seam allowances. You have drawn a square, which can be cut into two triangles, each with its seam allowance. The square is ⅞in (2.1cm) larger than the short side of the triangle.

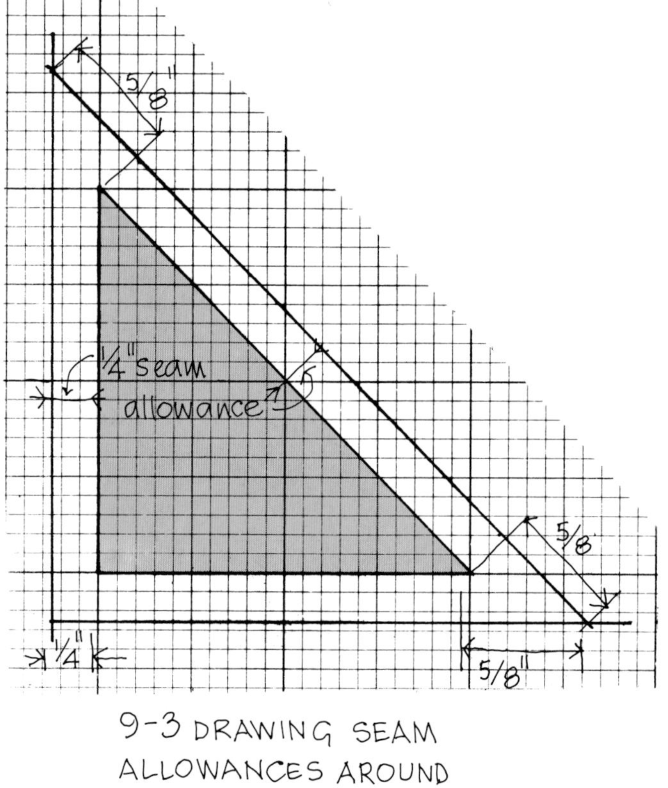

9-3 DRAWING SEAM ALLOWANCES AROUND TRIANGLE

HALF-SQUARE TRIANGLES

In Chapter 2 I talked about UNIT SQUARES, the subdivision squares of a patchwork block. Often, a unit square will have two triangles in it. They have the fairly obvious name of HALF-SQUARE TRIANGLES and, if you have just done the previous exercise, you will have drawn two... So the golden rule that you need to remember is **two triangles with their seam allowances can be cut from a square which is ⅞in (2.1cm) larger than the unit square** (9-4). These half-square triangles always have the grainline of the fabric in line with the short edge of the triangle, which will be the side of the finished square.

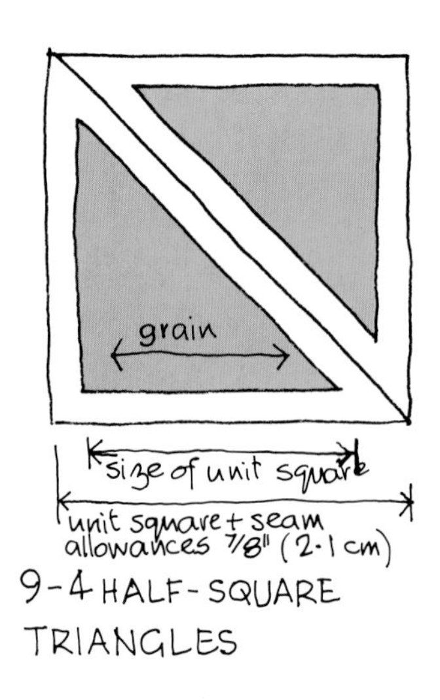

9-4 HALF-SQUARE TRIANGLES

QUARTER-SQUARE TRIANGLES

It would be boring to go through all the shapes, measuring the extra amount that is added on for seam allowances, but it is useful to know that four QUARTER-SQUARE triangles with their added seam allowances can be cut from a square which is 1¼in (3cm) larger than the UNIT SQUARE (9-5). The GRAINLINE will be parallel with the sides of the squares and the long sides of the triangles.

QUICK MACHINE-PIECED HALF-SQUARE TRIANGLES

To make two pairs of triangles for using in a quilt block, cut 2 squares of fabric ⅞in (2.1cm) larger than the UNIT SQUARE (say 3⅞in [9.6cm]). Draw one diagonal on the wrong side of one square. Pin the two squares together, right sides together, and edges all in line. Machine stitch a scant ¼in (6mm) seam on each side of the drawn line. Cut along the line, between the stitching lines. PRESS. You will have made *two* squares of half-square triangles (9-6).

MAKING MANY HALF-SQUARE TRIANGLES

When you need a lot of unit squares made of pairs of half-square triangles in the same combination of fabrics, you can sew them all at the same time. Draw a grid of squares on the wrong side of one fabric, half as many as the number of pieced squares you need, remembering to make them ⅞in (2.1cm) larger than the unit square. Draw all the diagonals in one direction. Pin fabric to second fabric, right sides together. Machine stitch a scant ¼in (6mm) seam on both sides of all the drawn diagonals (9-7). Cut along all the drawn lines, sides first and then diagonals. Unpick the few stitches remaining at the points of the triangles and press.

QUICK MACHINE-PIECED QUARTER-SQUARE TRIANGLES

The principle is much the same, but the square that you draw must be 1¼in (3cm) larger than the long side of the finished triangles. This is generally the same as the side of the UNIT SQUARE. Draw in BOTH diagonal lines. Check your block pattern to see how the finished triangles should look: depending on which side of the diagonal line you sew, you will get different results, although you will always finish up with four pairs of triangles:

A If you sew on each side of one diagonal only, you will get two pairs of triangles coloured one way, and two the other (9-8).

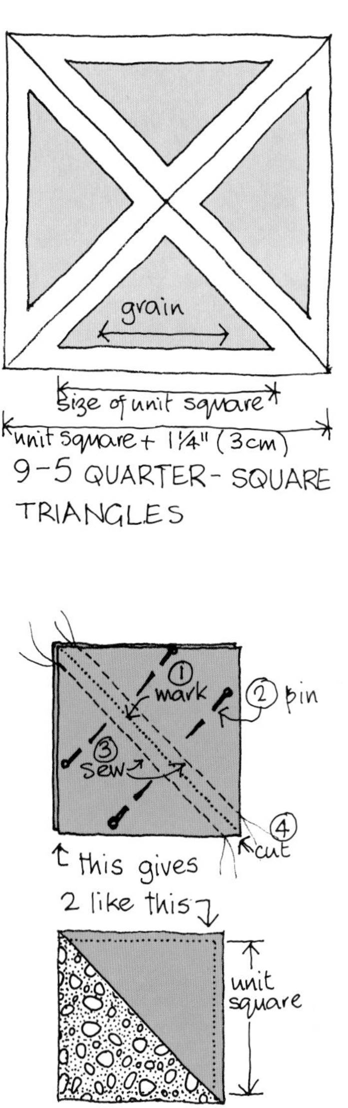

9-5 QUARTER-SQUARE TRIANGLES

9-6 QUICK HALF-SQUARE TRIANGLES

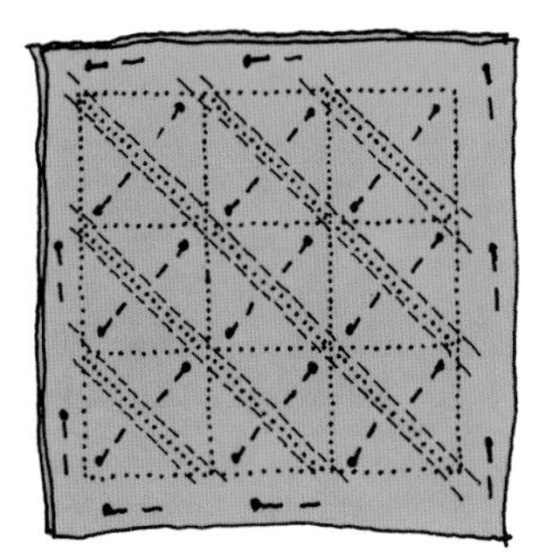

9-7 MAKING MANY HALF-SQUARE TRIANGLES

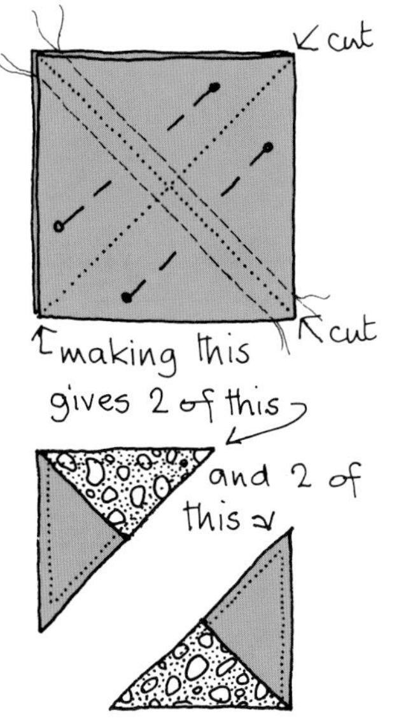

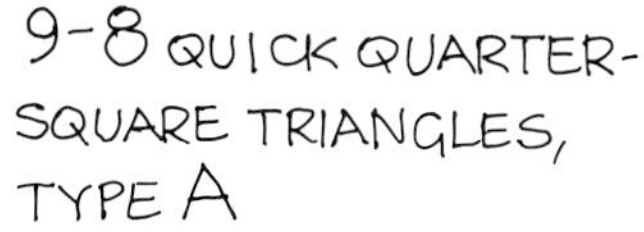

9-8 QUICK QUARTER-SQUARE TRIANGLES, TYPE A

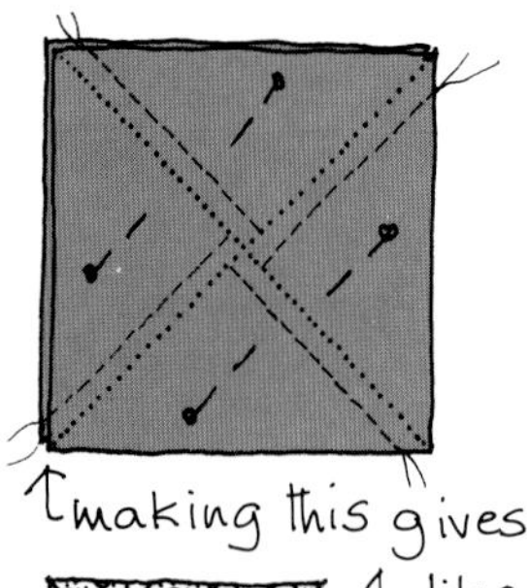

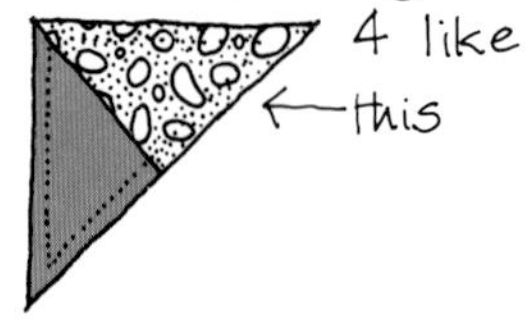

9-9 QUICK QUARTER-SQUARE TRIANGLES TYPE B

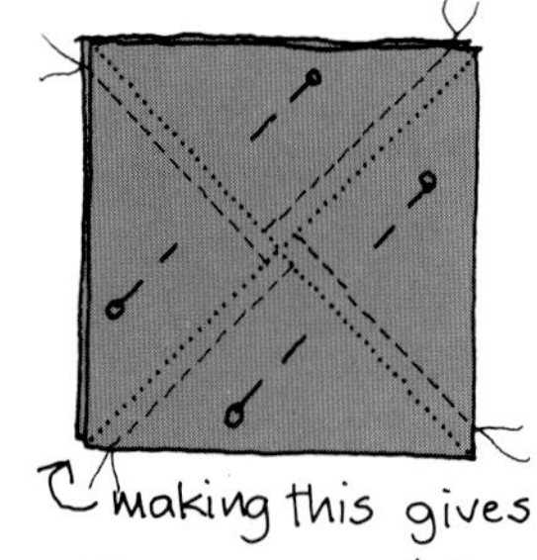

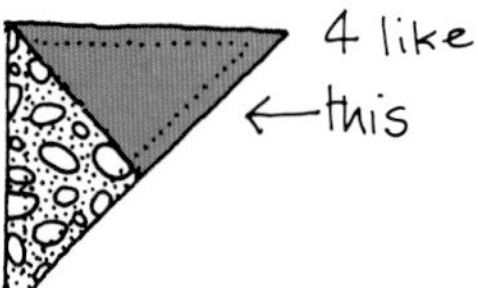

9-10 QUICK QUARTER-SQUARE TRIANGLES TYPE C

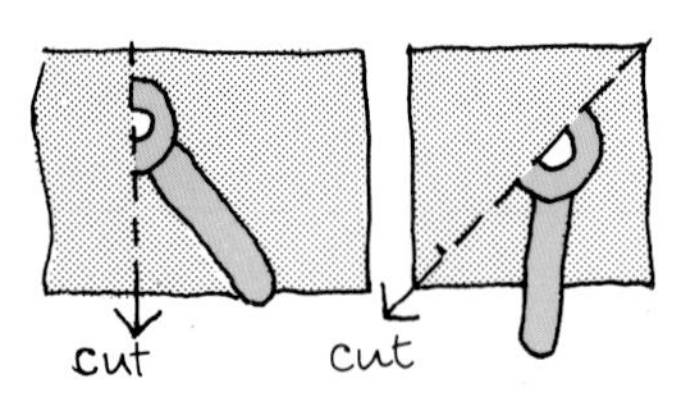

9-11 ROTARY CUTTING TRIANGLES FROM STRIPS

B If you sew on the clockwise side of each diagonal, you will get four pairs of identical triangles (9-9).

C If you sew on the anti-clockwise side of both diagonals, you will also get four pairs of identical triangles, but the colour arrangement will be the opposite of B (9-10).

MAKING MANY QUARTER-SQUARE TRIANGLES

These are made to exactly the same principle as the half-square triangles just described. Draw out the grid of squares with the correct seam allowance added (1 ¼ in or 3cm). Draw both diagonals on all squares and pin fabrics together. Depending on what colour arrangement is needed, stitch as in A, B or C above, a scant ¼ in (6mm) from the drawn diagonal. Cut out all the squares, then cut along both diagonals of each square.

ROTARY-CUT TRIANGLES

Some patterns, like FIREWORKS, call for single triangles to be sewn to, say, a pair of quarter-square triangles. It is no problem to rotary cut them once you know the secret of the STANDARD TRIANGLE SEAM ALLOWANCES, and have decided whether the triangles you need to cut are the half-square or quarter-square variety. Simply rotary cut strips the width of the square-plus-seam-allowance which contains your triangles, cut across into squares, and cut across the diagonal of the squares either once for half-square triangles or twice for quarter-square triangles (9-11).

FLYING GEESE

This is a pretty pattern, often used for borders or as a vertical motif in a quilt; it also appears in quilt blocks such as DUTCHMAN'S PUZZLE and FIREWORKS. Flying Geese are rather tricky to piece by machine, because of the small size of the pieces, and the difficulty of machining on the bias and near the points of triangles. One quick method was developed for bogus Flying Geese where you sewed two pairs of half-square triangles together. This meant that the main 'goose' triangle was split by a centre seam with the extra seam allowances at the point causing difficulties of accuracy and bulk. I have figured out a way of quick piecing genuine Flying Geese which is based on the principles behind quick pieced triangles.

QUICK MACHINE-PIECED FLYING GEESE

These instructions ('recipe') make a strip of four Flying Geese, with each goose finishing 4in (10cm) wide and 2in (5cm) high. Do not use striped fabric unless you want the stripes to run in different directions — prints, plains [solids] or checks work fine.

1 Cut one 5 ¼ in (13cm) square of 'goose' fabric. Mark both diagonals on the right side.

2 Cut four 2 ⅞ in (7.1cm) squares of 'sky' fabric. Mark one diagonal on the wrong side of each square.

3 Lay large 'goose' square right side up and pin one small 'sky' square exactly in one corner, wrong side up, with its diagonal line in line with the one it's lying on. Pin another 'sky' square in the corner diagonally opposite, in the same way. Trim off the corners of the 'sky' squares, just where they cross each other at the centre of the big square. Machine stitch a scant ¼in (6mm) seam on both sides of their diagonals (9-12). Cut between the lines of stitching.

4 Take one section and finger-press the 'sky' triangles away from the 'goose' fabric they are sewn to. Pin the third small square into its corner, as before, and stitch a scant ¼in (6mm) seam on both sides of the marked diagonal (9-13). Cut between the lines of stitching.

5 Repeat step 4 with the other section and last small square. Press the four pieces carefully to avoid distortion, with 'sky' seams pressed away from 'geese'.

6 In assembling the 'geese' into a strip, pin carefully at each end and in the centre, making sure that the point of the 'goose' will be exactly on the seamline for maximum accuracy and good looks. Trim off the projecting seam allowance triangle after the seam has been sewn. Press seam allowance towards the 'goose' above (9-14).

You may have noticed that the 'goose' square of fabric had the same seam allowance added as the quarter-square triangle square. This is because four 'goose' triangles were hidden inside it. Similarly, each of the four 'sky' squares hid two half-square triangles and therefore had the half-square triangle seam allowance. If you want to make Flying Geese to a different size, this is all you need to know to be able to quick-piece them to whatever size you wish.

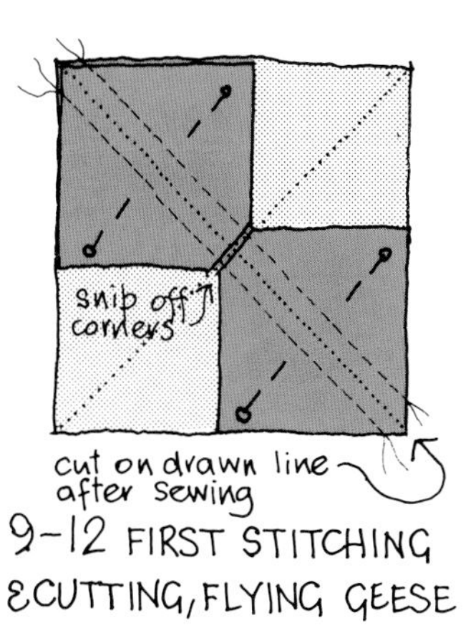

9-12 FIRST STITCHING & CUTTING, FLYING GEESE

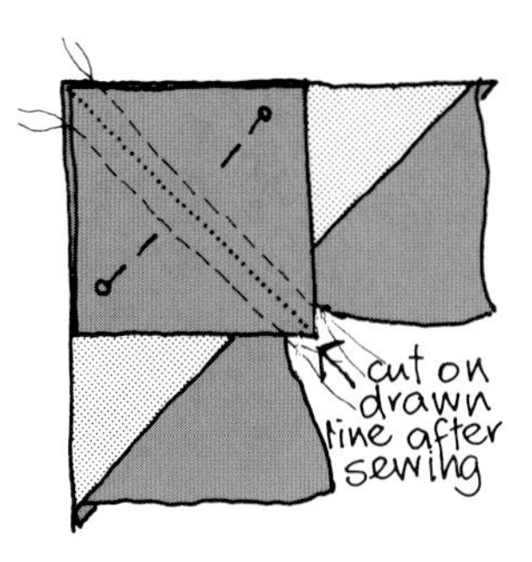

9-13 SECOND STITCHING & CUTTING, FLYING GEESE

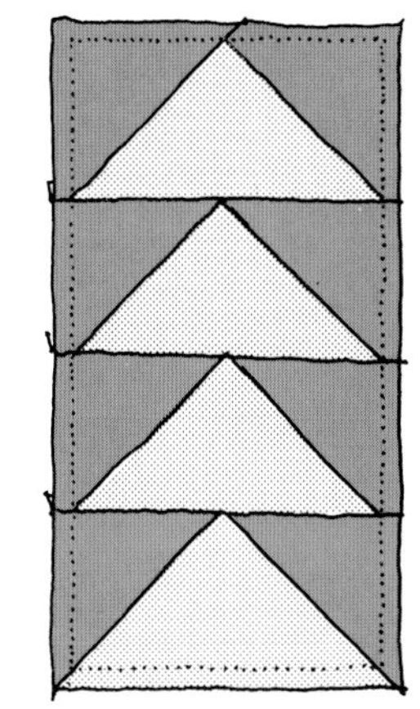
9-14 FLYING GEESE

DOUBLE X QUILTER'S TOTE BAG

This bag, using black as a background colour and four blocks of the old 9-patch pattern, DOUBLE X, came out rather more capacious than I was expecting. It holds a rotary cutting mat against one side and quilter's ruler on the bottom, and I think it would swallow up half a dozen quilts as well! Black is a marvellous foil to colours and makes them glow. Here the colours range from a rather sludgy green through a palish blue to much brighter royal blue and jade. The four blocks and the small black frame around them were made for a demonstration on quick machine-pieced triangles, and used up all the black fabric that I had, so the rest of the bag, including the lining, is made of dress-weight sailcloth. In the instructions, though, I have given fabric requirements for the same black cotton fabric to be used throughout. The 12in (30cm) blocks (9-15) are a good size for a first attempt at quick pieced triangles. You can see that the blocks are not all facing the same direction, but all face the centre and build up a larger patchwork pattern in the process. The front is machine quilted IN THE DITCH and the back in a diagonal square pattern.

MATERIALS: for bag measuring 26in (65cm) square with 7in (18cm) gusset

All fabrics 44in (112cm) wide.

3 ½yd (3.2m) black cotton fabric.

¼yd (15cm) in each of 4 plain (solid) colours cotton fabric.

2oz wadding (batting): 2 pieces 30in (75cm) square, one strip 9in (23cm) x 80in (200cm), and 2 strips 1 ½in (4cm) x 32in (80cm).

Black sewing thread.

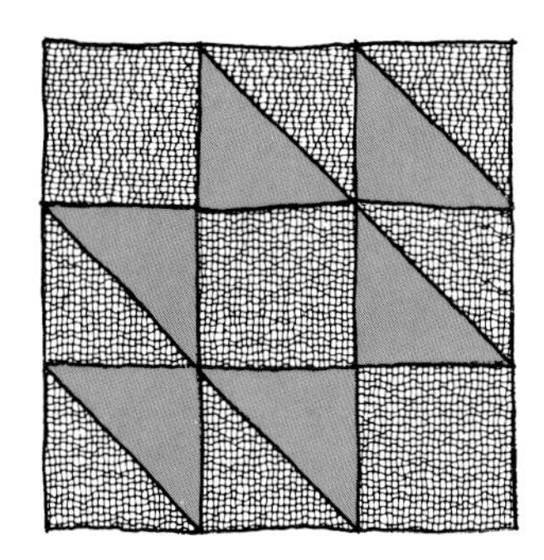

9-15 DOUBLE X BLOCK

2 handles (H) 4" x 33½" (10cm x 85cm)
12 squares (A) from 4½" (11·2cm) wide strips
12 squares (B) from 4⅞" (12.2cm) wide strips
2 strips (S.1.) 1½" x 26½" (3·7cm x 61·2cm)
2 strips (S.2.) 1½" x 28½" (3·7cm x 64·2cm)

9-16 CUTTING LAYOUT FOR DOUBLE X TOTE

PREPARATION

PREPARE fabrics, but cut 2 handle strips 4in (10cm) wide and 33½ in (85cm) long along selvages at one end of black fabric, before removing all other selvages.

Cut large squares, gussets and strips from black fabric (9-16).

Cut remaining black fabric into 4½ in (11.2cm) strips from which cut twelve squares; and 4⅞ in (12.2cm) strips from which cut twelve squares.

Cut three 4⅞ in (12.2cm) squares from each plain colour cotton.

MAKING

1 Make blocks first, to match Figure 9-15. For each block, make 6 HALF-SQUARE TRIANGLE units, sewing a scant ¼in (6mm) seam. PRESS seams towards black. Assemble in rows of three with plain squares and press. Join rows.

2 Join blocks together in pairs, and then join pairs of blocks together. Make sure that each block has a black square towards the centre.

3 Sew narrowest strips to blocks as a frame.

4 Machine quilt back and front before assembly: MARK diagonals on front, out from centre, through the black UNIT SQUARES. Mark a diagonal grid on the back, 3in (7.5cm) square. LAYER front and back. Machine quilt on all marked lines and IN THE DITCH around coloured triangles.

5 Pin wadding behind two handle strips. Fold long raw edges of handle strips over wadding and then fold selvage edges of strips over to cover raw edges (handles should finish 1½ in (4cm) wide). Pin, and MACHINE QUILT 3 rows along the length of handles. Trim excess wadding from ends of handles.

6 Pin wadding behind one gusset strip. Sew wadded gusset to bag front and back with ¼in (6mm seam). Trim away excess wadding. Sew lining squares to unwadded gusset strip.

7 Pin handles in position (9-17) on front and back of bag, with ends projecting 1¼ in (3cm) above raw edges of top of bag. Turn bag lining inside out, and slip bag into it. Match corners and pin all round before sewing ¼in (6mm) from top edge, leaving a gap to turn bag through. Turn right side out and slipstitch gap closed. Machine stitch twice right round top of bag, ½in (1.2cm) and 1in (2.4cm) from edge.

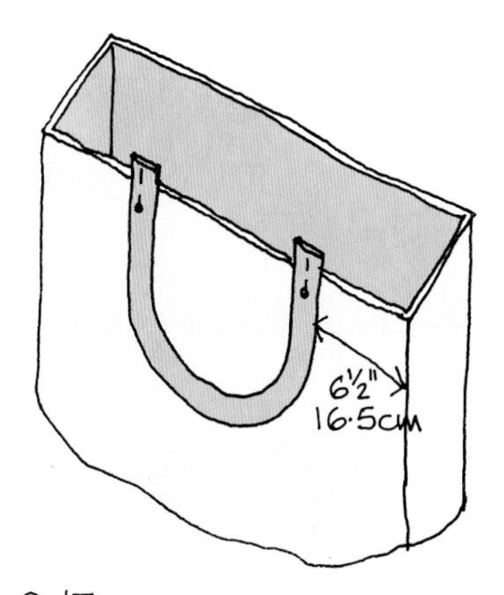

9·17 POSITIONING HANDLES

FLOTILLA QUILT

I made this quilt very quickly, so that we would have a bedcover in our Greek island cottage. The block is an old 4-patch favourite called SAILBOAT. Here it is set SOLID, with two borders, but you will notice that the sailboats in one row are sailing one way, while in the row below they are sailing the other way. There are many sailing boats among the Greek islands and, as the winds seem to blow in almost every direction at once, they often go in different directions. I used up lots of shades of light blues and grey blues for the sky, and deeper blues and greeny blues for the sea. In Greece, the light and sunshine are very strong and the island boats very brightly coloured, so pale wishy-washy shades would be quite lost. I took the opportunity of using checks, stripes and other bright or difficult fabrics for the boats. So that the quilt would be useable, I machine quilted IN THE DITCH around the boats, and on both sides of the inner border. Now, when we are on holiday, the quilt hangs on the wall as a decoration during the morning. I sit under a shady mulberry tree quilting it during the afternoon, and at night (still unfinished) it goes on the bed!

The quilting lines on the Sailboat blocks are all drawn freehand as I go along, but I had to make my own template patterns for the cable and Greek meander patterns to fit the border and block dimensions. All the quilting marking is done with a sliver of white soap. And because the hand quilting is only half-done, you can see the huge difference that quilting makes to the part that has been finished.

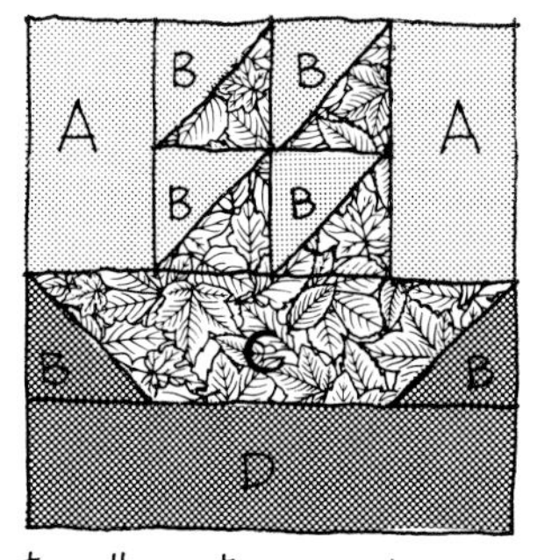

note: alternate rows have boats facing other way

9-18 12" (30cm) SAIL BOAT BLOCK

MATERIALS: quilt finishes 66in x 78in (165cm x 195cm) and has 20 blocks

All fabrics 44in (112cm) wide.

Borders (cut lengthwise) 2yd (1.7m) for inner border and 2 ¼yd (2m) for outer border.

One block sky fabric, 4 ½in x 22in (11cm x 53cm).

One block boat fabric, 4 ½in x 22in (11cm x 53cm).

One block sea fabric, 4 ½in x 18in (11cm x 43cm).

Backing fabric, 70in x 84in (170cm x 200cm).

2oz wadding, 70in x 84in (170cm x 200cm).

Sewing and quilting threads.

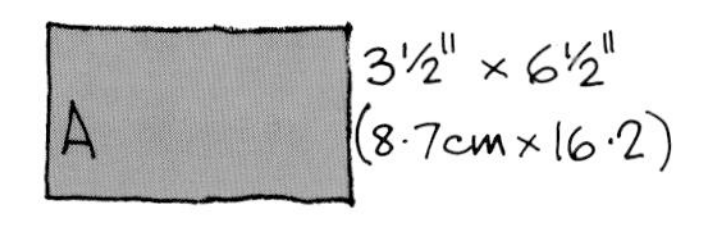

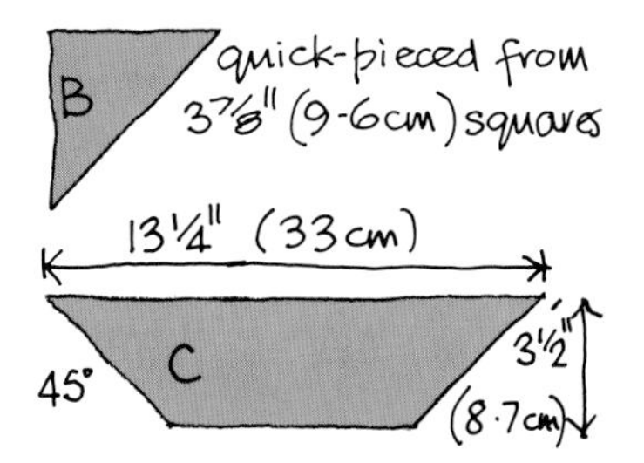

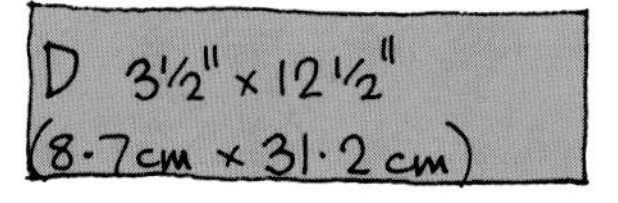

9-19 CUTTING SIZES, SAILBOAT BLOCK

PREPARATION

Select an assortment of fabrics. While each of the boats can be a different fabric, the sky and sea fabrics may be repeated on different blocks, and the border fabrics used also as sea. Block diagram 9-18.

PREPARE fabrics.

Cut inner border: 2 strips 3 ½in x 48 ½in (8.7cm x 121.2cm) and 2 strips 3 ½in x 66 ½in (8.7cm x 166.2cm).

Cut outer border: 2 strips 7in x 54 ½in (17.5cm x 136.2cm) and 2 strips 7in x 79 ½in (17.5cm x 181.3cm).

Cut block fabrics: refer to Figure 9-19 for sizes and ROTARY CUT if desired.

Arrange placement of fabrics in blocks, and arrangement of blocks.

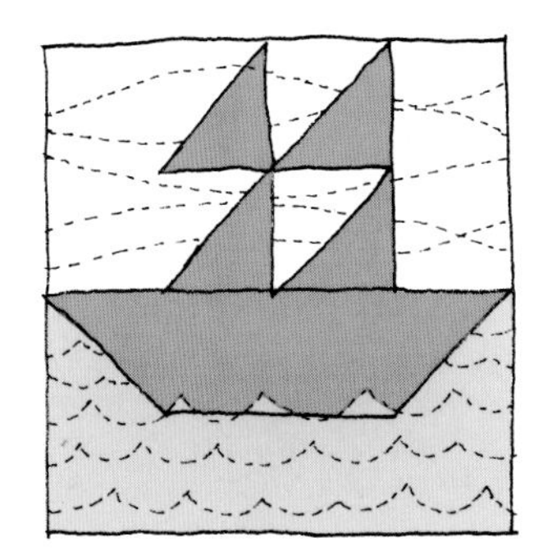

9-20 FREEHAND-DRAWN LINES FOR QUILTING BLOCK

MAKING

1 QUICK-PIECE (HALF-SQUARE TRIANGLE) sky/sails, using scant ¼in (6mm) seam allowance. PRESS. Sew into pairs of UNIT SQUARES. Sew pairs of squares together. Sew pieced sky/sails squares to sky rectangles.

2 Sew sea triangles to ends of boat.

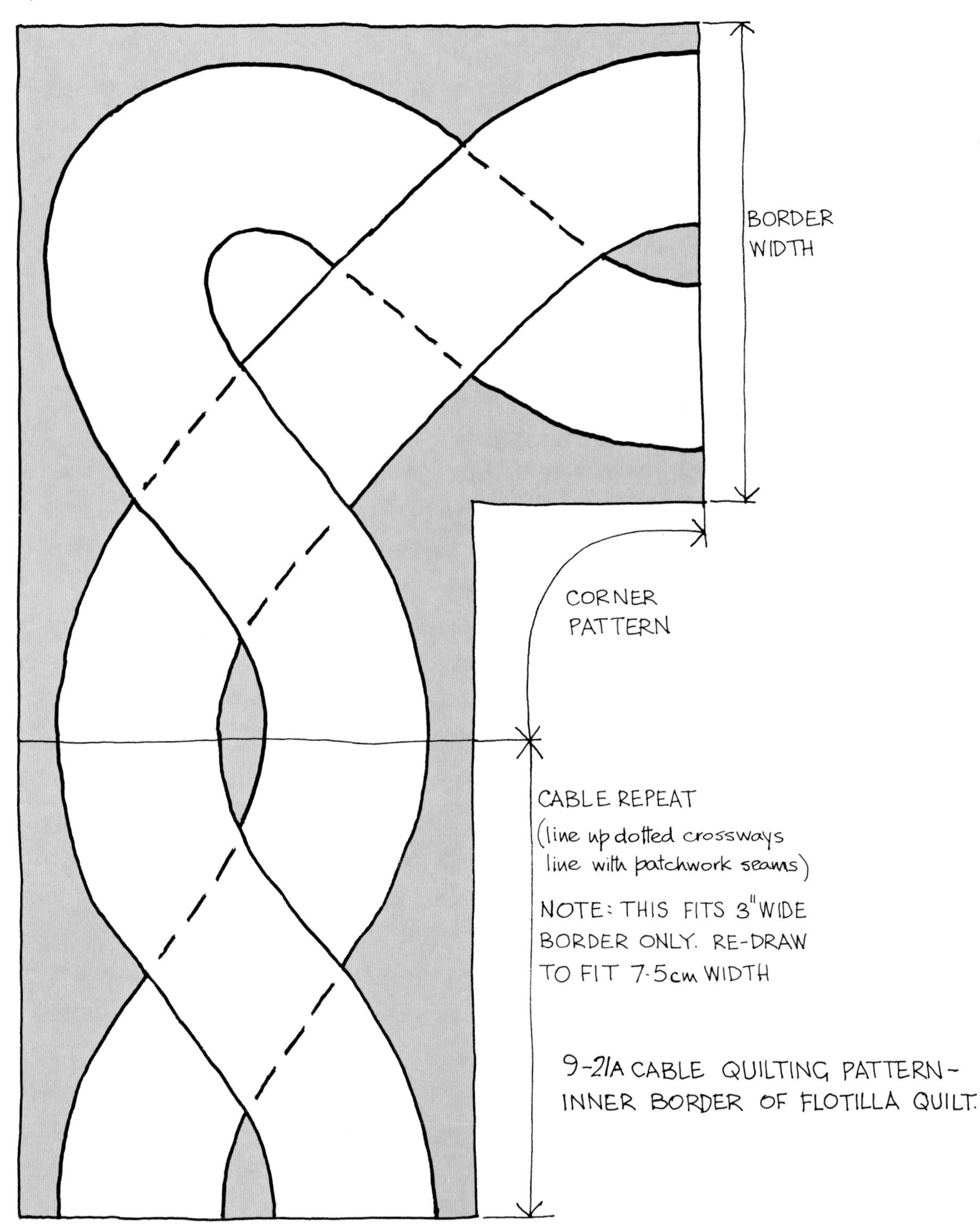

9-21A CABLE QUILTING PATTERN – INNER BORDER OF FLOTILLA QUILT.

3 Sew sea to boat and boat to sky/sails.

4 Make other blocks similarly. Sew into rows of 4. Sew rows together.

5 Sew on inner borders. Sew on outer borders. PRESS.

6 LAYER for quilting. Machine quilt IN THE DITCH around all patchwork pieces and on both sides of inner border *or* omit machine quilting and HAND QUILT only.

7 Hand quilt around profile of sailboats, IN THE DITCH between borders, and within the blocks with wavy lines for sky and wave shapes for sea (9-20).

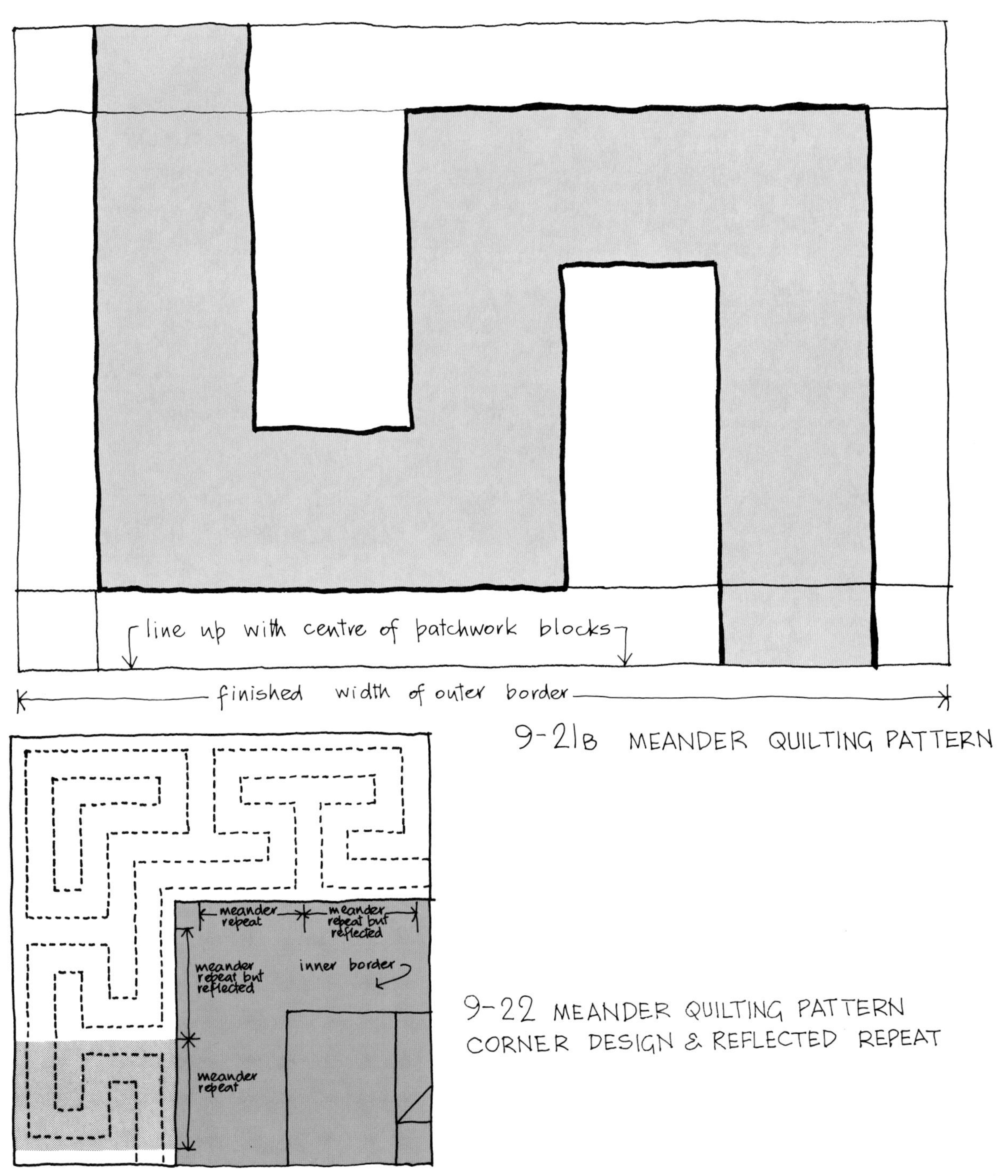

9-21B MEANDER QUILTING PATTERN

9-22 MEANDER QUILTING PATTERN CORNER DESIGN & REFLECTED REPEAT

8 Make quilting TEMPLATES (9-21A and 9-21B). MARK and quilt inner border, then outer border. Take care at corners with marking outer border — you will probably need to use a ruler to extend lines from the template. The corner meander pattern is shown in Figure 9-22.

9 Trim wadding to ¾in (1.9cm) smaller than raw edge of quilt top. Turn border edges back ¾in (1.9cm) to enclose wadding. Pin. Trim backing to ½in (1.2cm) larger all round than new quilt edge. Turn under ⅝in (1.5cm) on backing and hem to border.

- In working out complicated corner patterns on borders, whether in patchwork or, as here, in quilting, it is a great help to have a pair of mirror tiles hinged together with sticky tape, and use them to reproduce a corner repeat pattern.

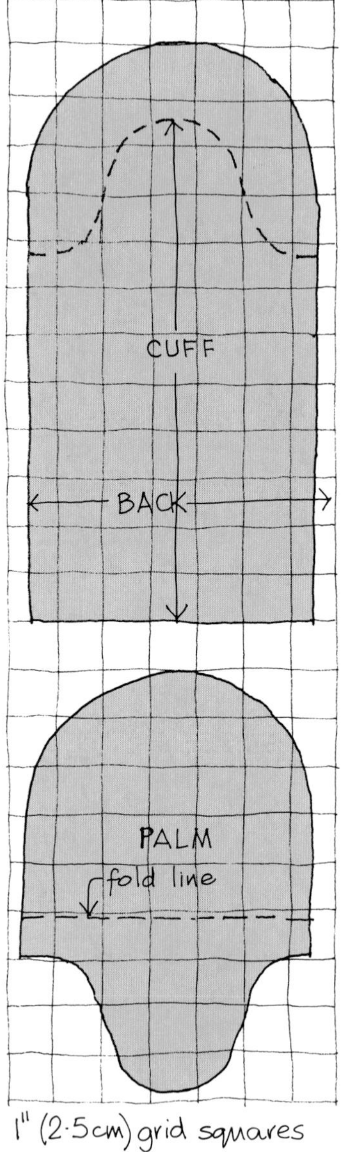

1" (2·5cm) grid squares
9-23 BARBECUE GLOVE PATTERN

FLYING GEESE BARBECUE GLOVES

This is a good way of using up practice Flying Geese, and makes a suitable present for a man who fancies himself as a barbecue chef. The extra-long cuff gives protection and the towelling wadding withstands heat well. The gloves fit either hand.

MATERIALS (for two gloves)
'Goose' fabric, 6in x 18in (15cm x 40cm).
Background fabric, ¾yd (70cm) of 44in (112cm).
Towelling, 9in x 40in (20cm x 105cm).

PREPARATION
Enlarge pattern pieces of back, palm and cuff onto squared paper (9-23).
PREPARE fabrics.
From background fabric cut 2 cuffs 6 ½in x 11in (16.2cm x 28cm); 2 palms 6 ½in x 9in (16.2 x 23); 4 strips 1 ½in x 12 ½in (3.8cm x 31.8cm); 12 squares 2 ⅞in x 2 ⅞in (7.1cm x 7.1cm) and 57in (145cm) of 2in (5cm) wide bias strip.
From 'goose' fabric cut three 5 ¼in (13cm) squares.
From towelling cut 2 pieces 7 ½in x 13in (19cm x 33 cm); 2 pieces 7 ½in x 12in (19cm x 30cm) and 4 pieces 7 ½in x 9in (19cm x 23cm).

MAKING
1 Make three 'recipes' of FLYING GEESE, using small squares of background fabric and large squares of 'goose' fabric. Sew the geese into 2 strips, each of 6 geese.
2 For one glove: sew a narrow strip of background fabric to each side of one strip of geese for the glove back.
3 Pin pieced glove back and cuff fabric onto single thickness towelling. Pin paper patterns on top and cut out. Pin palm fabric on double thickness towelling with paper pattern on top, and cut out.
4 Using DOUBLE FRENCH BINDING, bind each cuff edge. Bind thumb edges of cuff and palm together. Make fold in palm, so that length of glove back is the same as length of cuff and palm. Bind all round outside edge, making hanging loop of binding excess.
5 Make second glove in the same way.

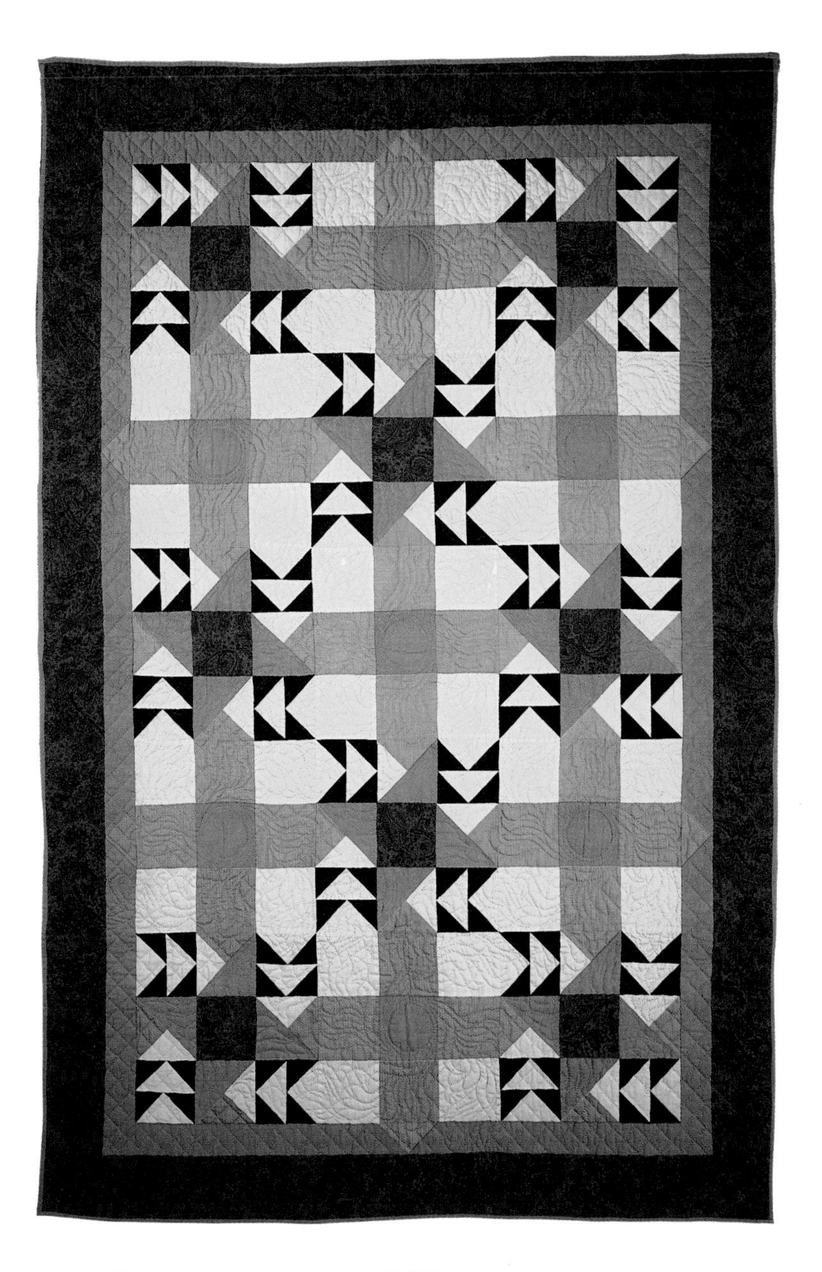

FIREWORKS WALLHANGING

This is a very fiery coloured wallhanging, large enough to double as a nap quilt. I started by doodling and found I had designed a brand new block. When this was combined with a plain 9-patch block it made definite turning patterns like catherine wheels. The choice of the first fabric — the Paisley pattern — set the colour scheme for the quilt, and the name helped to complete it.

The quilting took ages and about halfway through I decided that the quilting pattern, of small and intricate flame shapes, was much too complex and did not show up against the larger trellis pattern background quilting. Too late! This amount of quilting definitely makes a quilt both stiffer and less warm, because it compresses the wadding [batting]. Surprisingly, I found it also made the whole quilt a couple of shades darker, possibly because of the extra shadow tones from the quilting lines. Another learning experience for me. For you, I have designed a simpler quilting pattern. There is no reason, either, why you can't choose quite different colours of fabrics and make up your own quilting pattern.

MATERIALS quilt finishes 48in x 72in (120cm x 180cm)
All fabrics 44in (112cm) wide.
Orange cotton: 5¼yd (4.3m).
Orange/maroon print: 2¼yd (2.10m).
Grey cotton: 1yd (90cm).
Yellow cotton: 1¾yd (1.60m).
Navy cotton: ½yd (40cm).
2oz wadding: 52in x 76in (135cm x 195cm)
Sewing thread.
Orange quilting thread.

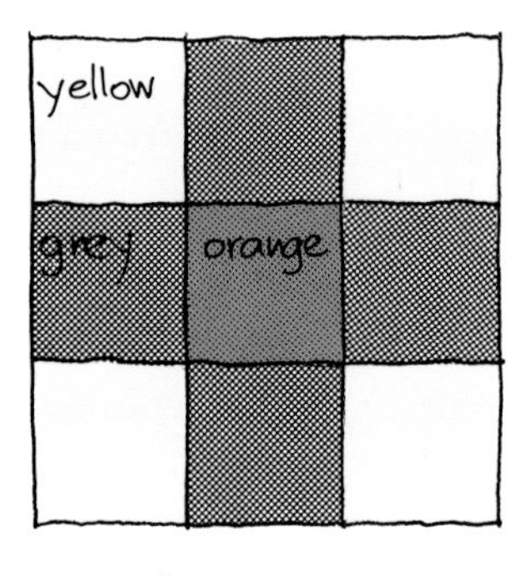

9-24 FIREWORKS QUILT, BLOCK B

PREPARATION
PREPARE fabrics.
From orange fabric cut backing: 76in (193cm) x whole width and a strip 9in x 76in (23cm x 195cm). Join, press and reserve.
From remaining orange fabric cut borders 2½ in (6.3cm) wide, with mitred corners: six 21¼ in (53cm) long and two 25¼ in (63cm) long. Cut sixteen 4⅞ in (12.1cm) squares and a strip 4½ in (11.2cm) x 31½ in (78.4cm). Cut 2in (5cm) wide bias strip from remnants, 6¾ yd (6.1m) long.
From print fabric cut borders 4½ in (11.2cm) wide and with mitred ends: two 49¼ in (123cm) long and two 73¼ in (183cm) long. Reserve.
From remaining print fabric cut eight 4½ in (11.2cm) squares.
From grey fabric cut four 4½ in (11.2cm) strips across the width, and ten 5¼ in (13cm) squares.
From yellow fabric cut sixteen 5¼ in (13cm) squares and 4 strips across the width, 4½ in (11.2cm) wide.
From navy fabric cut 64 squares, of side 2⅞ in (6.2cm).

9-25 FIREWORKS QUILT, BLOCK A

MAKING
1 Make 7 Block Bs first (9-24). This is a 9-patch, so STRIP PIECE yellow-grey-yellow strips and grey-orange-grey strips. SLICE SERIES across in 4 ½in (11.2cm) slices, 14 of yellow-grey-yellow and 7 of grey-orange-grey. RE-PIECE to make blocks.
2 Make 8 Block A's (9-25). Start with FLYING GEESE for the four corners. Two 'recipes' are needed for each block, with geese joined together in pairs. Make 8 'squares' of QUICK MACHINE-PIECED QUARTER-SQUARE TRIANGLES, having yellow fabric on top, and sewing on the anti-clockwise side of diagonals (9-10). Cut the 16 orange squares in half diagonally. Piece the resulting orange triangles to the smaller grey-yellow triangle pairs. Assemble block in three rows of three UNIT SQUARES. Join rows.
3 Join blocks in rows, following layout (9-26). Join rows of blocks.
4 Cut remaining grey squares twice across diagonally into 4 triangles each. Lay out inner border strips with 6 grey triangle pieces in place. Stitch grey triangles to border strips. Stitch inner borders to pieced top. Do not stitch mitred corners yet.
5 Sew outer borders to inner borders. Stitch MITRED CORNERS. PRESS.
6 MARK quilting pattern onto quilt top (9-27). (1in [2.5cm] diagonal quilting lines are drawn while work is in progress.) LAYER for quilting. QUILT.
7 Trim wadding and backing flush with edge of top. BIND with DOUBLE FRENCH BIAS BINDING.
8 If desired, sew a 3in (7.5cm) wide hanging sleeve on the back.

9-27 FIREWORKS QUILTING PATTERN

9-26 FIREWORKS QUILT LAYOUT

CHAPTER TEN

HAND-PIECING TECHNIQUES

So far, I have shown you methods which exploit quick cutting and quick piecing techniques. Some people prefer to hand piece, and there are occasions when it is relaxing, or more convenient, to have some hand piecing to do, such as on holiday or when you are away from home. Although the biggest breakthroughs in new patchwork techniques have been with machine piecing, it is still useful to understand hand piecing methods as well.

There are two distinct methods of hand piecing — the American, which joins patches with a small running stitch, and the English, which joins them with an oversewing stitch after they have been stabilised by tacking [basting] over paper shapes ('papers'). Of the two, the English method is probably the more accurate but it is slower. It is also, I think, more relaxing to do than American piecing because it is not necessary to pay careful attention to maintaining an accurate seam allowance, and the patch cutting does not need to be so accurate, either.

AMERICAN PIECING

In America, patchwork patterns were traditionally cut from a folded square of paper which was the size of the finished BLOCK. Using these paper patterns, PATCHES of fabric were then cut with an added seam allowance which was judged by eye. When the patches were sewn together, the seam allowances were again judged by eye. This often resulted in piecing which was very inaccurate indeed, as you will see if you look at old quilts. Even so, experienced quilters became able to judge their usual seam allowance very accurately.

In another method, cardboard templates were cut to the finished size of each piece, and these were used to draw the seamline on the wrong side of the fabric. But cardboard is rather soft, and repeatedly drawing round them wore them out (particularly the corners and points) so that the markings became more and more inaccurate.

However, marking round template pieces is still a very good way of starting for hand piecing, and a special see-through template plastic is now available from quilting suppliers which will last indefinitely. A good accurate alternative is to make the templates from graph paper glued onto the smooth side of sandpaper. This has the advantage that the materials are more easily obtained, and the sandpaper has a good gripping surface on the fabric. Sandpaper templates, although not as long-lived as plastic ones, should certainly last long enough to mark out the patches for a whole quilt.

When marking, the pencil should be kept sharp — or use a propelling pencil with a 0.5mm lead which will not need sharpening. Sewing on a pencil line drawn round a template is as accurate in its way as sewing a scant ¼in (6mm) seam by machine.

MAKING TEMPLATES

Study your desired block design to find out how many different template shapes will be required, and whether any will need reversing. Draw out enough of the block full size on paper to include all the pattern shapes once. If you use graph paper it will be easy to be accurate. Figure 10-1 shows the FIREWORKS block from the last chapter, with a heavy line drawn round one piece of each shape or size. Notice that you have three different triangle shapes, and that the FLYING GEESE in the corner square are the same size triangle as the

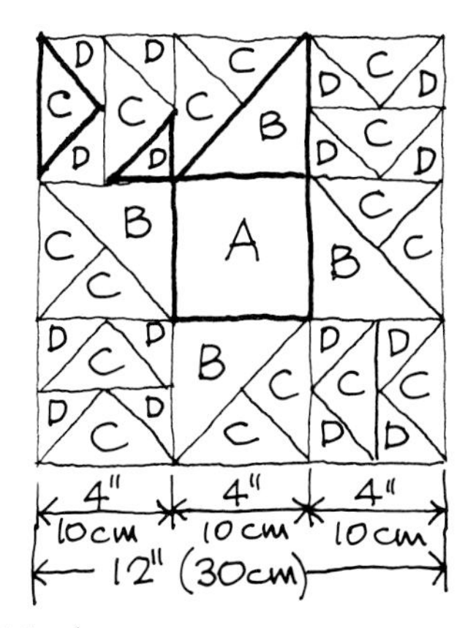

10-1 DRAWING-OUT PATCHWORK BLOCK

quarter-square triangles marked C.

Either lay a piece of template plastic over the drawing and trace each piece required onto the plastic, **or** glue the graph paper onto the smooth side of fine sandpaper.

Before cutting the templates, be sure to mark GRAINLINES; and, remembering that the templates will be used to mark the back of your fabric, make sure you know (or adjust for) any asymmetrical or reversing templates by marking accordingly or by cutting other side up. On a piece of paper note how many times each piece will be used for each colour in the block.

Cut out the templates with a craft knife and steel rule (or with strong paper scissors if you can cut straight enough).

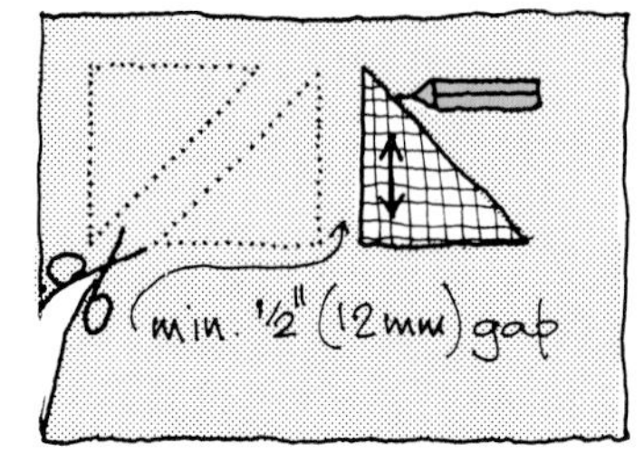

10-2 MARKING AROUND TEMPLATE

MARKING AND CUTTING

For marking, use whatever shows best (but never ballpoint pen). A soft 0.5mm propelling pencil, or silver or white coloured pencil, are all likely to be right at one time or another, and should be kept sharp.

PREPARE fabrics and lay one piece on a firm surface, wrong side up. If you wish to cut more than one layer, they should be stacked wrong side up and pinned to prevent shifting when cutting.

Lay template on fabric, allowing ¼in (6mm) margin on all sides. Draw round template, holding it down firmly meanwhile to prevent it shifting (10-2). Do not press or drag the pencil too much, or the fabric may cockle and shift. Place template as economically as possible, but at least ½in (1.2cm) from any shape already drawn. If you are unsure about judging a seam allowance, mark it too, using either a brass ¼in roller guide or a ¼in wide seam marker while the template is still in position on the fabric. So far there are no equivalent metric tools.

Scissors are now obtainable from quilting supply stores which will cut through up to 6 or more layers of dress-weight cotton fabrics. This can save time and effort in cutting out for a large project, although cutting with scissors can never be as accurate as with a rotary cutter, especially on the bias.

Cut out all patchwork pieces, and store carefully awaiting use.

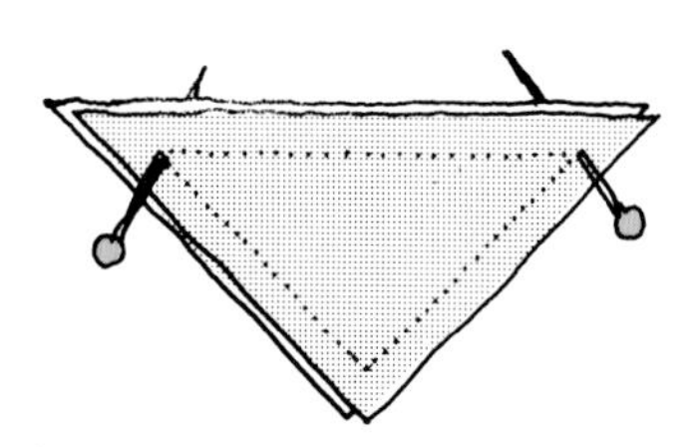

10-3 PINNING THROUGH SEAM CORNERS

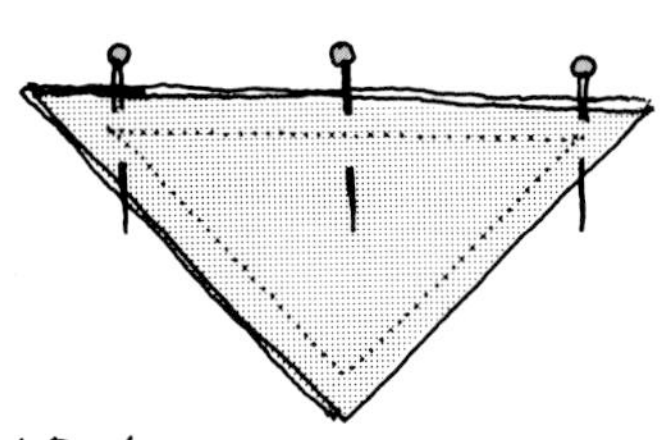

10-4 EXTRA PINNING

ASSEMBLY AND SEWING

The block is assembled in the same order as in machine piecing, with patches being joined to make subsections, always with the idea of only sewing straight seams.

Take your first two patches. Make sure that all the seam lines have been drawn on the wrong side, and put pins vertically through both pieces at each end of both seam lines (10-3). Check alignment and pin more fully (10-4) if the seam is a long one. Use a thread matching darker fabric (cotton on cotton, otherwise synthetic). Make a small backstitch at the first corner, and sew with a RUNNING STITCH (10-5), finishing with a couple of backstitches at the other corner. Check as you go that your sewing remains on the drawn line on both front and back patches. This can be a remarkably fast method, using the hand holding the fabric to wiggle it onto the needle. Stopping the seam short of the edges of the fabric enables choices to be made later as to which way the seams are to be pressed. Never press handsewn seams open, as the wadding will show through and may tuft out.

The seam allowance may be judged by eye ('eyeballed') when sewing but I wouldn't recommend it unless you are very experienced.

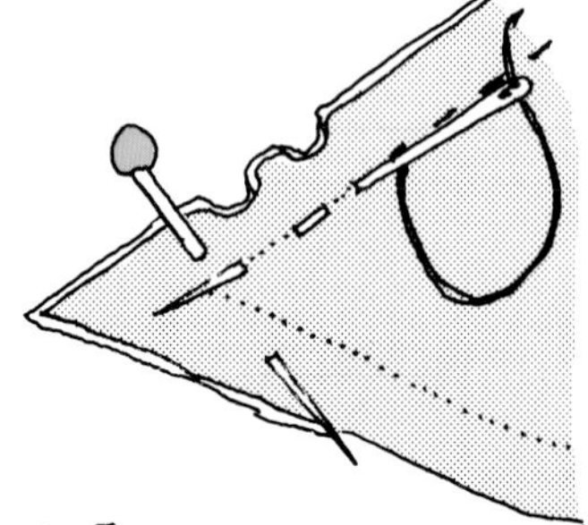

10-5 RUNNING STITCH

ENGLISH PIECING OVER PAPERS

The best known shape pieced by this method is the hexagon, which is difficult to sew by conventional straight seaming because it has shapes where the corner of one piece has to be sewn into the corner made by two other pieces. The method is also used for diamonds, squares, octagons etc, and also for conventional blocks or curved seam patchwork.

You will need an accurate template for each shape, which will be used as a pattern for cutting thick paper or thin card 'papers'. Templates should be robust enough to stand up to being repeatedly drawn or cut around. They must also be highly accurate, because any slight inaccuracy in size or shape will make piecing difficult, and the final patchwork less attractive. For this reason I recommend buying ready-made metal templates. These often come with a companion 'window' template, which is used to lay over patterned fabric to select where motifs should go, before cutting out patches, and which can also be used to mark out seam allowances. If you cannot get a template in the size or shape required, draw it out very carefully onto template plastic, and cut it out equally carefully.

Prepare a quantity of papers. You do this either by drawing round the template with a sharp pencil (10-6), and then cutting out with paper scissors, or holding the template firmly to the paper and cutting with the scissors pressed close to the edge of the template (10-7). This second method is really only suitable when the template is made of metal, otherwise bits could be shaved off it when cutting papers, and it would end up inaccurate!

10-6 DRAWING ROUND TEMPLATE BEFORE CUTTING

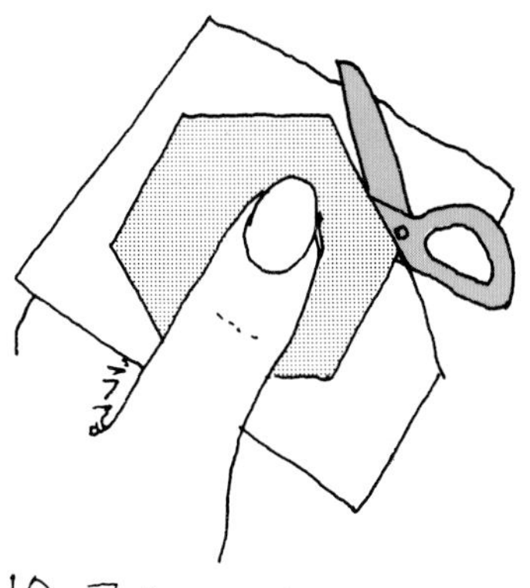
10-7 CUTTING FROM TEMPLATE DIRECTLY

CUTTING

Cut patches ¼in (6mm) larger on each side than the template (10-8). Make sure any motifs are correctly placed, and stripes run in the right direction on the patch to get the effect you intend. Sort and store patches by threading all those for a block or motif onto a knotted thread.

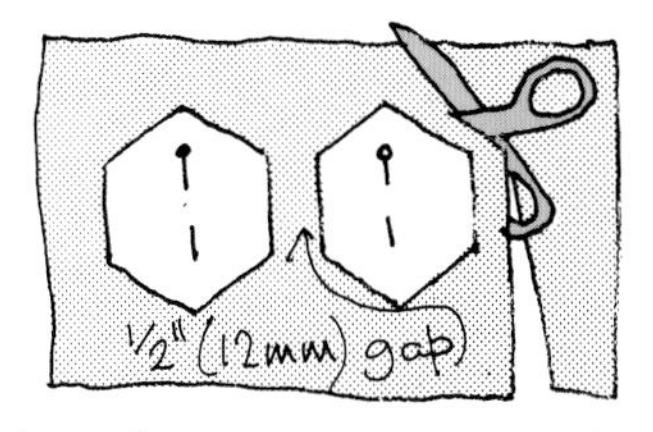

10-8 CUTTING OUT PATCHES

TACKING OVER PAPERS

Prepare patches by laying a paper centrally on the wrong side of a patch; then, holding both together (pin if you wish), turn the seam allowance on one edge over to the back and tack [baste] it down (10-9). Continue folding down and tacking each side in turn. Be careful that the fabric is snugly turned over, particularly at corners. Diamonds and triangles may need the seam allowance beyond the point turned over before the side allowances are tacked onto it.

SEWING

Take two tacked patches and hold them face to face, with corners and edges even. Stitch together using thread matching the darker of the two, with a small oversewing stitch (10-10). The aim is to go through the threads of fabric on the very edge of the fold, not through the paper at all, with stitches which should hardly be visible from the right side. Whenever a patch is completely surrounded by other patches, its tacking thread can be removed and the paper lifted out for re-use.

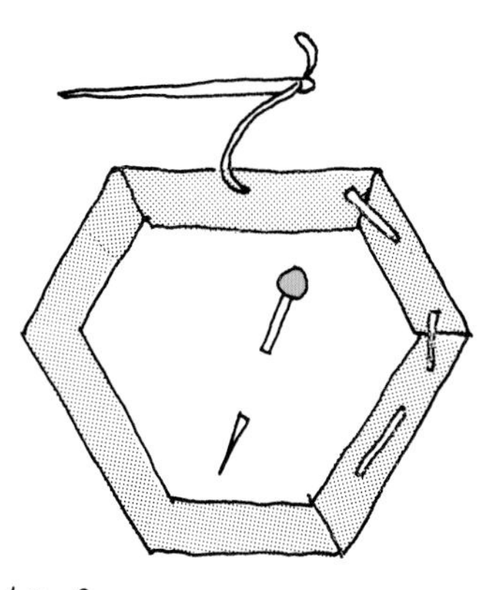
10-9 TACKING PATCH AROUND 'PAPER'

DESIGN

The commonest pattern made in this way is the hexagon 'flower' (10-13). This consists of one central hexagon surrounded by six others. Generally, the central patch is yellow or coloured, with the others patterned, striped or contrasting. A flower can be surrounded by another ring of hexagons, when the pattern is called Grandmother's Flower Garden, or it can be set with a single row of background colour hexagons between flowers. One of the difficulties of dealing with hexagon flowers is that if you start with a central one,

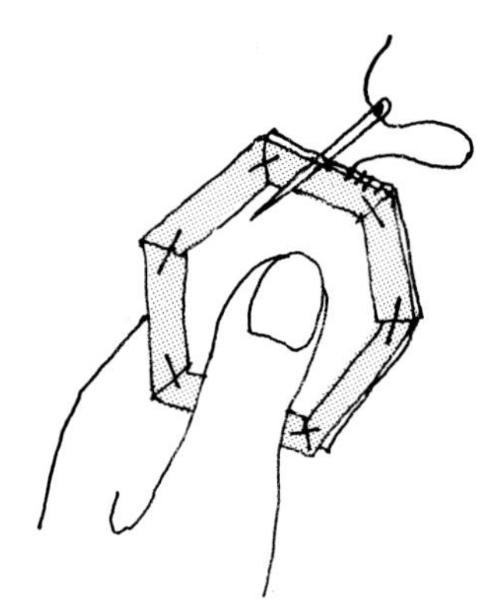

10-10 OVER-SEWING PATCH EDGES TOGETHER

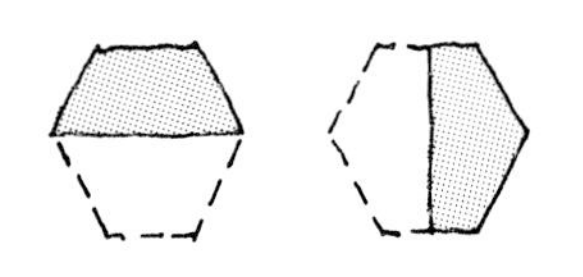

10-11 HALF HEXAGONS WILL FILL IN QUILT EDGES

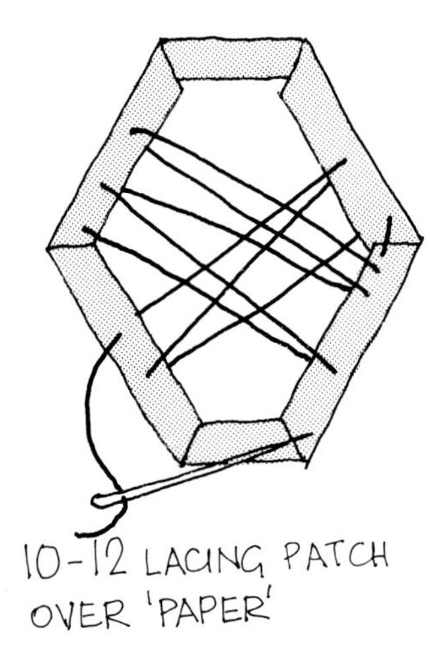

10-12 LACING PATCH OVER 'PAPER'

and make successive rings of flowers, you will end up with a large hexagon. This is not a good shape to have to cope with if you are trying to make a rectangular object like a quilt. But hexagon flowers can also be arranged in rows to run the length of a quilt, or they can be joined without any background pieces at all.

Hexagon and these other mosaic types of designs are difficult to envisage or draw. Therefore, it is a good idea to experiment with some coloured arrangements of shapes before starting to make anything. The best way to do this for hexagons is with isometric paper which should be obtainable from good quilting or draftsman's suppliers. It is like graph paper, but with lines at 60°, making an all over pattern of equilateral triangles. Six of these triangles make one hexagon.

THE EDGES

When joined together, hexagons, octagons and diamonds all finish with uneven edges. One solution is to APPLIQUÉ the patchwork onto a background fabric. This saves making some patchwork, but I don't think it looks nearly as good as running the patchwork to the edge of the quilt. Paper pieces to fill in the edge gaps can be made by halving the normal papers (10-11). If you aim to BIND the edge, don't forget to unpick [rip out] the edge tackings and press the seam allowances out before binding (or just don't tack the outside edges of any outside patches). The quilt can be completed in any of the ways shown in Chapter 14.

WORKING WITH SILK

Some of the most exciting patchwork made during the Victorian era used silks, satins and velvets. These pieces were for show rather than utility wear, and patterns such as Baby Blocks, Grandmother's Flower Garden and Crazy Patchwork were especially popular. I would not recommend trying to work with velvet over papers, because its thickness makes sharply turned corners almost impossible, and the different tones which show when the direction of the pile is altered make design complicated. Silk looks particularly lustrous, and comes in rich colours, but it is easily marked by pinning and tacking. It is better, instead, to use card rather than paper for the 'papers' and to 'lace' the turnings across the back of the card (10-12). Be careful to allow extra wide seam allowances when working with silk or similar fabrics which fray [ravel] easily. 'Changeable' silk has the warp and weft threads of different colours, making the silk itself seem to change colour depending on which way you look at it. It is beautiful but very tricky to use, and a colour layout should be drawn before cutting out patches.

FLOWER PINCUSHIONS

These pincushions are pretty, easy and quick, and make attractive gifts. They are also good practice in English piecing, before deciding whether you want to embark on a larger project. The template used can vary in size from ½in (1.2cm) to 1in (2.5cm) which is what I used for the example, or even more.

MATERIALS
Hexagon template.
Thick paper or thin card.
Scraps of cotton dress-weight fabrics.
Scraps of wadding for stuffing.
Matching thread.
Embellishments if desired

PREPARATION:
PREPARE fabrics.
Cut out 14 'PAPERS'.
From chosen fabric, CUT OUT 2 hexagons for centres and 12 for 'petals', centring any patterns, or lining up stripes as desired.

MAKING
1 Tack [baste] patches to papers (10-9). Oversew patches together (10-10) to make two 'flowers' (10-13).
2 Place 2 flowers together face to face, and oversew together round their edges, leaving part open. PRESS.
3 Remove tackings and papers and turn flowers right sides out. Make sure corners are fully turned.
4 Stuff cavity with shreds of waste wadding, filling the corners first, until well filled. Stitch the opening closed.
5 TIE just inside the corners of the centre hexagons with double thread. Small beads may be caught in the ties for decoration.

- The photograph shows one finished pincushion and two flowers waiting to be sewn together. You can see some of the different ways stripes can be used.
- Pincushions can be made with more hexagon pieces and/or other shapes such as diamonds (based on the hexagon) can be incorporated.

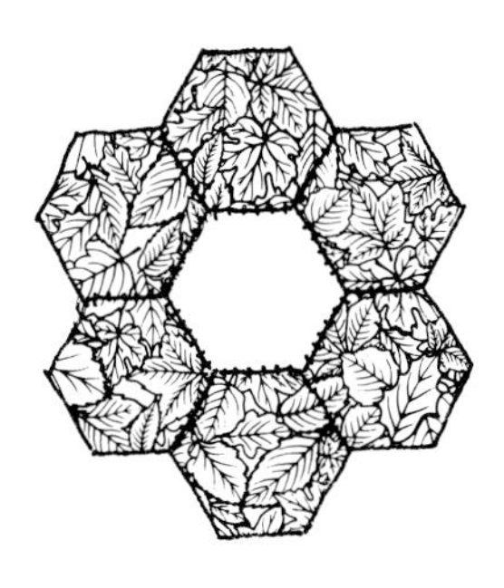

10-13 HEXAGON FLOWER

TANGRAM RAINBOW WALLHANGING

The TANGRAM (10-14) is an ancient Chinese puzzle — a square made up of seven separate black pieces which are rearranged to make many different silhouette shapes such as dogs, swans or people. It has two large triangles, one middle-sized one, two small ones, one square and one trapezoid. Sometimes it is quite a puzzle to make up the square correctly again, especially if the trapezoid has been turned upside down!

Here I had the idea of using seven rainbow colours on the seven pieces, and making a small English pieced wall picture in silks, with the templates remaining inside for stiffness. Silk marks when it is tacked, so it is generally LACED across the back of each template. Here I used pelmet Vilene® as my template material and found that the silk could be tacked if I took stitches from the back which only went part-way through the thickness of the Vilene®. Because silk frays [ravels] badly, I doubled the seam allowance to ½in (1.2cm).

MATERIALS: for wallhanging 18in (46cm) square, silks 44in (112cm) wide.
Scraps of slub silk in seven rainbow colours; the two largest triangles need ¼yd (20cm) each.
¼yd (30cm) white slub silk for 'frame'.
⅝yd (50cm) pelmet Vilene®.
White tacking [basting] thread.
Silk sewing threads to match silks.
Mounting card 18in x 18in (50cm x 50cm).
White cotton fabric, 19in (52cm) square.
White glue.

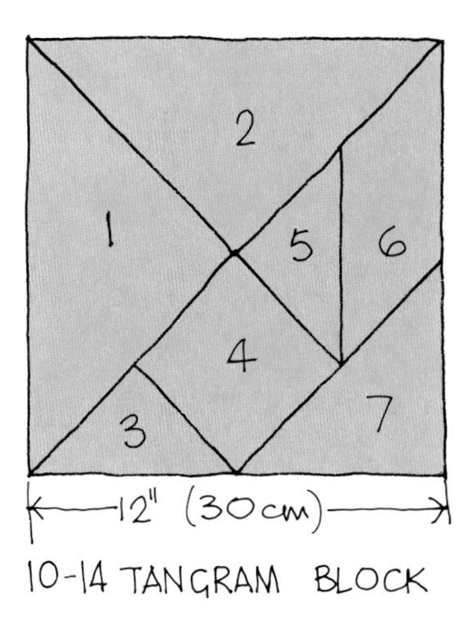

10-14 TANGRAM BLOCK

PREPARATION
Press Vilene®. Draw a 12in (30cm) square on it and draw division lines on the square as in Figure 10-14. Draw a 3in (7.5cm) border all round, with mitred corners. So that the differently shaped pieces will fit, you must cut each piece a fraction smaller, so draw new lines 1mm on each side of the first lines, and cut out carefully on the new lines. Mark the reverse side of each template piece. I didn't do this trimming down of templates on the example, and had great difficulty forcing and wrestling pieces to fit.

Press silks. Put Vilene® pieces on the wrong side of silks, with their marked sides upwards. Direction of grainline is not important for this project, as variation makes the sheen of silk more effective. Cut out, allowing ½in (1.2cm) or larger seam allowances.

MAKING
1 TACK silk pieces over Vilene® 'papers'.
2 OVERSEW together in the order 1 to 2; 3 to 4 to 5 to 6. Sew 7 to strip 3-4-5-6. Sew 1-2 to strip 3-4-5-6.
3 OVERSEW borders onto Tangram. Unpick tackings at each outside corner of border, to enable you to trim the fabric point off slightly before folding it in, followed by the two side seam allowances. Re-tack them all down.
4 Measure one side of border. Cut a square of mounting card, ½in (1.2cm) smaller than that measurement. Cut white cotton fabric into a square 2in (5cm) larger than that measurement. Lay card onto wrong side of cotton, and glue edges of cotton over onto card, mitreing corners.
5 Holding wrong sides of Tangram and backing together, sew through edge of cotton fabric into seam allowance of Tangram border. Make a HANGING LOOP.

KALEIDOSCOPE CUSHION

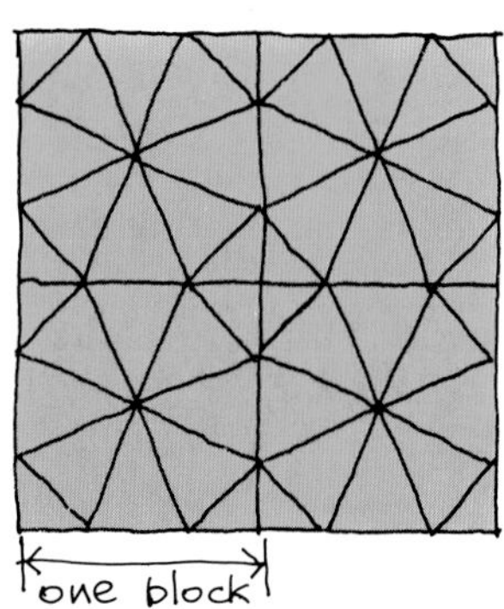

10-15 KALEIDOSCOPE PATTERN

The Kaleidoscope is a fascinating pattern with exciting possibilities for swirling colour-movement. My dictionary describes the kaleidoscope as "an optical instrument in which one sees an ever-changing variety of beautiful colours and forms", which I think just about sums it up. This cushion was started at a workshop with Mary Golden, who is an expert on the pattern. I'm afraid I was a bad student and didn't keep to the rules, so my cushion is really only loosely based on the real pattern (10-15). I took cut-out patches of the two shapes, the octagon triangle and the corner triangle, and played around with them until I had something interesting (10-16). If this block was going to be repeated many times, you could simplify it by eliminating some of the seams (10-17). The cushion [pillow] is small so, to set off the pattern, I made a little projecting border for it.

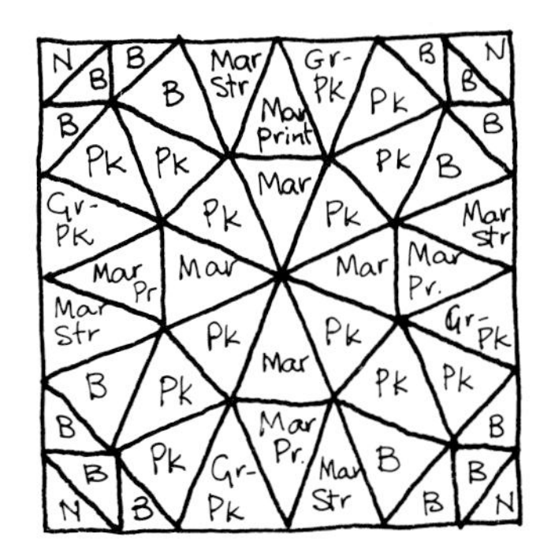

10-16 KALEIDOSCOPE CUSHION LAYOUT

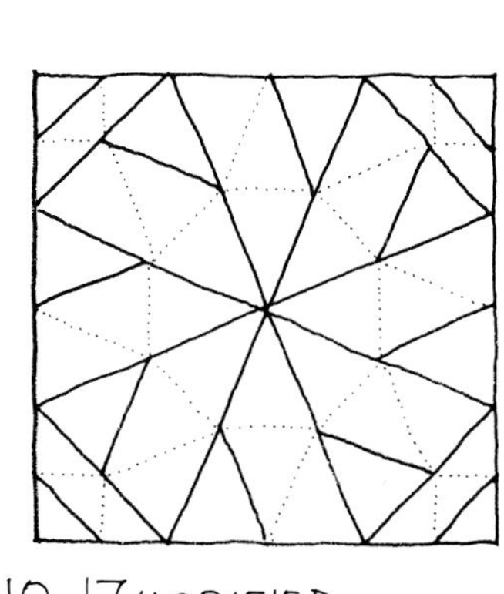

10-17 MODIFIED CUSHION BLOCK

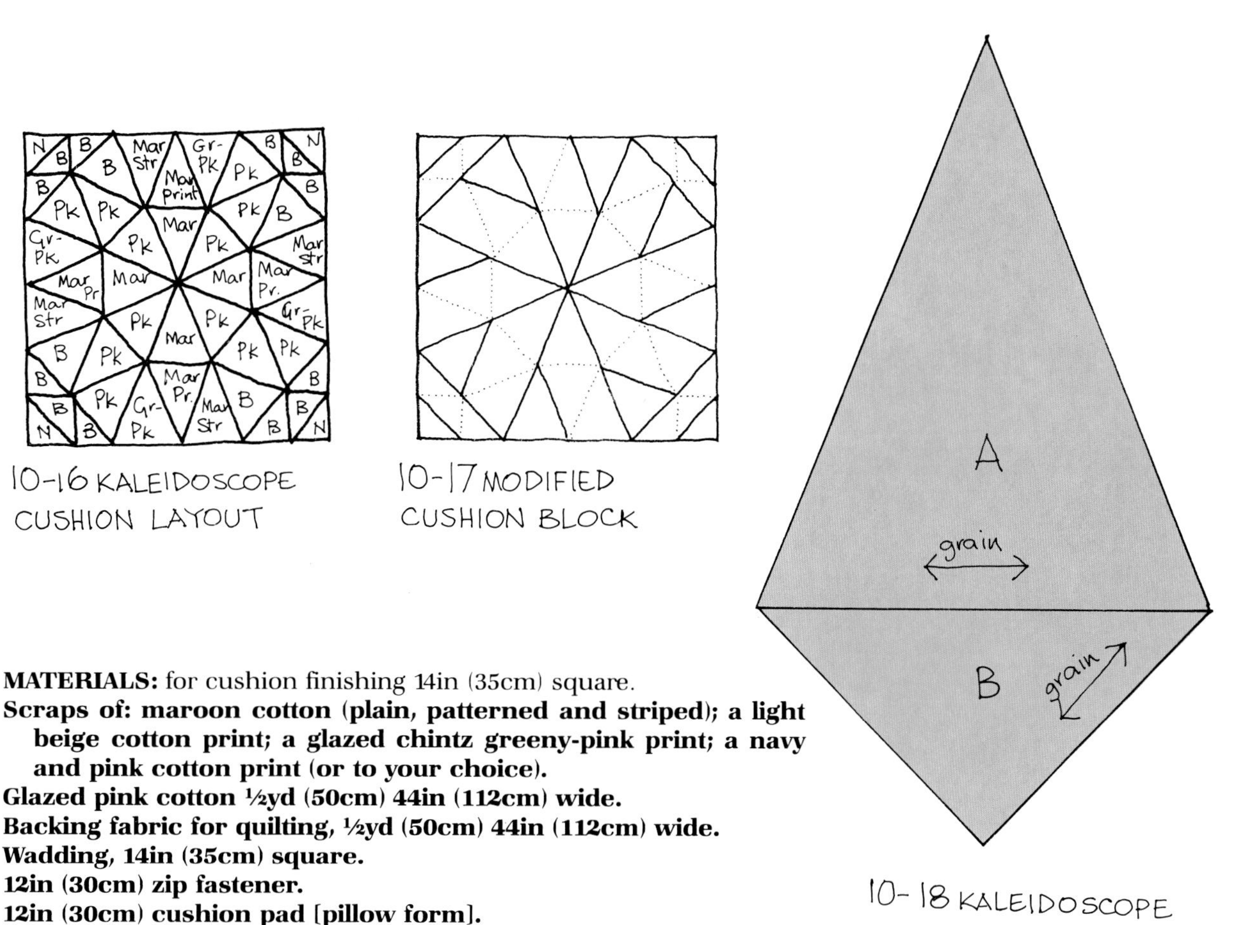

10-18 KALEIDOSCOPE TEMPLATES

MATERIALS: for cushion finishing 14in (35cm) square.
Scraps of: maroon cotton (plain, patterned and striped); a light beige cotton print; a glazed chintz greeny-pink print; a navy and pink cotton print (or to your choice).
Glazed pink cotton ½yd (50cm) 44in (112cm) wide.
Backing fabric for quilting, ½yd (50cm) 44in (112cm) wide.
Wadding, 14in (35cm) square.
12in (30cm) zip fastener.
12in (30cm) cushion pad [pillow form].

PREPARATION
Trace triangle templates (10-18 A and B) onto template plastic and cut out.
PREPARE fabrics.
MARK and cut (shape A) 12 pink, and 4 each in maroon, maroon print, maroon stripe, greeny-pink print and light beige print, adding seam allowances.
Mark and cut (shape B) 12 light beige print and 4 navy/pink print.
From pink, cut out borders, 4 strips 2in x 16in (5cm x 40cm), and cushion backs, one 14 ½in x 13in (37cm x 35cm) and one 14 ½in x 2¾in (37cm x 5cm).
From backing fabric cut one 14in (35cm) square.

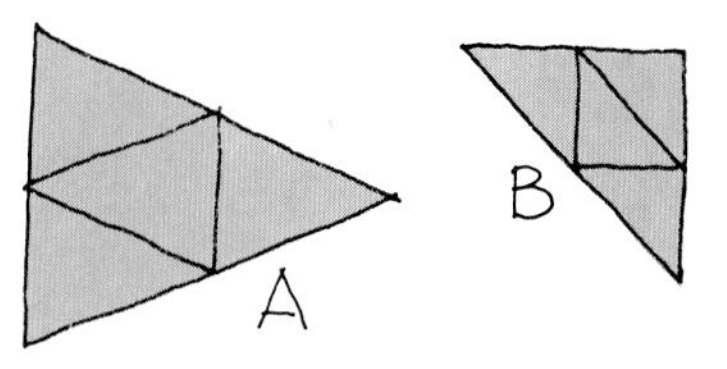

10-19 SECTIONS OF KALEIDOSCOPE

MAKING
1 Lay out patches in pattern (10-16). HAND PIECE into triangular centre sections (10-19A) and corner sections (10-19B). Join centre sections into pairs, pairs into fours and two sets of fours together, remembering not to sew beyond marked corners at the end of lines. Sew B sections to pink As to complete corners of block.
2 PRESS from back, making seams spiral around centre, and then as they seem to prefer.
3 LAYER patchwork and wadding for quilting. QUILT ¼in (6mm) inside seamlines, or as preferred. (I MARKED concentric octagons at 1in (2.5cm) spacings).
4 Attach borders to patchwork, by machine. MITRE corners.
5 INSERT ZIP FASTENER into backing pieces.
6 SEW back to front (trim if necessary) with ¼in (6mm) seam. Turn right side out. Stitch again ¾in (2cm) from outside edge of border. Insert cushion pad.

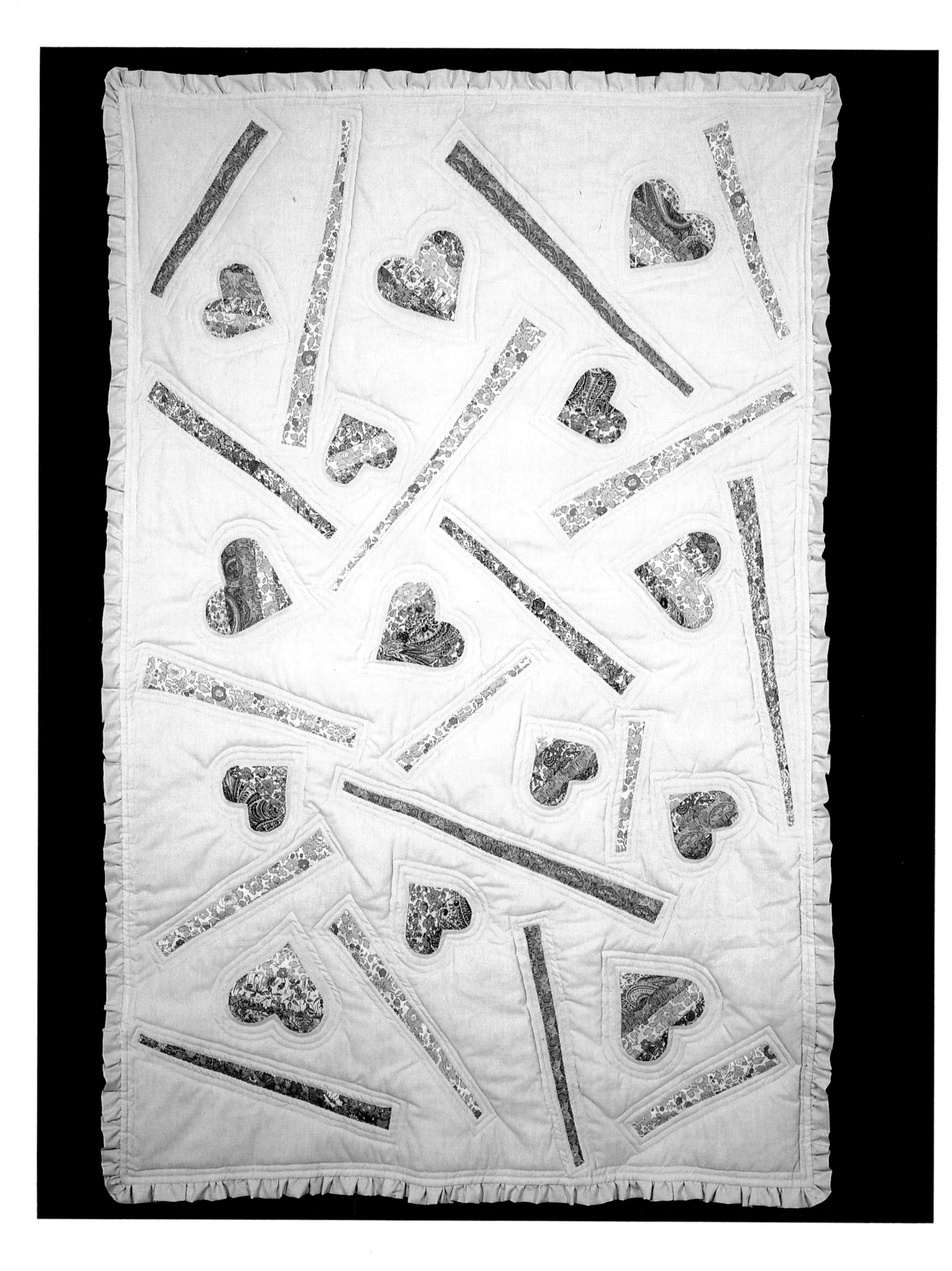

CHAPTER ELEVEN

APPLIQUÉ

Appliqué is the technique of sewing shaped pieces of fabric to the surface of a background fabric (onlay) or, in reverse appliqué, behind a shaped hole in the background fabric (underlay). Appliqué is mostly used pictorially, as it lends itself to curved and intricate shapes which would be difficult if not impossible to piece. Appliqué can be done by hand or machine in several different ways. Some methods need seam allowances added to the motifs, others don't, and some even combine hand and machine sewing.

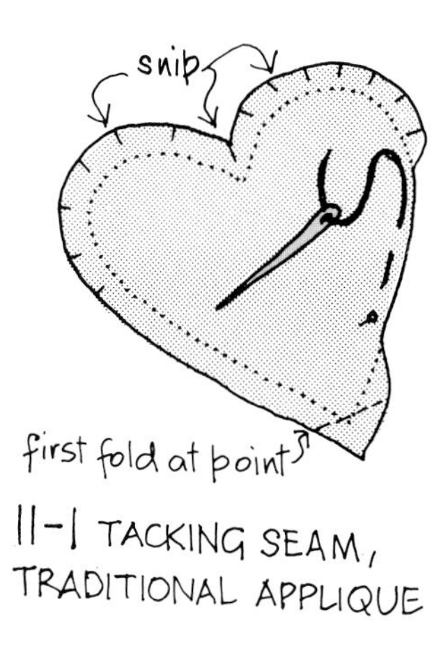

11-1 TACKING SEAM, TRADITIONAL APPLIQUE

BEFORE YOU START

The best fabric to use for appliqué is a fine pure cotton, as it holds a folded edge well. The background fabric in onlay and any underlay fabric which does not have to be cut and hemmed, can be a blend.

Some patterns involve lapping one appliqué piece over part of another. On any patch, there is no need to turn under any seam allowance on any part which will be covered by another patch.

Make sure to PREPARE all fabrics before starting and, when you have finished, press from the back, over thick padding, to prevent shine on the seams.

It is traditional to align the GRAINLINES of background and appliqué pieces. This is not always possible if, for instance, printed motifs are being appliquéd on the splay. Billowing or puckering of the appliqué pieces can be prevented by snipping out the background fabric inside the seam allowance, after the pieces have been stitched on. If you plan to QUILT over the motif, then this snipping out will help by reducing the number of thicknesses of fabric that have to be quilted through.

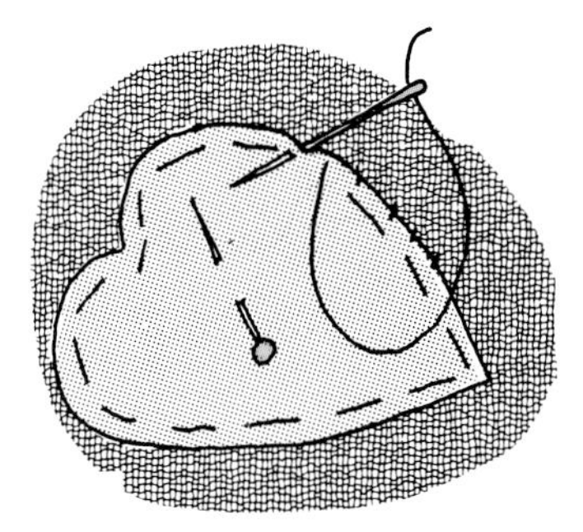
11-2 HEMMING STITCH

TRADITIONAL HAND APPLIQUÉ 1

1 TRACE pattern shapes onto the right side of the fabric, leaving ½in (1.2cm) space between motifs. Cut pieces ¼in (6mm) larger than drawn.

2 Turn seam allowances under on the drawn line and tack [baste] them. In order to get smooth curves, you will find that the seam allowance will need to be clipped at intervals, nearly to the drawn line. At inside corners, you must clip almost fully into the corner and, on outside corners, fold the point under before turning the sides in (11-1).

3 If the pattern is complicated, trace the whole of it onto the right side of the background fabric. Otherwise mark sufficient guide points to enable you to place the appliqué pieces correctly.

4 Position the prepared pieces on your background fabric. Pin (tack if desired) and appliqué the first layer of pieces. Use a small HEMMING stitch (11-2) or BLIND HEMMING (slipstitch) (11-3) and match thread to upper fabric. Follow with further layers of pieces if the design calls for them. Take out tacking threads. PRESS from the back.

11-3 BLIND HEMMING

TRADITIONAL HAND APPLIQUÉ 2

The appliqué pieces are cut exactly to their finished shapes, and pinned, tacked or lightly glued (use a washable fabric glue stick) to the background fabric. Sew them down with a close BUTTONHOLE (11-4) stitch, using a matching or contrasting thread, or decorative embroidery thread. This encloses and protects the raw edges.

11-4 BUTTONHOLE

11-5 FREEZER PAPER APPLIQUE

11-6 MACHINING ROUND FREEZERPAPER PATTERN

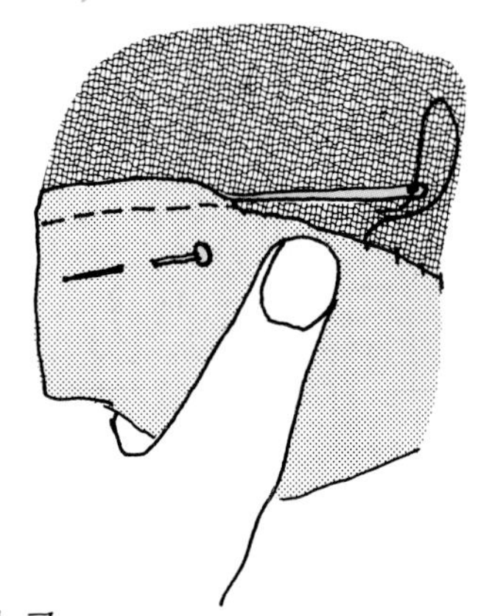
11-7 NEEDLE-TURNING SEAM ALLOWANCE UNDER

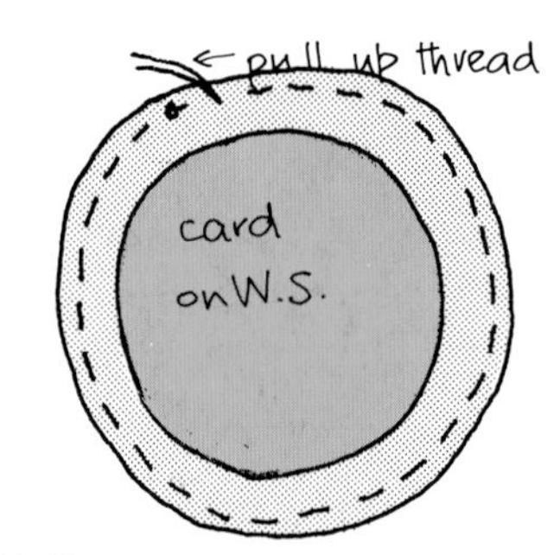

11-8 GATHERING SEAM ALLOWANCE

MODERN HAND APPLIQUÉ 1

Anne Oliver invented this very precise freezer paper method. It was used (with her dogwood design) in the centre of PENNY'S DOGWOOD TRAIL.

1 Draw or trace the appliqué shapes onto the dull side of freezer paper. Pin the dull side of the paper pieces to the wrong side of the appliqué fabrics and use as patterns for cutting out. Make sure to cut out ¼in (6mm) bigger all round for the seam allowance.

2 Using the tip of a dry iron, carefully press seam allowance over onto the paper, where it will be held (11-5). Curves and corners will need to be clipped, as before. If the seam allowance doesn't go down evenly, it may be gently lifted off the paper and re-pressed. Remove pins.

3 Position the appliqué shapes on the background fabric. Press again so that the freezer paper sticks the shapes lightly to the background. Hem down. From the back, carefully cut out the background fabric *only* behind and within the appliqué shape, and remove freezer paper pattern. Or if you don't want to cut the background fabric, sew nearly all round the piece, then ease out the paper through the unsewn gap with a long needle or pin before completing sewing. PRESS.

MODERN HAND APPLIQUÉ 2

This is my freezer paper method. It is a little unorthodox in that it combines machine stitching with hand appliqué, but I think the end justifies the means. It is very quick and accurate, and the machined line makes it easy to do smooth curves. Choose this technique if you don't see so well (trust the machine stitched line!) or if your hand control is not so good. I did the hearts in HEARTSTRINGS COT QUILT by this method.

1 Trace pattern shapes onto the dull side of freezer paper. Cut out. Iron them lightly onto the right side of the appliqué fabric, leaving at least ½in (1.2cm) between pieces. Cut out fabric ¼in (6mm) larger all round than pattern pieces.

2 Using thread which matches appliqué pieces, machine stitch all round the paper patterns, with the needle just off the edge of the paper, but touching it (11-6). Peel off the paper (which can be re-used several times) and pin pieces in position on background fabric.

3 Hold the work with the seam allowance facing away from you, and turn a short length of seam allowance under with your needle, using the stitched line as a help and guide, but making sure that it ends up hidden just under the fold. Hold the turned length down with your thumb, and stitch it down before continuing 'NEEDLE TURNING' and stitching. Curves and corners will need clipping, as before (11-7).

MODERN HAND APPLIQUÉ 3

This is specially good for round patches, even quite small ones.

1 Cut a card template the finished size of the patch. Cut a patch with ⅜in (10mm) seam allowance. Run a gathering thread round the patch, ⅛in (3mm) in from edge.

2 Lay the card template centrally on the wrong side of the patch. Pull up the gathering thread, making sure the gathers are even all round (11-8). PRESS well. Ease off the gathering thread tension and remove the card for re-use. Trim off ¼in (6mm) of seam allowance. Position the patch (11-9) on the background fabric, pin and stitch down.

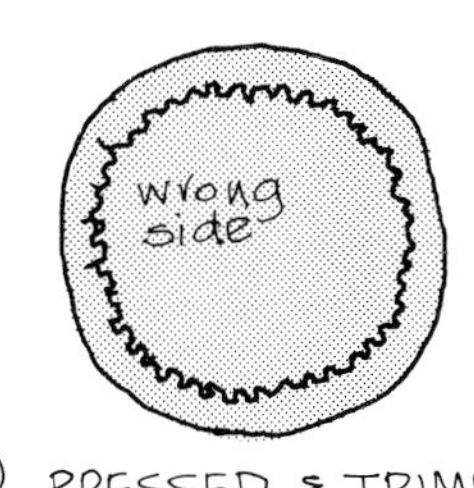

11-9 PRESSED & TRIMMED CIRCULAR PATCH

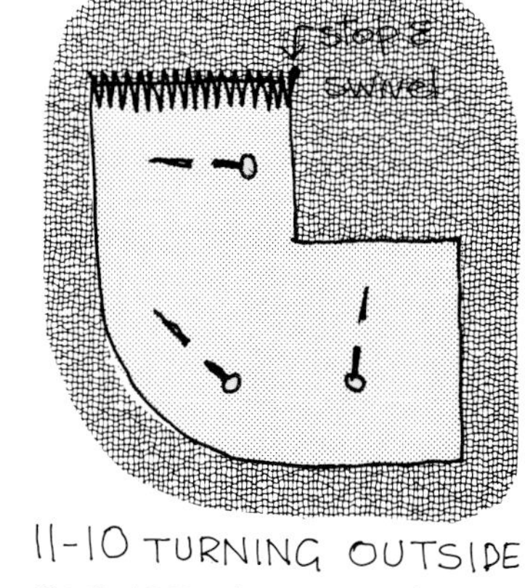

11-10 TURNING OUTSIDE CORNER, MACHINE APPLIQUE

MACHINE APPLIQUÉ 1 (swing-needle machine)

This is the simplest method and, done by experts, is suitable for the finest work, particularly when stabilised with fusible webbing. It will withstand laundering and is good for motifs and patches on children's clothes or wallhangings. The CHILDREN'S SHOEBAGS were made using this method.

1 Cut out the appliqué pieces without any seam allowance. Position them on background fabric and pin or tack. For difficult shapes use fabric glue stick or fusible webbing to hold them in place.

2 Set your sewing machine to satin stitch — generally a stitch length of nearly 0 with a width of less than ⅛in (about 2mm). Most makes of sewing machine have slightly different quirks, so check the instructions in your sewing machine handbook for settings, threads, needle type and size etc, and do a bit of practice on spare fabric.

3 Satin stitch around appliqué patch so that the outside edge of the satin stitch just covers the cut edge of the patch. To turn at outside corners, stitch to the edge of the fabric. Stop, with the needle down in the outside position. Lift presser foot and swivel fabric (11-10). Lower presser foot and continue sewing. For an inside corner, sew ⅛in (2mm) past the corner, and stop with the needle down in the inside position. Lift presser foot and swivel fabric (11-11). Lower presser foot and continue sewing. For curves, do not try to wrestle the fabric round, but sew in a series of short, straight runs; on outside curves stop with the needle down in the background fabric outside before making an adjustment in direction, and on inside curves stop with the needle down in the appliqué fabric before changing direction. When complete, trim away any whiskery appliqué threads if necessary.

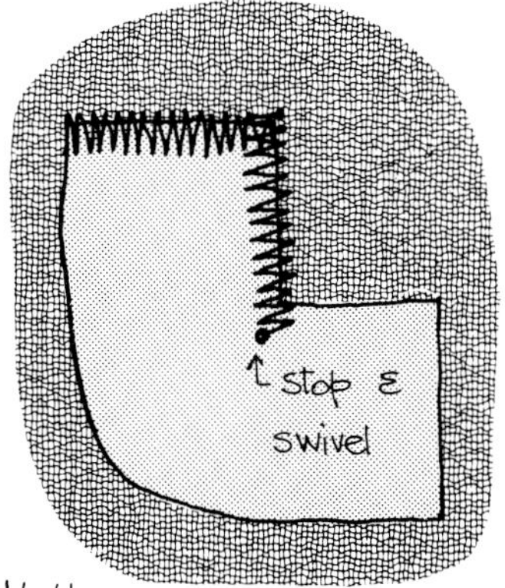

11-11 TURNING INSIDE CORNER, MACHINE APPLIQUÉ

MACHINE APPLIQUÉ 2

This is another of my own techniques and I much prefer it to the last method, as the freezer paper is a temporary stabiliser for the patch and does not permanently stiffen it. I used it for the TULIPS TOTE.

1 Cut pattern shapes from freezer paper. Press onto right side of fabric, leaving ½in (1.2cm) between shapes. Cut out patches with ¼in (6mm) seam allowance.

2 Position papered patch on background fabric and pin in place. Machine stitch all round paper pattern, through fabrics only but as close as possible to paper (11-12). Peel off paper (which may be re-used several times). With small, sharp-pointed scissors, carefully trim off almost all of the seam allowance from the patch. Set machine to satin stitch and appliqué patch on, covering machined guide-line and raw edge.

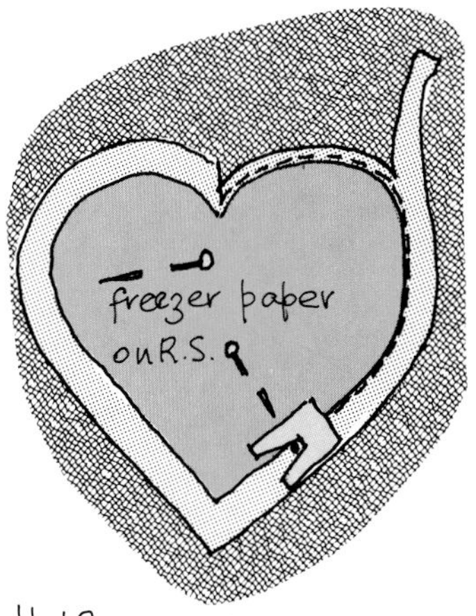

11-12 SEWING FREEZER-PAPERED PATCH TO BACKGROUND

MACHINE APPLIQUÉ 3

This one is good for squares, rectangles or easy curves, but not so easy for intricate shapes, because of the difficulty in keeping the needle exactly the right distance from the fabric edge. To do it, you must have a sewing machine that can 'blind hem'. I used this technique to appliqué the strings in HEARTSTRINGS COT QUILT.

1 Cut out patches with seam allowance added. Turn under seam allowances by whichever method you find easiest. Press.

2 Pin or tack patch to background fabric. Set sewing machine to blind hem (see machine handbook). Use thread to match background fabric, or invisible thread. Position needle so that straight stitches are sewn on background fabric and jump-sideways stitches catch the edge of the appliqué patch (11-13).

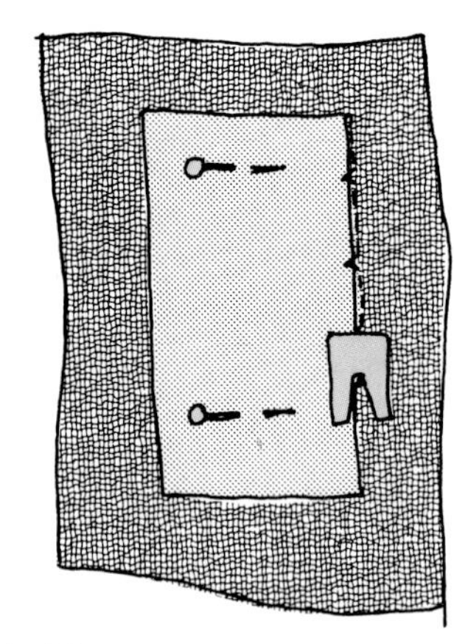

11-13 BLIND HEMMING MACHINE APPLIQUÉ

REVERSE APPLIQUÉ USING GREASEPROOF PAPER

This is Herta Puls' method which she developed for reproducing Kuna Indian work. Their blouses (or Molas) are decorated with panels of colourful and complicated multi-layered appliqués. The panels are now often (and wrongly) called Molas as well. This is a particularly useful technique for similar complicated reverse appliqué designs, as the pattern is marked and the layers of fabric held all at the same time. It is also very good for pointed leaf shapes, which are easier to sew in reverse appliqué than regular appliqué. This was the technique I used in making JUNGLY PUSSY.

Greaseproof paper is transparent enough to trace through, robust enough to stitch through, and easy to remove afterwards by scoring the surface with the point of a needle or pin. Alternatives could be tissue paper, or thinnest drafting or tracing paper. Try them if you can't obtain greaseproof paper.

Use fine pure cotton fabric for best results, and do not have any part of your design motifs narrower than ¼in (6mm) unless you are capable of handling a seam allowance of less than ⅛in (3mm)! The ⅛in (3mm) seam allowance is standard for this technique. You may feel you need a larger seam allowance, but the method is so easy and exact, I think you will find you can manage it.

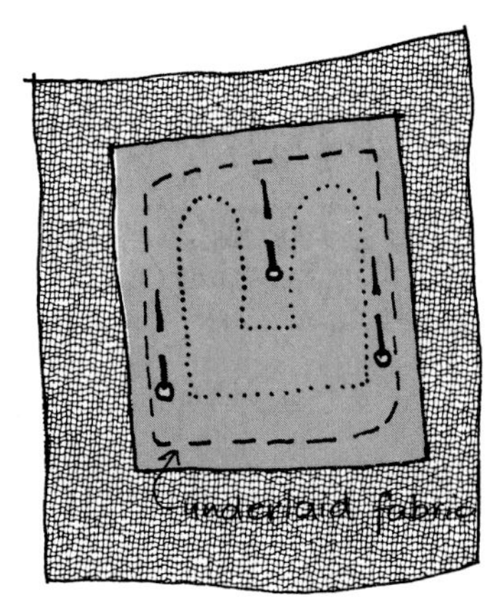

11-14 POSITIONING GREASEPROOF PAPER PATTERN

1 Draw out your pattern carefully on paper, and colour it with crayons or felt pens to keep for reference. Trace all the pattern onto greaseproof paper. With care in handling the greaseproof paper, only one tracing should be necessary, even if you plan to use several colours.

2 PREPARE all fabrics. Cut background fabric large enough to include finishing seam allowances. Cut underlay motif fabrics to the rough shape of the motifs, but a little larger all round, say ½in (1.2cm). Pin the traced design on the right side of the background (i.e. top) fabric, and locate and pin first motif fabrics underneath its motif (11-14).

3 With ¼in (6mm) long stitches, and using a thread colour to contrast with both motif and background fabrics, tack [baste] along all traced lines of the motif to be stitched first, and through all thicknesses of paper and fabrics. Make sure that any corner or point has a stitch right into it. Remove pins, and remove greaseproof paper by needle-scoring it under the tacking threads but not in the spaces between threads. Then lift paper gently off without disturbing stitching. Because the paper will remain intact, it can be repositioned to mark subsequent layers (11-15).

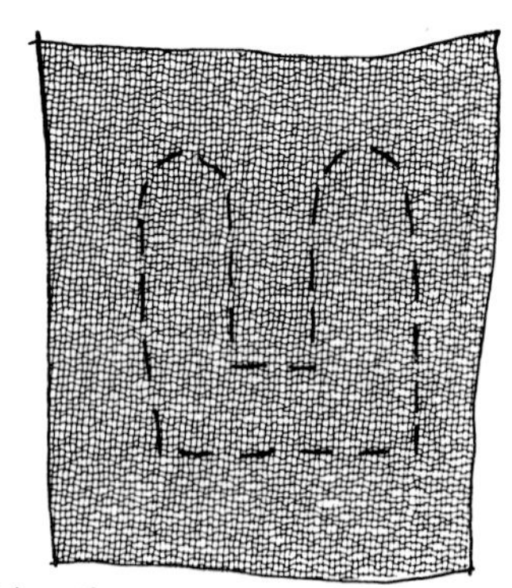

11-15 PAPER REMOVED LEAVING TACK-MARKED PATTERN

4 With small, sharp-pointed scissors, and referring to your coloured diagram, carefully snip out background fabric (i.e. top layer only) in centre of motif ⅛in (3mm) from tacking line. On narrow elements of the design, such as stems, this may mean cutting centrally between tacking lines (11-16).

5 Choose a straightish edge to start stitching, and use a thread to match top fabric. Snip the tacking stitches on the right side along a 2in (5cm) length at your chosen starting point. Gently separate the fabric layers so that the threads pull down out of the top layer but remain in the bottom layer of fabric to indicate the motif edge. Hold the work with the seam allowance away from you and turn it under with your needle, so that the turned edge lines up with the cut tacking threads. Hold the turning down with your thumb and hem it down with small stitches. As you come towards the end of the 2in (5cm) length, snip more tackings over a further short length, and continue turning and stitching (11-17).

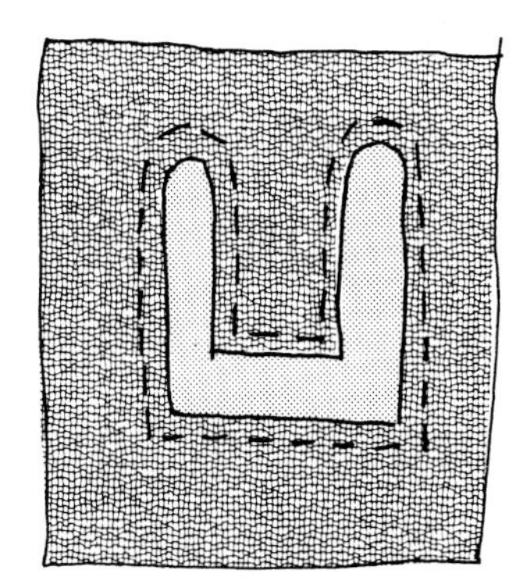

11-16 SNIPPING OUT MOTIF CENTRE

6 Where you come to a very sharp inside curve it may be necessary to snip into the seam allowance in order to be able to roll it under fully. On outside curves, any fullness will have to be eased under evenly so as not to produce unwanted corners on the curve. On inside corners, snip fully into the corner and, when stitching, take closer and deeper stitches right in the corner to hold it securely and prevent fraying. On outside corners, anything above a right angle can easily be stitched by first turning under the seam allowance across the tip, followed by turning under and stitching up to the point before turning under and stitching the other side. On smaller angles, or where a motif comes to a very fine point, it may be necessary to trim away a sliver of the seam allowances on each side of the point.

7 Remove tacking threads from the back. Tweezers are a big help here!

8 If your design incorporates more layers, replace the tracing paper pattern accurately on the appliqué and tack the outline of the new motif through the fabrics as before, following steps 2 through 7. When all the appliqué work is finished, press from the back.

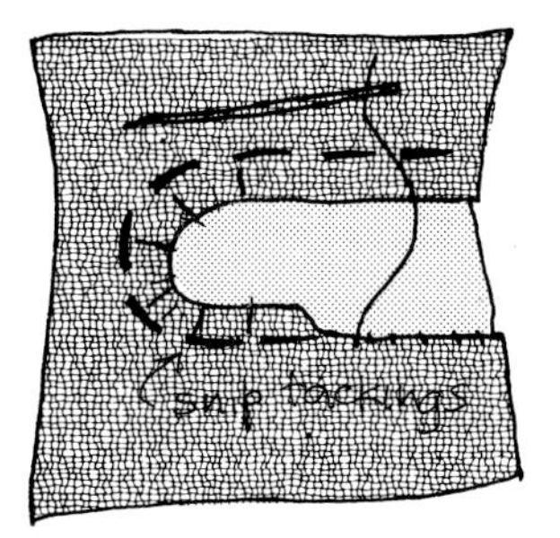

11-17 NEEDLE-TURNED & STITCHED ON TACKED LINE

STEMS AND STRIPS

There are three ways of making stems or strips. All work best with bias fabric, which you must use if the stems are to curve at all. Method 3 was used for the stems in TULIPS TOTE.

STEMS 1

Cut bias fabric strips, the width of the stem plus ½in (1.2cm). Press ¼in (6mm) seam allowance under on each side. Position strip, pin and stitch down (11-18).

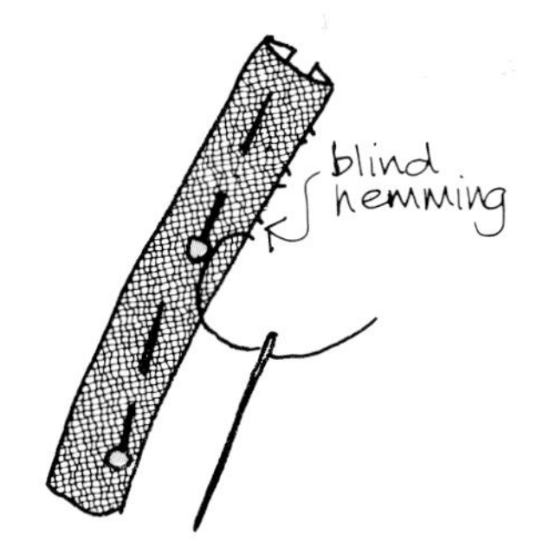

11-18 BIAS STEMS 1

STEMS 2

Cut bias fabric strips twice the width of the stem, plus ½in (1.2cm). Fold strip lengthwise, wrong sides together. Machine stitch a scant ¼in (6mm) from the raw edge. Press so that the seam is centred on the back of the strip. Position strip with the seam allowance underneath, pin and stitch down (11-19).

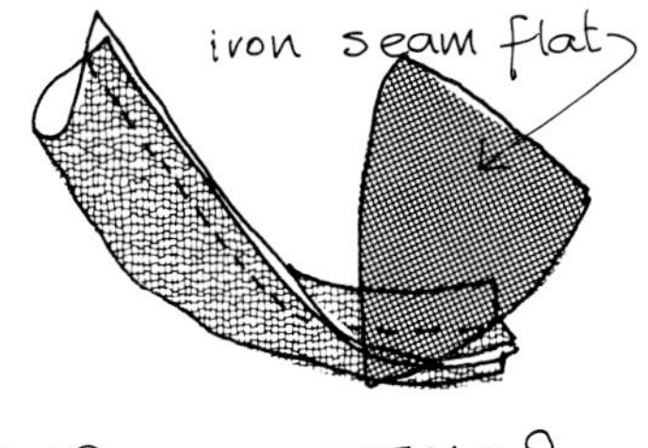

11-19 BIAS STEMS 2

STEMS 3

Elly Sienkiewicz explained this very neat method of getting extra fine stems in her book, *Spoken Without a Word*, and Rosemary Muntus showed me how. These stems come out nicely plump, and you can even taper them. I have managed to make them as narrow as 1/16in (1.5mm) by using a Liberty lawn and a short machine stitch, and trimming the seam allowance to the bone, but ⅛in (3mm) is a more comfortable aim. I used this method, but with wider stems, in TULIPS TOTE.

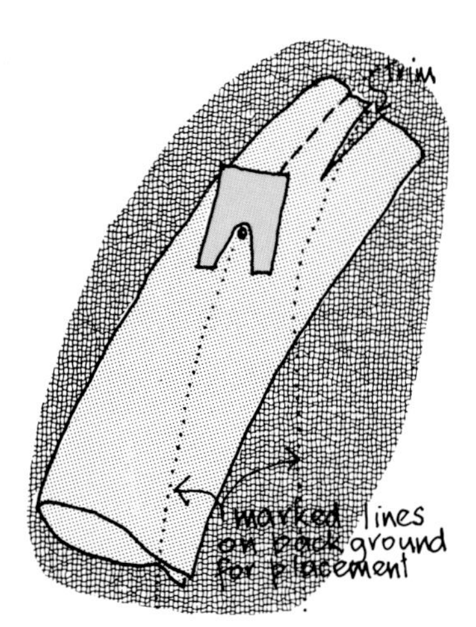

11-20 BIAS STEMS 3
PLACEMENT & STITCHING

1 Cut bias strip allowing ½in (1.2cm) plus at least twice the width of the widest part of the stem. Even for very narrow stems don't cut narrower than ¾in (2cm) because it becomes too small to handle. Fold in half lengthwise, wrong sides together, and press. Draw both sides of the stem on your background fabric. NEEDLE-MARK another line to the left of the stem, the width of the stem away. Position the folded edge of the strip touching the needle-marked line and pin or tack. Sew by hand or machine along the drawn left-hand line. If the stem is narrow, use a short machine stitch (11-20).

2 Trim seam allowance. Turn the folded edge of the stem strip over, and stitch down onto the right-hand drawn stem-line, enclosing the trimmed edges (11-21).

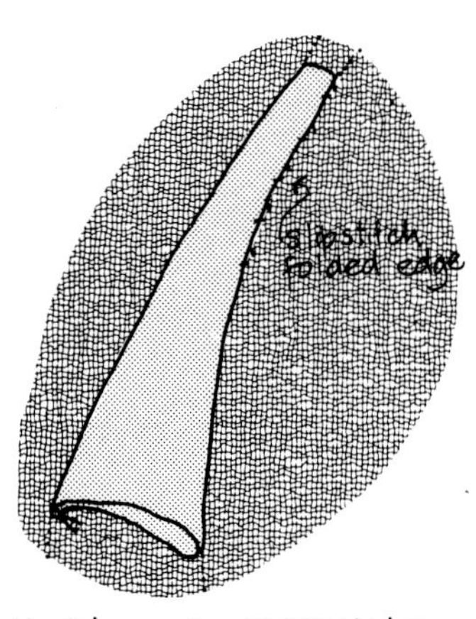

11-21 SLIPSTITCHING
STEM

CLAMSHELLS

These are a pretty, old-fashioned appliqué and quilting pattern, traditionally drawn by marking round a glass. The pieces can, with difficulty, be sewn together to make up a new fabric, but the usual method is to stitch in rows to a background fabric. It helps to mark this fabric in a cross-grid to show the rows and the verticals of the clamshells where they stagger in alternate rows. The following method helps considerably with accurate placement.

1 Cut freezer paper patterns of clamshell. Iron onto right side of clamshell fabric. MARK round the lower, stemlike part and, using MODERN HAND APPLIQUÉ 2, machine stitch around top curve and appliqué in place on the marked grid (11-22).

11-22 CLAMSHELL

SCHOOL SHOEBAGS

These are quick and easy and always a popular item for the Primary School fundraising sale. When little children start school, they all need shoebags, but can't read their names. What better than a bag with an individual appliquéd motif? Bags I made more than 20 years ago are still going strong and nostalgically cherished by the now-grown-up original owners. Size is not critical within an inch or two.

MATERIALS: (for one bag)
Heavy cotton or denim, 16in x 33in (40cm x 85cm).
Scraps for appliqué.
Machine appliqué thread.
Sewing thread.
1yd (90cm) tape, ribbon or cord.

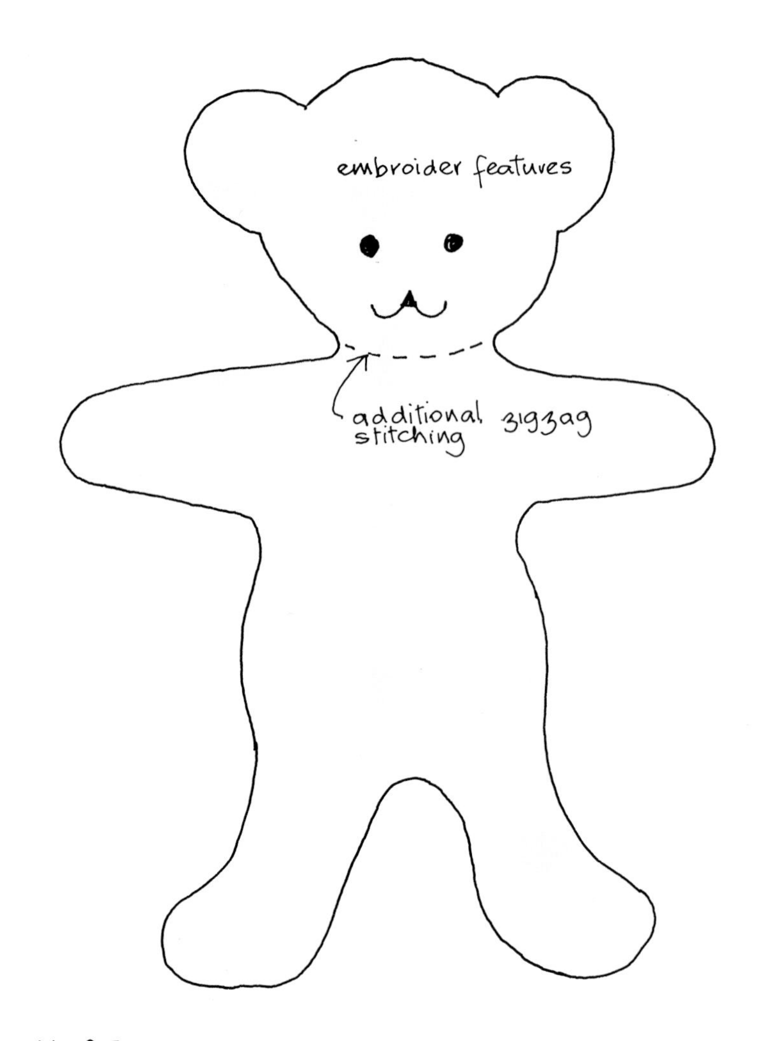

11-23 TEDDY PATTERN

MAKING

1 Decide on appliqué motif. Very simple shapes, which are easily recognised, are best. Sometimes children's colouring books have large simplified pictures which can be traced. The three bags illustrated have an assortment of motifs — the red bag has a humming bird cut from an exotic furnishing fabric remnant, the striped bag has a simple red apple and green print leaf cut straight from the fabric, without a pattern, and the blue bag has a yellow teddy (I was going to use a cookie cutter, but the teddy on it was too small (11-23)). Draw or trace, if necessary, and cut out motif (the bird was cut slightly outside the print outline, so that the satin stitch would not obscure the print).

2 Following instructions for MACHINE APPLIQUÉ 1, position motif on one side of the bag and apply. I used fusible web to hold the bird, because of its complex shape, but the others were held with fabric glue stick. The bird was more stable, but the appliqué stitching not so good because my sewing machine decided to play up.

3 Sew up sides of bag. Press over ½in (1cm) fabric around the top, and then another 1in (2.5cm) for the hem. Machine stitch hem, starting and finishing with some reverse stitches, and leaving a 1in (2.5cm) gap at one side, through which you thread the tape. Knot the tape ends together.

4 Add any embroidered features called for — eyes, nose and mouth for the teddy, for instance.

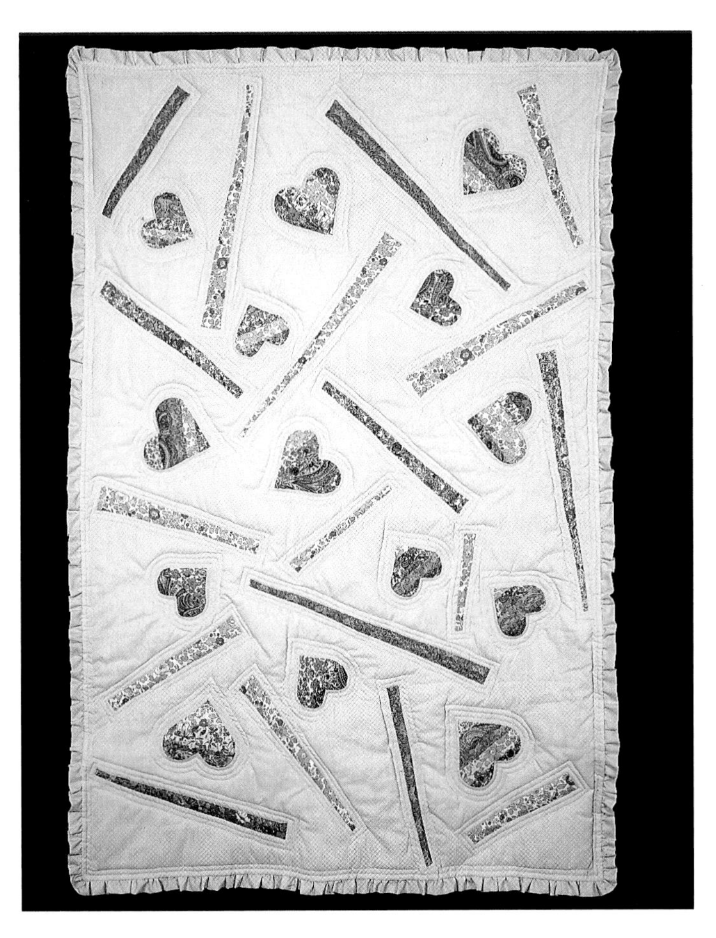

HEARTSTRINGS COT QUILT

Hearts are a very good shape for practising hand appliqué, as they have two straight edges, two half circle curves and inside and outside corners. Here I made use of some narrow tapered strips of Liberty Tana© lawn to piece a square of STRING PIECING, from which the hearts were cut. Because of all the seam allowances on the backs of the hearts, I thought that my method of MODERN HAND APPLIQUÉ 2, where the freezer paper goes on the right side of the patches, was likely to be easier then Anne Oliver's freezer paper MODERN HAND APPLIQUÉ 1 method where it goes on the wrong side. After I had randomly placed, appliquéd, stuffed and machine quilted once around the hearts, I decided they looked rather lonely. There was some lawn left over, already cut into tapered strips, and I machine appliquéd it by MACHINE APPLIQUÉ 3 between the hearts. If I was doing it all over again, I would have appliquéd the strips on before starting to quilt, as it was difficult to stop the layers of fabric and wadding from shifting. The quilt was CONTOUR MACHINE QUILTED and finished with a RUFFLE.

MATERIALS: for quilt finishing about 34in x 54in (86cm x 137cm)

3 ¼yd (3m) fine cotton or cotton blend 44in (112cm) wide, for background, ruffle and backing.

Strips fine cotton prints, at least 6 different prints, ¼yd (20cm) of each.

2oz wadding about 58in x 39in (122cm x 100cm) and some small scraps.

Matching thread to background fabric.

Freezer paper or substitute.

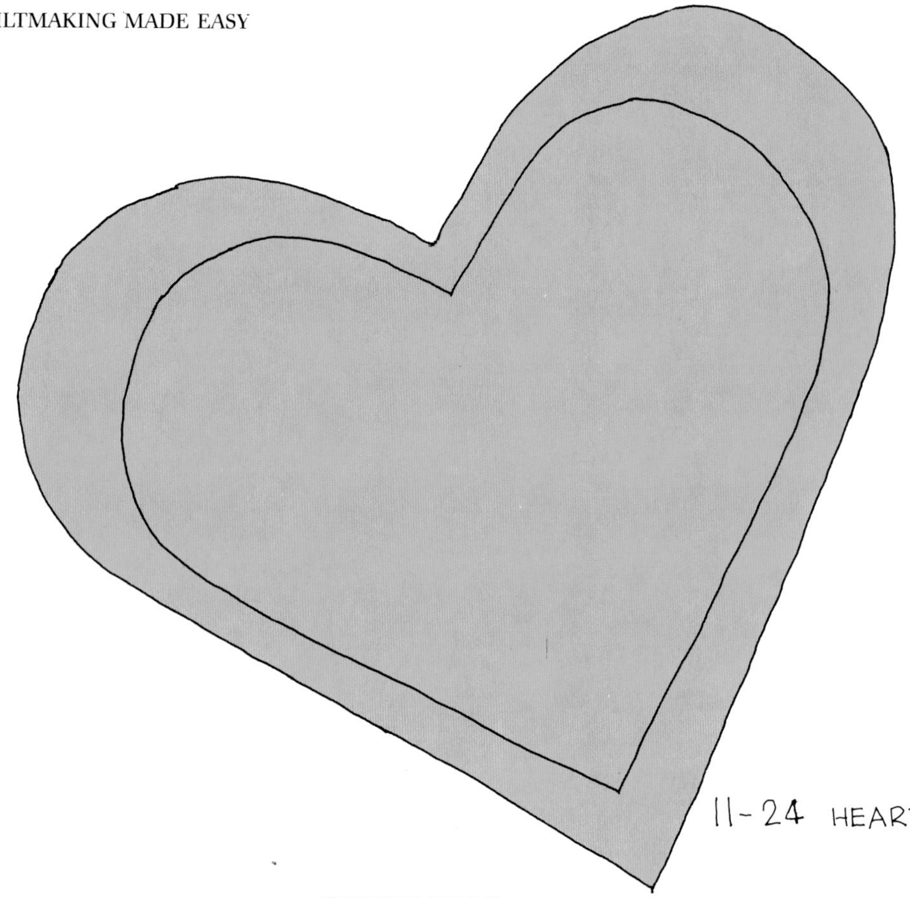

11-24 HEART PATTERNS

PREPARATION

Cut 7 heart shapes (11-24) of each size from freezer paper.
PREPARE fabrics.
Cut three strips from length of main fabric, each 2 ½in (6.5cm) wide, and cut one strip in half.
Cut remaining main fabric into two pieces each 54in (137cm) long. (The remnant can be used for practising machine quilting.)
Cut cotton prints into 18in (45cm) widths, and cut these into tapered strips (rotary cutter useful here). The strips should vary both in width and taper, but narrow ends should not be less than ¾in (2cm) wide.

MAKING

1 Machine piece enough strips together to make an approximate 18in (46cm) square. Press.
2 Lay freezer paper hearts randomly on stripping, leaving at least ½in (1.2cm) between them. Follow steps 3 through 6 of MODERN HAND APPLIQUÉ 2, arranging hearts on background fabric in a pleasing arrangement.
3 Test placement and adjust lengths of additional strips between appliquéd hearts before pressing under their ¼in (6mm) seam allowances and pinning and stitching in place.
4 Cut 7 heart shapes of each size from wadding. Cut slits in background fabric behind hearts, large enough to insert wadding hearts behind applique. Stitch slits up again by hand.
5 LAYER quilt, attach ruffle (made of the 2 long strips and the half length strip), and finish edges.
6 MACHINE QUILT twice round the edge of the quilt and round all appliqué shapes, using the machine foot as a guide. The widths between lines can be varied by changing the position of the needle. I did two rows of this CONTOUR QUILTING round the strips and three round the hearts. Where pieces come close to each other, and there is no space for a row of quilting in between, turn and go round the obstructing piece.

TULIPS TOTE

This bag always has people puzzling about how it is made, and it is certainly very eye-catching with its brightly coloured appliqué tulips bursting out of a Log Cabin basket. In fact, it is three blocks sewn together. The bottom one (which you can't see) is a plain Log Cabin block, and the other two are half Log Cabin and half appliqué. The Log Cabin is made from all dark fabrics, rather than being half dark and half light, which is the traditional way. The bag is an 'old faithful' which I have used a great deal. It holds a surprising amount and I have to remember not to overload it, because it puts a strain on the curtain rings that carry the cord. I had great difficulty with the appliqué, possibly because the right colour thread I was trying to use was too thick for the sewing machine needle. Do remember to follow the instructions with your sewing machine to avoid this sort of problem.

MATERIALS
Scraps dark cotton prints to make 3 Log Cabin blocks.
14in (35cm) square cotton fabric for background behind tulips.
Scraps plain [solid] cottons for tulips, and green for leaves and stems.
¾yd (70 cm) cotton fabric for lining, 44in (112cm) wide.
2oz wadding
2 small curtain rings.
1 ¼yd (1m) coloured cord.
Sewing thread.
Nylon quilting thread.
Machine embroidery threads to match tulip and leaf colours.

PREPARATION
PREPARE all fabrics.
Cut three 12 ½in (31.2 cm)squares of lining fabric.
Cut three 14in (35cm) squares of wadding.
Cut one 13 ⅜in (33cm) square of background fabric, and cut in half diagonally.
From prints, cut strips for Log Cabin 1½in (3.7 cm) wide, and three 2½in (6.2cm) centre squares.
From freezer paper cut 8 of tulip pattern and one each of each leaf shape (11-25).
From stem fabric cut bias strip 1 ¼in (3cm) wide and about 28in (71cm) long.

MAKING
1 Make 3 LOG CABIN 2 blocks, machine pieced with scant ¼in (6mm) seam, and central large square, measuring 12 ½in (32cm) square when finished.

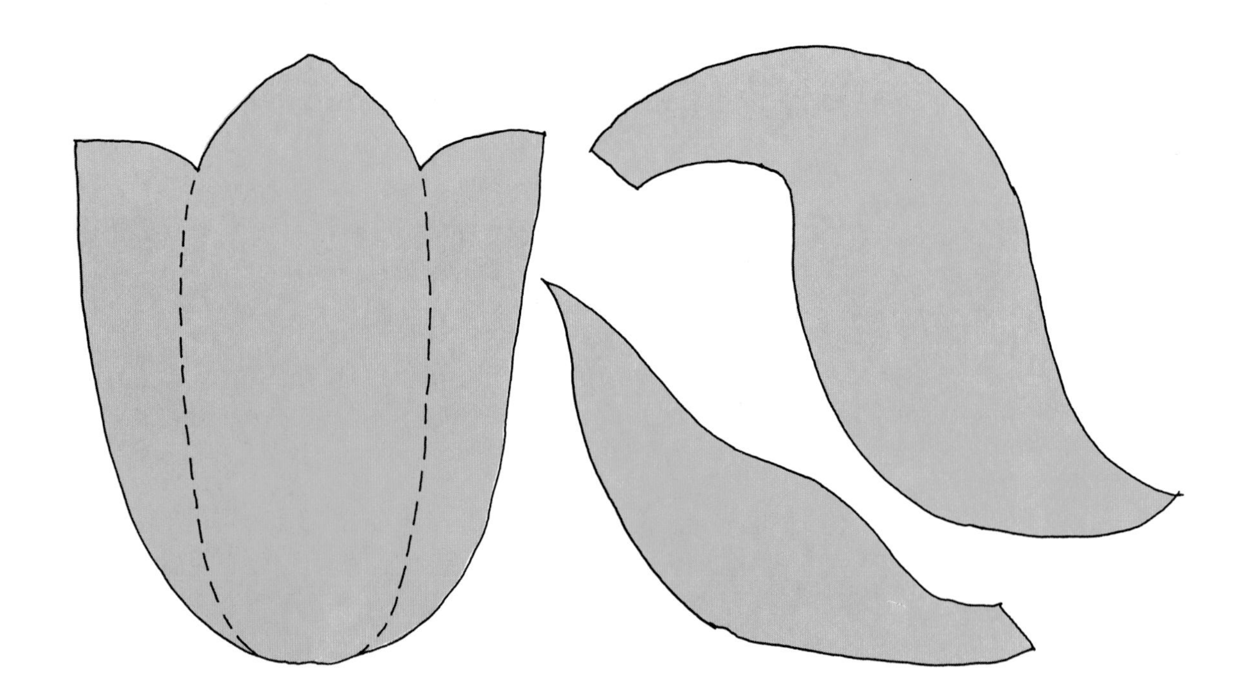

11-25 TULIP & LEAVES PATTERNS

2 Draw one diagonal on 2 Log Cabin blocks. Mark a line ¼in (6mm) away from it, and cut on this line. You will be using the larger pieces — the others can be kept for another project.
3 Pin one piece of background fabric in the corner of a square of wadding.
4 Lightly iron tulip shapes onto tulip fabrics, spacing them at least ½in (1.2cm) apart. Cut out, allowing ¼in (6mm) seam allowances. Do the same for leaf shapes. Work one tulip arrangement first, and re-use freezer paper patterns for the second arrangement.
5 Pin tulips in position on triangle of wadded background fabric, keeping them at least ½in (1.2cm) from the edges. Note that the stems have to be appliquéd on and then the Log Cabin piece sewn on *before* the tulips and leaves are attached. So...
6 Following instructions for STEMS 3, MARK position of stems, cut lengths of stem bias and position to go under bases of tulips and reach diagonal edge of background fabric. Some may be curved. Appliqué in position.
7 Stitch Log Cabin half blocks to tulip half blocks, matching diagonal raw edges. Pin remaining Log Cabin block onto wadding.
8 MACHINE QUILT Log Cabins IN THE DITCH with nylon thread on spool.
9 Pin tulips in final positions, starting with those that will be covered by others later on. Using matching machine embroidery thread, follow instructions for MACHINE APPLIQUÉ 2, and tapering machine satin stitch (11-26). Apply leaves in the same way.
10 Machine stitch the three blocks together, using ¼in (6mm) seam (11-27), sewing the base block first to the Log Cabin basket of one tulip block and then the other. Join the 3 lining squares to each other in the same way.
11 With right sides together, stitch patchwork and lining together, leaving a gap on one side.
12 Turn right side out through gap. Stitch gap closed. Firmly stitch tulip blocks together 2 ½in (6.5cm) up each side edge. Machine or hand stitch through all layers close to free edges of tulip background fabric.
13 Sew one curtain ring 1in (2.5cm) below and behind each top corner. Thread cord through rings and knot ends.

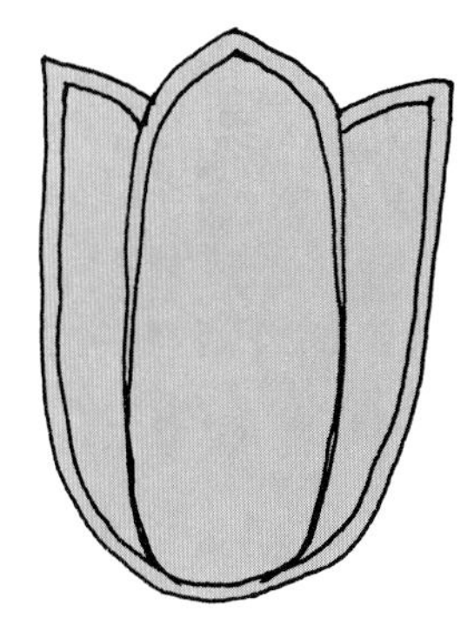

11-26 TULIP ZIGZAG STITCHING

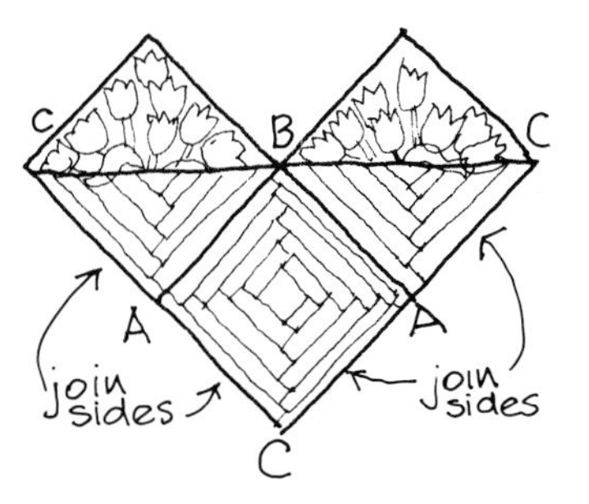

11-27 ASSEMBLING BLOCKS - TULIPS TOTE BAG

JUNGLY PUSSY

This picture was sparked off by a particularly enticing piece of batik and memories of television pictures of striped tigers in the jungle, made nearly invisible because their stripes blended with the jungle shadows. But I couldn't find any suitable pictures of tigers, and decided instead to do a picture of a striped tabby cat among jungle grasses. The REVERSE APPLIQUÉ USING GREASEPROOF PAPER technique is one I was shown in a workshop about Mola making (Kuna Indian work). I didn't get enthused enough about these panels to complete my sample piece, but remembered the technique when I thought of making the picture. You will see that I have slightly simplified the design from the original (see photograph) to eliminate some of the narrower pieces where seam allowances were reduced to less than ⅛in (3mm).

MATERIALS: for picture 12in (30cm) square
2 pieces of plain cotton fabric 14in (36cm) square.
1 piece of cotton print 14in (36cm) square for cat and grasses.
Small scraps of black cotton for ear linings, mouth and nose
2 small pieces of yellow leather for eyes.
Small length of black yarn for pupils.
Thread to match plain fabric.
White pva glue.
12in (30cm) square piece of heavy card.
2 small curtain rings.
Length of fine string for hanging.
Greaseproof paper (or substitute).

PREPARATION
PREPARE fabrics.
Enlarge pattern from diagram (11-28) onto graph paper. Each square represents 1in (2.5cm). Colour inside stripes and grasses.
Trace in ink onto greaseproof paper.
Put masking tape over edges of background fabric square to prevent fraying [ravelling].

11-28 JUNGLY PUSSY , one square equals 1" (2·5 cm)

MAKING

1 Re-read [review] instructions for REVERSE APPLIQUÉ USING GREASEPROOF PAPER, and follow them.

2 The plain fabric will be on top, as the background, with the print underneath as the first layer of reverse appliqué. Sewing thread should match plain fabric.

3 If you start appliquéing at a foot, you will be less likely to get muddled when cutting out the insides of the stripes. So do each leg in turn, and then start from the tip of the tail and work along the body to the head.

4 When all the stripes have been done, appliqué black patches for ears, nose and mouth by the same method, behind the print fabric. The thread should match the print fabric. Remove masking tape. Press the work well from the back.

5 Make cat's eyes: cut 2 diamonds each 5/8in (1.5cm) long from yellow leather (or substitute), put into position, and hold each in place with a single stitch of black yarn.

6 Mount by laying picture right side down on table. Lay card centrally over design. Bring spare fabric to the back, either glueing it down with white glue (hold with clean plastic clothes pegs [pins] until it is set), or lacing from side to side with stout thread.

7 Turn in edges of second piece of plain fabric, so it is just smaller than picture. Sew it down neatly over the back.

8 Sew on 2 curtain rings on the back, 4in (10cm) down and 1in (2.5cm) in from the edge.

9 Tie a length of fine string about 15in (40cm) long to the curtain rings. Adjust length so that no string shows at the top of the picture when hanging.

10 Stand back and admire your handiwork!

CHAPTER TWELVE

QUILTING

Once your patchwork or appliqué has been made, the question arises — what next? While it is sufficient just to finish the edges of APPLIQUÉ which has been sewn onto a backing fabric, all PATCHWORK needs the protection of at least a backing, as the narrow seam allowances are very vulnerable to wear, in use and when being washed. The use of some form of wadding [batting] behind it makes the patchwork warmer. The wadding also supports the surface fabric and helps to prevent it from creasing and wearing. But the wadding itself is fluffy and fragile and has to be sandwiched between the decorative front and a backing fabric. Then the three layers must be held together to prevent them from shifting, and especially to prevent the wadding from disintegrating under the onslaughts of wear and wash.

Some quilts are traditionally TIED through the layers. LOG CABIN 1, for instance, which is sewn onto a fabric backing, becomes too thick to quilt easily and so is stabilised in this way. Tying is very quick, and ideal for utility quilts.

QUILTING combines the practical advantage of holding the layers of the quilt together, with an added aesthetic and design dimension given to the quilt by the play of light and shade over the quilting pattern. It really brings a quilt to life. Look at the picture of FLOTILLA, and see the difference between the bottom half which has only been machine quilted round the patches, and the top half which has hand quilting to give extra meaning, subtlety and a counter-decoration to the patchwork.

The choice of fabric for BACKINGS and the types of WADDING available are discussed in Chapter 2.

Traditional cotton and wool waddings had to be quilted in such a way that no spaces larger than 1in (2.5cm) were left unquilted, otherwise the wadding shifted and bunched when washed and the quilt lost its warmth. Polyester wadding purposely has its fibres so entangled in manufacture that this does not happen, and ties or quilting can be spaced as far as 4in (10cm) apart. Mostly, though, quilting looks better if it is not too sparse, and the quilt will also not crease so much. On the other hand, too much quilting will make the quilt thinner, stiffer and not as warm, because less insulating air is trapped in it.

If you decide to quilt part of a patchwork top, then it should all be quilted, to a fairly even density; an unquilted border looks puckered and floppy and unquilted central areas look uninteresting and droopy.

Quilting is generally done before the quilt edges are finished off, as fabrics sometimes 'creep' during the process, and take up more backing or wadding. QUILTING PATTERNS may be marked on the quilt before assembling or after. CONTOUR QUILTING should not need marking at all, as it follows the outlines of appliqué shapes in parallel circuits.

MARKING FOR QUILTING

You will need quilting patterns and markers. If the patchwork or top fabric is thin enough to see through, the quilting pattern can be traced directly from the design. The use of a light table helps — you can improvise a light table by supporting a glazed picture frame over a table lamp, or putting a lamp under a glass coffee table. I have never succeeded with the idea of taping the quilting pattern and quilt to the inside of a window and using daylight to show up the pattern for tracing.

Types of MARKERS — pencil, coloured pencil, soap etc — were dealt with in Chapter 4. Your choice will vary depending on whether you are marking a whole quilt before LAYERING it (choose coloured pencil or fine propelling pencil) or just marking for a small area which will soon be quilted, when a sliver of white soap is hard to beat and easily removed. As soap is slightly shiny, it will even show up on white fabric.

Traditionally, wholecloth quilts — those with no patchwork — were often needle-marked. The top of the quilt was laid on a table which was covered with a thick cloth. Templates of the quilting patterns were held down firmly and marked round with the blunt point of a large yarn needle held nearly flat. This left a visible dent in the fabric which could easily be followed. Finer details were added as the quilting progressed.

Often it is necessary to mark quilting patterns after the quilt has been LAYERED. This is more difficult because of the squashiness of the wadding, and it helps to have a hard surface under the part to be marked. Of course, you will not be able to trace through the layers, and will need a QUILTING TEMPLATE of the pattern.

Straight lines can be marked with MASKING TAPE. This may be ¼in (6mm) wide, and placed butting against the patch edges for the traditional quarter-inch-in-from-the-edge quilting. Or wider tape can be used to mark parallel lines of quilting. The lines of stitching are done right against the edge of the tape, which is then removed. Do not leave the tape in position for more than an hour or two, for fear of adhesive residues sticking to the quilt surface. The strips of tape can be re-used several times.

Possibly a good compromise is to trace on the complicated pattern parts, and then LAYER, leaving background marking to be put on while quilting is in progress.

QUILTING PATTERNS

All the projects in this book which are hand quilted have their quilting patterns with the instructions. The patterns I use are either drawn freehand (the sky and waves of FLOTILLA), drawn with a straight edge or ruler (the furrows of TRIP AROUND THE WORLD and the background of FIREWORKS) or traced around my own templates (the borders of FLOTILLA, the flames of FIREWORKS). The cable pattern used in FLOTILLA is a traditional quilting pattern, which I redrew to fit the particular border width and unit square repeat of that quilt.

If you want to use bought patterns for your quilts, you will find that they are available either as drawings on sheets or in books, which have to be traced onto the quilt or onto template plastic, or as plastic templates rather like stencils, where you draw the lines through slots. Traditional templates were more often silhouettes, with sometimes a guide or two for internal features. Often quilting would be set out entirely freehand, with coins, cups, glasses and plates pressed into service for marking circles (CLAMSHELL, WINEGLASS, and the small curves of feather patterns). Straight lines were marked with a straight-edge and pencil, or a chalked string was held tautly across the quilt, lifted up and released smartly to 'snap' down and mark a line.

If you are making a wholecloth quilt, then you should mark the vertical and horizontal centre lines and any other points (such as the width of a border) which locate the position of motifs. This should be done before marking out any of the patterns.

American quilters now often quilt ¼in (6mm) away from all seamlines of PIECED blocks. This is easy because it does not involve quilting over seam lines, and gives good stability to the patchwork, but I think it gives the wrong emphasis to the patchwork pattern. Use the narrow masking tape as a guide.

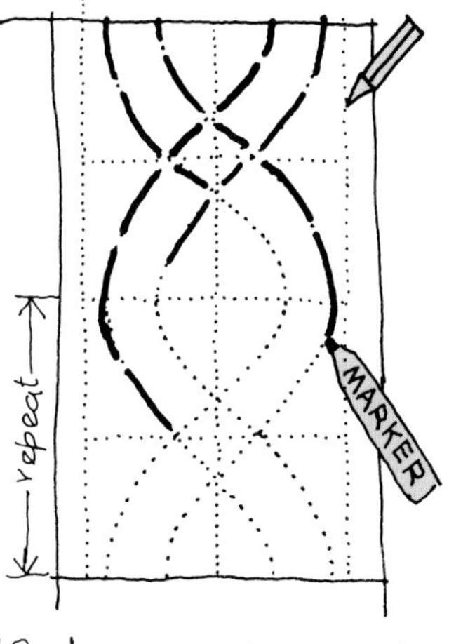

12-1 DRAWING QUILTING PATTERN FOR STENCIL CUTTING

MAKING A QUILTING TEMPLATE

1 Use template plastic if you can. It is robust and as it is transparent you will be able to place it accurately on your patchwork. Simple shapes can be cut with small, strong scissors, or use a craft knife for more complex shapes.

2 Mark your patchwork grid pattern onto the plastic before tracing the patchwork pattern. This will help in positioning the template accurately later on. If you are quilting with a hoop, it will also show whether you have stretched the quilt evenly in the hoop.

3 Design or decide on your quilting pattern. Trace it onto the template plastic with a permanent marker pen (width about $\frac{1}{16}$in [2mm]). If you are cutting channels, mark the position of 'bridges' which will remain uncut, and cut across the marker line at each end of each bridge before cutting the channels the full width of the marker line (12-1). This wide channel gives space for a soap sliver or crayon. If you are cutting a silhouette shape (which can be an outside or an inside shape) cut to the inside of the marker line for a silhouette (12-2), and the outside edge of the marker line for an inside shape (12-3).

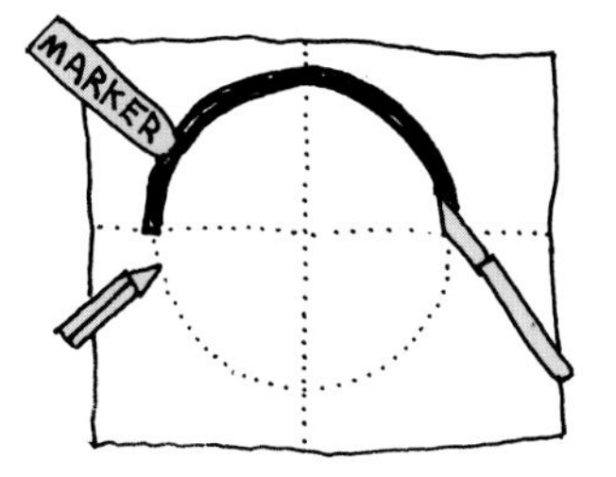

12-2 CUTTING SILHOUETTE QUILTING TEMPLATE

QUILTING PATTERNS

There is a wealth of traditional quilting patterns in Britain and in America. Some of the favourites are variations on roses, leaves, feathers and hearts (hearts are traditionally used only on bridal quilts) and cables. They may be individual motifs or form a repeating decorative border pattern. A quilt completely covered with curving patterns would be excessive — the best thing to show up the curved patterns is a straight line background, and the easiest and most effective of these is the DIAGONAL CHEQUER, where lines are MARKED at, say, 1in (2.5cm) spacings diagonally in both directions.

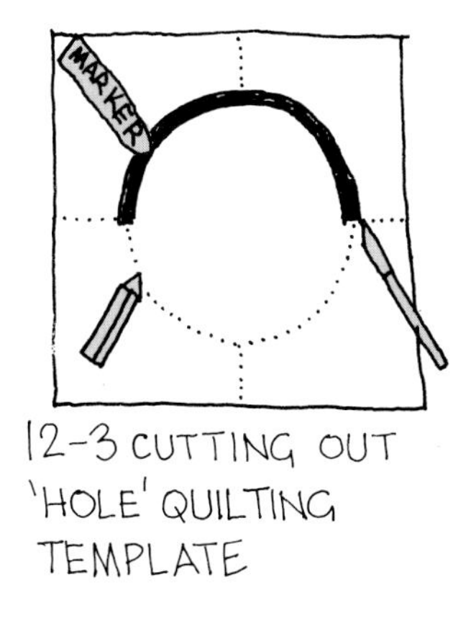

12-3 CUTTING OUT 'HOLE' QUILTING TEMPLATE

LAYERING THE QUILT

This is the final preparation before quilting or tying, when all three layers are assembled.

1 If the wadding has been packed up small, release it and open right out for several hours to remove creases. Join the wadding if necessary with a loose ladder stitch. It should be at least 2in (5cm) larger on each side than the TOP of the quilt.

2 Join lengths of backing fabric if required to make a piece the same size as the wadding. Be sure to have the WARP threads (parallel with the cut off selvages) running lengthwise, and arrange seams so that a central seam is avoided. PRESS all seams open.

3 PRESS top for the very last time (a quilt should never be pressed after washing or dry cleaning). Make sure beforehand that any loose threads or frays have been removed, and seam allowances trimmed to prevent dark fabrics shadowing through light ones. MARK the quilting pattern on the top (or positions for ties).

4 Lay the backing out smoothly, wrong side up, on a large table or large clean clear floor. It helps to anchor it where possible with masking tape. It also helps to have two people doing this job!

5 Unroll the wadding and centre it on the backing, smoothing out any wrinkles. Pin round the edge. Lay the patchwork centrally on top,

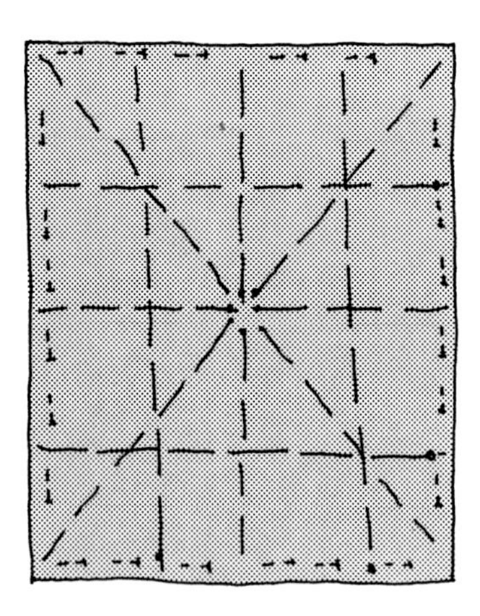

12-4 TACKING LAYERED QUILT

right side up, again smoothing out creases. Backing and wadding should both be larger than patchwork by at least 2in (5cm) on each side. This is insurance in case of extra take up or shifting of layers.

6 Anchor all three layers together by tacking [basting] or safety pinning. I much prefer safety pinning as it's quicker and makes a more positive anchor. Use 1in to 1 ¼in (2.5cm to 3cm) pins (see Suppliers) and space them 4in (10cm) or so apart. You will need 300-400 for a whole large quilt. If tacking, pin temporarily with ordinary straight pins and tack using a long needle and long thread. It helps sometimes to hold the bowl of a tablespoon under the backing to help the needle up. Start from the middle and work out to sides and corners (12-4).

ALL-IN-ONE LAYERING

This is useful for small quilts and very quick, if rather unorthodox. It was used for BABY BLOCKS PRAM QUILT.

Lay out wadding. MARK quilt for quilting, then lay it right side up on top of wadding, and safety pin or tack. Lay backing on top, right side down. Pin all round edges. Trim wadding and backing to size of top. Stitch all round, ¼in (6mm) from outside edge, except for a gap large enough to turn the quilt through. Snip off points of corners. Turn quilt through gap, pulling out corners. Hand stitch gap closed. Re-pin through all three layers for quilting.

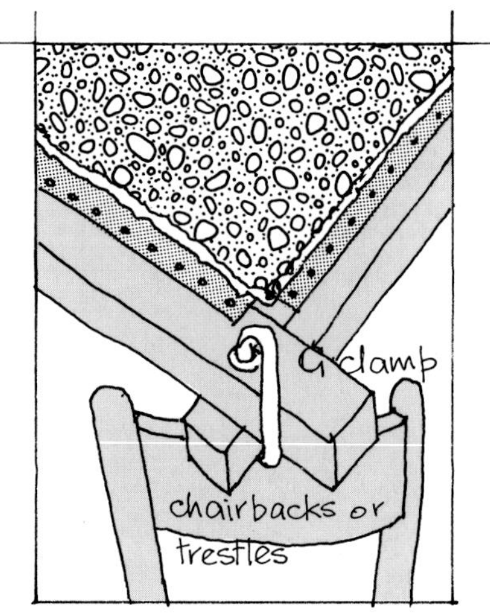

12-5 CORNER OF LARGER QUILTING FRAME

QUILTING FRAMES

Most people quilt better if the work is held firmly. There are three types of traditional large quilting frames. The simplest is made of four long lengths of 1 ½in x 2 ½in (4cm x 6cm) planed timber, each with a strip of strong fabric stapled or nailed to one face. Two must be the length of the quilt, and two the width, plus about 6in (15cm) on both. They are connected with four large G-clamps [C-clamps] at the corners, and supported by trestles or chairbacks. Naturally, although simple, this frame takes up a lot of space (12-5). It permits eight or more people to quilt around it at first, with progressively few quilters as the outside areas are worked and the quilt rolled on. It can also be used as a TACKING FRAME, when the backing is stretched out in the frame and wadding and top laid on for tacking. This is less back-breaking than crawling over the floor.

The second frame has two long bars, with fabric strips, and slots cut through near their ends. Two short, thinner stretcher bars (2in x ½in [5cm x 1.2cm]) called 'swords' slide through the slots and are held taut with pegs. This frame is also supported by trestles or chairbacks (12-6). It does not take up as much room as the first frame, and can be stored propped against a wall when not in use.

The third frame is free-standing and self-supporting. The long bars again have the fabric strips, but they revolve, and tension in the quilt is maintained by ratchets (12-7).

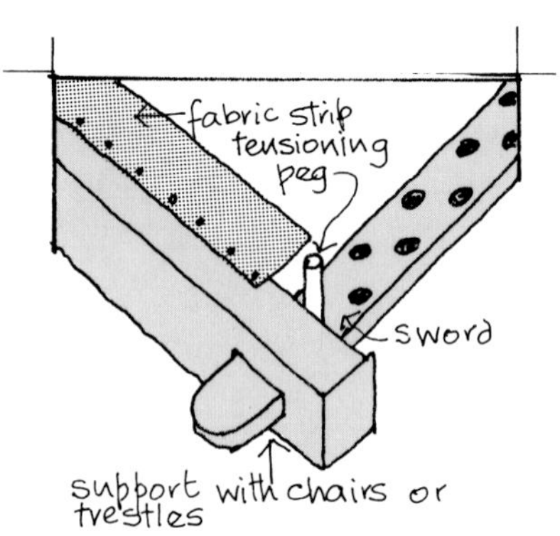

12-6 CORNER OF QUILTING FRAME

QUILTING HOOPS

These are made of wood, but are deeper and more robust than embroidery hoops. I use a 14in (35cm) diameter circular one, which is a good all-purpose size. They are made as large as 23in (57.5cm) across. You can also get oval hoops, and a new collapsible plastic tube frame, which is rectangular and good for borders or when travelling.

'DRESSING' THE FRAME

This means putting the quilt into the quilting frame.

The most usual method is to take the LAYERED quilt, and tack the backing firmly to the fabric strips fixed to the back and front bars of the frame, roll up the slack smoothly and tension the quilt with pegs or rachets. The side edges of the quilt are held taut by pinning tape to the quilt and looping it round the side frame or sword (12-8).

One traditional method dispenses with tacking the three layers together, and can be used on the second and third types of frame. Tack the backing (wrong side up) firmly to the webbing strips on the frame. Roll all the spare backing onto the back bar and tension with pegs or rachets. Pin one edge of wadding and marked 'top' to the nearer edge of backing, and smooth them over backing on back bar, fastening layers with pins or safety pins. Loop the spare wadding and patchwork up off the floor. By having only the backing stretched in the frame, the finished quilt is given higher relief or puffiness once it is out of the frame and the tension in the backing relaxes.

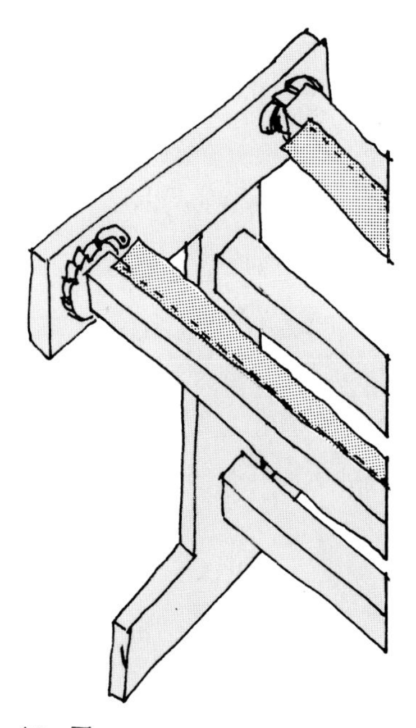

12-7 FREE-STANDING QUILTING FRAME WITH RATCHETS

USING THE FRAME

The quilting stitch is described below. If you quilt with a frame, it is essential to sit in good light and with a chair of the right height *for you*. Quilt from the near edge, as far as you can comfortably reach, taking out any pins no longer needed. You may work with several needles in progress at the same time, particularly if you are working a background. When you have worked a comfortable reach, remove side tapes and slacken ratchets (or take out pegs and side bars) and wind some of the completed quilt onto the front bar. Replace side bars and tension with pegs or re-tension with ratchets. Replace tape tensioning.

USING THE HOOP

Have good lighting and a comfortable quilting position. Some people like to support their hoop on a table edge. You may wish to wrap cotton bandaging round the two parts of the hoop. This will increase the frictional hold of the hoop, and prevent the possibility of the wood staining the fabric. Do not leave your quilt in a hoop after you have finished a quilting session, for fear of creasing the fabric.

When you are quilting the edge of your quilt with a hoop, tack an extra strip of fabric to the backing, otherwise part of the hoop will be trying to hold air and the patchwork won't be properly tensioned.

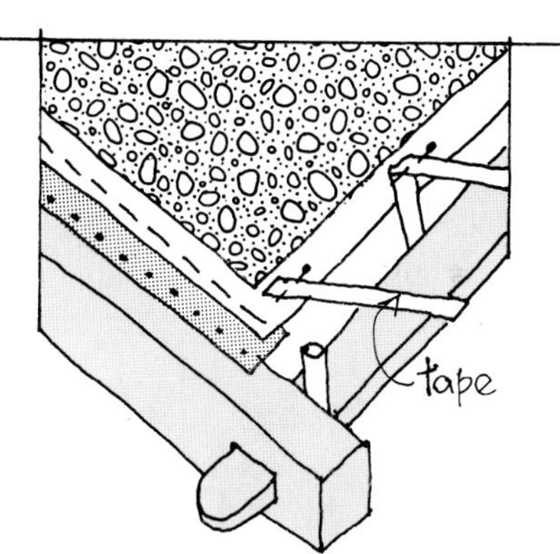

12-8 TAPE-TENSIONING QUILT SIDES TO SWORDS

TYING

Mark the points for tying at about 4in (10cm) spacings. Use doubled crochet cotton or cotton knitting yarn and a stout sharp large-eyed needle. The following knot, which takes far longer to explain than to do, is much better than a reef [square] knot, which needs a lot of 'tail' to tie and so is wasteful of yarn. Take a stitch through all three layers, pull yarn up until a tail of only 2in (5cm) or so is left. Loop the yarn and needle right round the back of the tail, passing the needle under and up through the front of this loop, while grabbing hold of the tail with the left hand. Pull with both hands and the knot tightens (12-9).

12-9 KNOTTING QUILT

QUILTING

It has been said so many times, but the quilting stitch *is* only a running stitch. So if you can sew, you should be able to quilt. The aim is to sew very even stitches, and for a beginner this is more important than making tiny ones. The hand with the needle is naturally above the work, the other hand is held below, with a finger pressing up under the quilt to feel the needle point as it goes in, and then to help turn it up again. Don't try to quilt without a thimble on one or both hands (the underneath finger gets quite sore with continued small prickings). The underneath thimble should have a flattish top to help the needle turn (flatten it with a hammer). Use a small 'between' needle, size 9 or 10, and preferably quilting thread. If you are quilting on silk, then use silk thread. Experiment with the tension of your quilt in the frame or hoop until it suits your method of working. It is necessary to have some 'give' in order to make the stitches.

SINGLE STITCH QUILTING

Take one stitch through the three layers, using the underneath finger to help the needle up again. Pull the needle out and take several more single stitches before pulling the thread through. This stitch is much helped with a flat ended thimble on the underneath finger. The sharper edge of the thimble is used to turn the needle upwards.

STAB STITCHING

This is most often done by embroiderers, who become adept at working in this way. The work should be held very tautly. Put the needle in vertically, and pull it out underneath the quilt, then insert vertically upwards with the other hand, and pull out. I find it difficult to make even stitching by this method, but it is useful when sewing across seam allowances where the thickness forces your normal stitch length to become much longer.

ROCKING STITCHING

It helps to use as small a needle as you can manage. Insert it into the quilt and feel it from underneath. Now, having the right hand's thimble against the needle head, rotate the hand alternately outwards and inwards. This changes the angle of the needle — on the inwards rock, the needle goes in, and on the outwards rock the needle is at a flatter angle and comes out again. You are still all the time pushing on the end of the needle, because it is still travelling forward through the fabric layers. The left hand still maintains pressure and contact from underneath the quilt. Aim to get two or three stitches on the needle at first before pulling it through. When you have the rhythm established, you will be able to take more stitches. But don't forget, wadding and fabric thicknesses and densities all make a difference to stitch length, ease of stitching and the number of stitches you can make at one time.

12-10 STARTING QUILTING (KNOT)

12-11 STARTING QUILTING (LOCKING THREAD)

STARTING QUILTING

Thread the needle with no more than an 18in (45cm) length of thread. Cut off at the spool and make a single knot at the cut end. Insert needle about ¾in (2cm) away from the point where quilting is to start, and run it through the wadding to emerge at your start point. Pull gently and the knot should 'plop' into the wadding (12-10).

Or Insert the needle ¾in (2cm) along the line to be quilted, through the wadding layer and out at the start. Make your first few stitches with the aim of stabbing through the hidden thread. You will find out whether you have succeeded when you pull the needle out — if all the thread comes out too, try again; if it stays in and resists a slight tug, it's locked in and safe (12-11). I always use this method, because I don't like the idea of knots inside my quilt.

FINISHING QUILTING

Try to finish at a seamline or other inconspicuous place. Either make a single knot, running it down the thread to within ½in (1.2cm) of the fabric surface, and then take a long stitch (as when you started) to 'plop' the knot and bury it in the wadding (12-12).

Or Take a backstitch into the last space and bring needle up ¾in (1cm) ahead. Take another small backstitch before running thread off into the wadding. The next piece of quilting will cover the second backstitch.

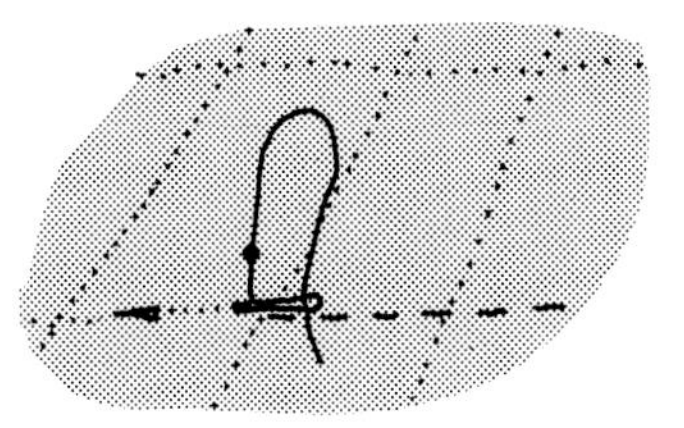

12-12 FINISHING QUILTING (KNOT)

MACHINE QUILTING

This is not as easy as it seems, because of the tendency of the sewing machine to slide the quilt layers over each other and cause puckers. Various things can help:

1 Tacking (or pinning) very closely; this means every 2in (5cm).

2 Using an even-feed foot or darning foot. When using an even-feed foot, do not help or hinder the fabric going through, but let it go at its own pace smoothly under the needle. When using the darning foot the feed-dogs of the machine must be lowered or made inoperable. Once they are not working, any forward (or backwards or sideways) movement of the quilt through the machine comes from you pushing or pulling it. Do not sew too fast or the stitches will be too tiny, and do lots of practice before starting on an important piece.

3 Sewing diagonally seems to be more successful than sewing on the straight, particularly when lines of quilting are crossing each other.

4 Quilting a large quilt in sections and joining them up later, to avoid having to struggle and push the bulk through the sewing machine. LUCY'S QUILT was done like this. When working on a section, it helps to roll up the ends and secure them with (believe it or not) bicycle clips! You would need 5 or 6 pairs for a small quilt. Hold the rolled-up quilt on your right shoulder and feed it through the machine. Re-roll and re-clip as needed.

5 Having a large table to support the quilt while it is going through the machine.

QUILTING IN THE DITCH

This is the easiest form of machine quilting and almost unnoticeable. For greatest invisibility, it is best done with a nylon thread in the spool and a synthetic thread in the bobbin. The line of stitching goes right along the seamline. If the seams have been pressed open, then the stitching goes on top of the seam stitching. If the seams have been pressed to one side, then stitch as close as possible to the seam line, without running up onto the top fabric.

CONTOUR QUILTING

This is quilting (hand or machine) which is sewn an even distance outside a (generally) appliqué shape. The foot of the sewing machine makes a useful width guide. There may be several lines of contour quilting, or only a few, as in HEARTSTRINGS COT QUILT.

'TAKE UP'

All quilts, when they are quilted, end up slightly smaller than they were before quilting started. This 'take up' will be only about 2in (5cm) over a large quilt unless the quilting is very densely done or unless you pull the quilting thread very tight. It is not critical although, if making a quilted garment, leave the cutting out until after the quilting is finished. This was one element of quilting that really worried me before I plucked up courage to quilt — I couldn't work out how much bigger I needed to make my quilt to allow for take up, and consequently didn't even attempt it.

BLOODSTAINS

Inevitably, you will prick your finger at some stage. This is no problem, provided you deal with it quickly, as your own saliva has the useful property of dissolving your own blood. Take some white cotton thread and scrunch it up into a little ball. Moisten well with saliva and rub the bloodstain with it. It may need re-moistening, but works well on fresh stains.

QUILTED CUSHION

This quilted silk cushion [pillow] has a pattern derived from an Art Nouveau motif changed just enough to make it repeat around a circle. The cushion back is quilted in the traditional Wineglass design. I started the quilting using a silk buttonhole twist which was in my workbox, only to find halfway through that it was no longer manufactured. Luckily it doesn't show unless you look very closely.

MATERIALS: for cushion 16in (40cm) square.
Fine silk, 36in (90cm) wide, ⅝yd (50cm).
White cambric, ¾yd (50cm).
Wadding, two pieces 18in (50cm) square.
Silk thread.
Silky cord, 2yd (1.8m).
16in (40cm) square cushion pad [pillow form].

PREPARATION
PREPARE fabrics.
Note that the silk is cut oversize to allow for fraying, so cut 2 pieces 18in (45cm) square, and lay masking tape on all silk edges.
On the cushion top, mark centre and quarters by light finger-pressing. TRACE the quilting pattern motif onto opposite sides of the centre point, on the straight grain, and space the motif twice more on each side and evenly spaced (12-13).
Make TEMPLATE for Wineglass pattern (12-14). MARK 2in (5cm) square grid on cushion back, and then mark Wineglass pattern.

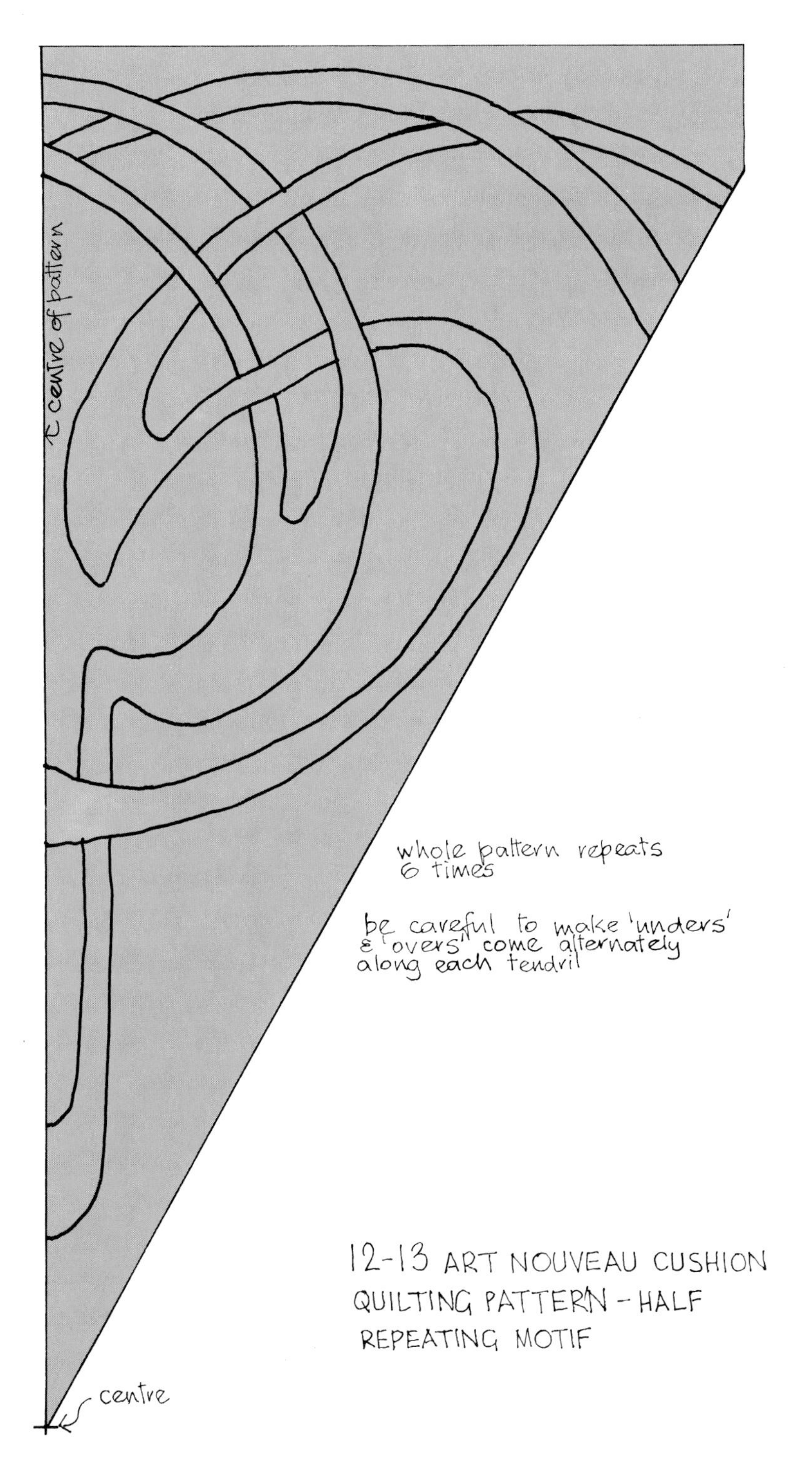

12-13 ART NOUVEAU CUSHION QUILTING PATTERN – HALF REPEATING MOTIF

MAKING

1 LAYER cushion front and back. Attach extra strips around sides to hold in quilting hoop.

2 QUILT front. Make sure that pattern 'unders' and 'overs' come out correctly. QUILT back, and note that the Wineglass can be sewn as long diagonal wavy lines of quilting — there is no need to quilt each circle separately.

3 Trim cushion top and back to 16 ½in (41.2cm) square. Mark with a 1in (2.5cm) radius quarter circle in corners, and trim corners to this line. Pin right sides together and stitch ¼in (6mm) from edge, leaving 12in (30cm) open on one side. Turn through opening and insert cushion pad before hand stitching opening shut.

4 Hand stitch cord all round on seam line, knotting ends at a corner.

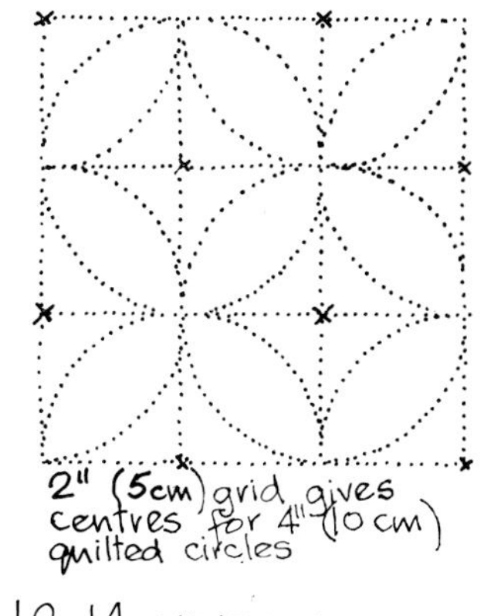

12-14 WINEGLASS QUILTING PATTERN

CHAPTER THIRTEEN

COMBINED TECHNIQUES

In this chapter I illustrate three group quilts, which are all very different, and which all contain more than one technique — and I don't mean just patchwork *and* quilting! I also include two quilter's chatelaines, which can be mini-samplers of techniques, to be worn around the neck for holding needles, threads, glasses, etc, and an unusual sampler quilt.

Many quilters belong to quilting groups. Some groups regularly make quilts as a joint effort, with members taking it in turn to initiate the concept and design of a quilt, and receive it when completed. Most groups from time to time want to make a group quilt, usually for fundraising for charity or to show off at an exhibition. The usual format is for each participant to make one block (generally 12in [30cm]) and then for all the blocks to be put together, with or without sashing and borders. The blocks may all be the same design, or within a general subject or colour range.

The assembly of such a quilt can be a very difficult design exercise, which can be further complicated by variations in the sizes of so-called 12in blocks. I have seen them smaller or larger by as much as 1in. Then there is the awkward decision: do you trim some blocks down or add narrow borders to the small ones? Often, such difficulties in putting a quilt together mean that next time the group probably opts for making appliqué blocks, with pre-cut background squares. This is certainly a way out, but it means that the whole vast field and opportunity of pieced work will be ignored. One way of partly overcoming this is for all the participants to practise the exercise for ACCURATE SEAM ALLOWANCES. It helps also, when members are making the same block pattern, for the organiser to make up a test block first and write out detailed instructions.

One other area of difficulty is the time it takes to quilt a group quilt. This is when enthusiasm flags. Consider doing QUILT-AS-YOU-GO blocks, which would leave just sashings and borders for the final quilting.

THE OAKLANDS WALLHANGING

For several years, Alban Quilters of St Albans were given space at the Oaklands Agricultural College's open day, and we wanted to make a wallhanging to give to the college as a thank-you present. The group is only about 16 strong, and many members felt very diffident about trying something new but they were happy to make blocks. Liz Sherburn and I designed a 6ft (2m) square wallhanging, where the central feature was an oak tree cut out of a solid set of pieced blocks which were made in many shades of greens and browns and quilted with an oak leaf pattern. Because this was before I had worked out the ¼in (6mm) seam allowance test, the blocks came in a whole variety of 12in (30cm) sizes. One or two had to be trimmed and another one or two, which were made of shiny fabrics or were just too small, were made into cushions [pillows].

The design was drawn to scale on gridded paper and then enlarged to its full 6 feet on sheets of card taped together. Each section was numbered and cross-seam balance marks made between all sections, for matching up when assembling. Apart from the tree of pieced blocks, the hanging incorporates a handsewn eight-pointed star cut to form the sun, appliqué clouds, strip-pieced tree trunk,

clamshell flowery bank in the foreground, SOMERSET FOLDED trees on the skyline and an appliqué tractor. The yellow field of rape flowers was made from Liz's towelling bathroom curtains and the ploughed field from lots of striped pieces from leftover curtaining. The card drawing was cut up and used as templates for MARKING and cutting all the pieces, which went together beautifully. Quilting was fairly minimal, mostly long wavy lines across the background.

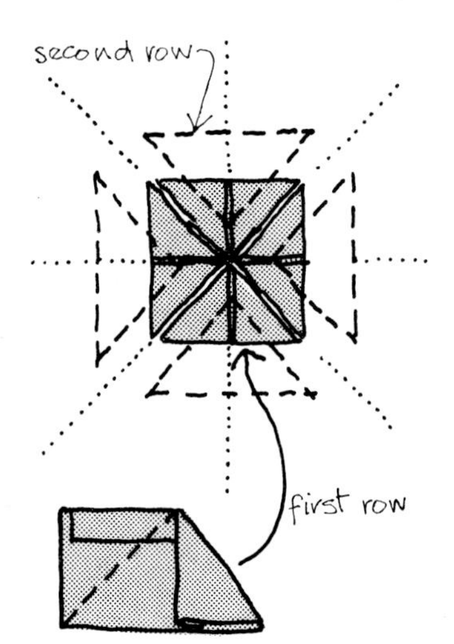

13-1 'SOMERSET' FOLDED PATCHWORK

SOMERSET FOLDED TREES

This is the only technique we used that hasn't already been explained. It is sometimes called Mitred or Folded Patchwork and may be made on a square or round background. In the wallhanging the two trees are round, and different sizes.

1 Cut background fabric. MARK diagonals and horizontal and vertical lines. Cut fabric into pieces 1 ½in x 2 ½in (3.8cm x 6.4cm). Fold down ¼in (6mm) along one edge, and fold corners down to make a triangle.

2 The first circuit will take 4 of these triangles, the second and third 8 each, and progressively more, round by round. Lay the first four with points to the centre (13-1), and carefully lined on the marks. Pin and tack the bases of the triangles.

3 In the second circuit, the first 4 go on top of the first circuit triangles, but a little further out and the second 4 in between.

4 Continue making circuits, with each round a different fabric. Trim the edge to a circle and bind.

PENNY'S DOGWOOD TRAIL

Penny Roberts organised and looked after a group of one Swiss and 22 British members of The Quilters' Guild on an exchange visit to America. As a 'thank-you' the group made her this wallhanging. I based the design on things we had been shown in Atlanta, Georgia. There was a central dogwood flower from a demonstration of Anne Oliver's FREEZER PAPER APPLIQUÉ (and the dogwood was one of Anne's patterns). This was set inside a Carpenter's Square block, copied from a very beautiful old quilt we were shown. The quilting pattern was dogwood blossoms (designed from postcards) and sand dollar shells. On our way from Atlanta to Raleigh, North Carolina, for a quilt convention, I calculated how much fabric we needed and when we stopped for a (brief) three hours at a fabric discount store Penny chose the fabrics — peachy colours because Georgia is the Peach Tree State.

Each participant sewed one block, which I sent out with full instructions — except that I forgot to put in the little word 'scant' and, in spite of advising practice seaming to gain accuracy, participants believed the instruction which said '¼in seam', rather than the one which said 'make sure your strips measure 8in across after stitching'. It was very hard to put together because of the resulting variation in block sizes. Then it went on a circular tour around Britain and was quilted. The kink in the border comes, I think, from trying to cover up a slit in the fabric which appeared somewhere in transit.

The diagram shows a quarter of the quilt (13-2). Although it was divided up into blocks for group making, it would lend itself very well to rotary cutting and strip piecing. The inside corners of the central cross-shaped piece of fabric were lightly coated with Fray Check™ to prevent problems of fraying during appliqué.

13-2 PENNY'S DOGWOOD TRAIL (QUARTER DESIGN)

WELWYN WALLHANGING

Mimram Quilters (Mimram is the name of a little river which runs through the village of Welwyn) wanted to make a village wallhanging, to include the river and pictures of local buildings. I think they chose a very interesting way of going about the difficult business of representing the buildings. First they took lots of photos; these were then whittled down to a few special views which were enlarged several times in a good photocopier until they were the right size. Then the blown-up pictures were simplified and traced to make the patterns for the appliqué pieces. For the sake of consistency, it was agreed to use one sky fabric only. A brown print is also used almost throughout for roofs or walls of buildings, but otherwise each person chose what looked best.

The edges of the appliqué pictures are softened by trees and shrubs and the winding river enlivened by its white ducks, which are a feature of the village. In the quilting are portraits of the local Muntjac deer.

The final feature is the Welwyn Viaduct, an early, very high and famous brick railway viaduct spanning the valley. This was cleverly used as part of the header for hanging the wallhanging. The group was the proud recipient of a Highly Commended rosette at the National Patchwork Championships in 1989, and the hanging will be displayed in the village Civic Centre.

TILLY'S AUTUMN SAMPLER

One very common way of starting to learn how to do patchwork and quilting is to go to classes. And the usual way of teaching beginners is to have them make a sampler quilt. In theory, this is a great idea — you start with very simple blocks, learning how to make templates and to piece, and how to choose colours. Then you progress to more difficult patterns, maybe with curves or sharp points. Finally, the whole collection of blocks (varying in quality of skill and design complexity) has to be assembled into a coherent quilt. And this is where I think the greatest difficulty lies, because it is so hard to achieve a satisfactory balance between the simple and complex, straight and curved, sparse and dense shapes of the blocks.

Tilly Campbell, textile artist, was faced with an even more difficult problem. She was the lucky winner of 20 patchwork blocks at a Quilters' Guild Area Day — each participant had been asked to make one 12in (30cm) block in autumn colours to put into the draw, and by winning first prize Tilly got first choice of blocks.

You can see from the picture what a variety of blocks there were — some light, some very dark, some appliqué, most patchwork, one house block, one Log Cabin, one pineapple, one window, one leaf etc. The obvious SET is to add sashing between the blocks, and 20 blocks would have made a single-sized quilt set four by five. Tilly's solution was most ingenious. No sashing, and no alternate blocks in the conventional sense, but alternate blocks of Attic Windows. This is a three dimensional block which, used in this way, makes all the patchwork blocks seem to stand proud of the background. This also gave her the possibility of adding narrow borders to some of the blocks to make them all the same size.

And finally, having used all her blocks, Tilly made the quilt with stepped corners at the bottom, but she manages to make it look intentional and I think the whole thing is very successful.

QUILTER'S CHATELAINES

Some quilt groups have formal meetings with speakers, and others meet informally. Alban Quilters meets twice a week to sew, and these chatelaines are becoming quite a vogue within the group. They are portable sewing tidies which keep thread, scissors and other bits and pieces to hand. Of course, they are also a way of showing off different patchwork techniques. The number, shape and placement of pockets is as you choose, and so is the shape of the bottom ends. Add a pincushion but put a piece of card behind it to prevent stabbing yourself, or have a free-hanging one. Optional extras are an embroidered name and quilted badges and brooches [pins]. You could incorporate zip fasteners inside the pocket tops to prevent everything falling out when you take the chatelaine off. Or decorate the back with further goodies — newly pieced or leftovers.

Peta Breeze's chatelaine was decorated with leftover samples of Seminole piecing on the pockets, and a strip-pieced pincushion. Margaret Freeman's (made by Mary Jeffreys) has one pocket decorated with RE-PIECED STRIP PIECING, one with a SOMERSET FOLDED disc, the third with CANADIAN PLAIT and a Cathedral Windows pincushion.

CHATELAINE

No fabric requirements are given because of the great variety of ways this could be made, but the scarf pieces will need a 12in (30cm) length of 48in (122cm) wide fabric, or equivalent. Binding is extra. The pockets are lined and mounted on the double thickness scarf shape (13-3) before being bound.

CANADIAN PLAIT

Peta was shown this pretty pattern in Canada but we don't know who invented it. Use three fabrics (A, B and C). These are cut into rectangles 1 unit by 3. Mark 1 unit up one side and 2 units up the other side. Cut from mark to mark (13-4). Sew the end of one A piece to the long side of one B piece. Sew the long side of one C piece to the end of B and short side of A. Continue adding pieces in order on alternate sides, pressing after each addition. Trim ends across (13-5).

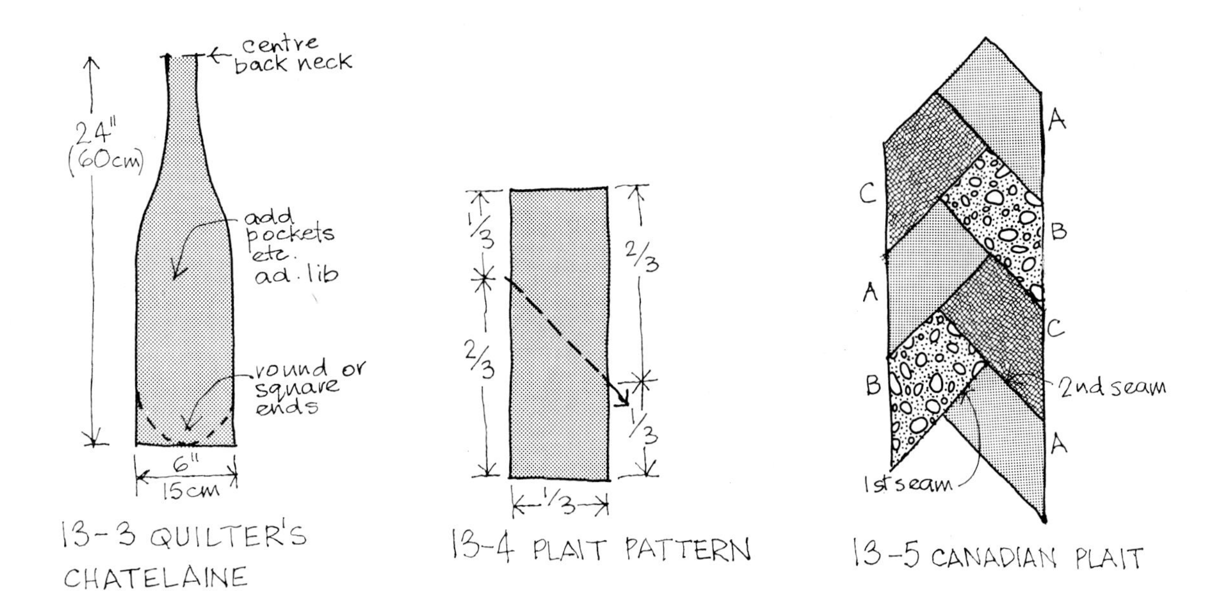

13-3 QUILTER'S CHATELAINE

13-4 PLAIT PATTERN

13-5 CANADIAN PLAIT

CHAPTER FOURTEEN

BORDERS AND FINISHING

The border is really a part of the quilt top, but difficult to allocate to any particular chapter. It is not necessary for quilts to have borders — it depends on the design effect you want. If you do have a border (or more than one) then the widths should have some relationship to any block size in the top. It could be the width of the unit square, for instance, as in FLOTILLA. Borders may be pieced or plain, and apart from QUILT-AS-YOU-GO they should be sewn on before LAYERING or QUILTING.

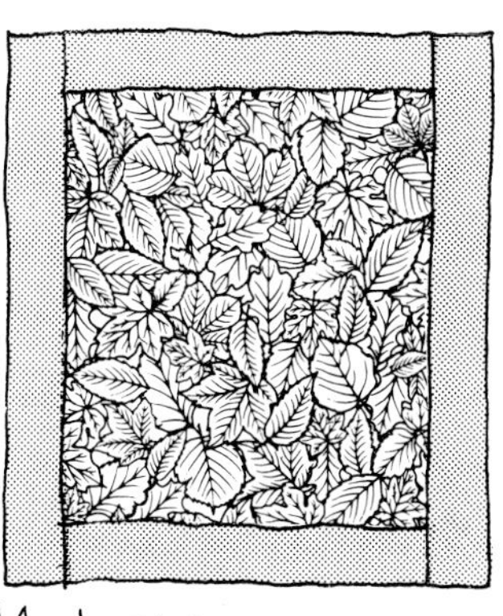

14-1 PLAIN BORDER

PLAIN BORDER

This is the easiest border (14-1). Measure the width of the quilt top. Cut 2 border strips as long as the measured width, and sew them on. Measure the length, including the top and bottom borders, and cut 2 border strips as long as that length. Sew them on.

MITRED BORDER

FLOTILLA has double borders with mitred corners. Cut the border strips the width of the quilt plus borders, and the length of the quilt plus borders. In both cases add on 4in (10cm) for ease of handling. Mark the centre points of quilt top and borders, and pin in position. Also mark ¼in (6mm) in from each corner of the top, on the right side. Sew borders on from marked spot to marked spot. PRESS the seam but not the corner. Lay out each corner in turn, right side up, and fold the excess ends under so they stick out at right angles. This will make a diagonal fold at the corner, which you should press in. Pin, matching fold lines, and stitch on the fold lines from the 'spot' to the edge. Trim excess and PRESS again (14-2).

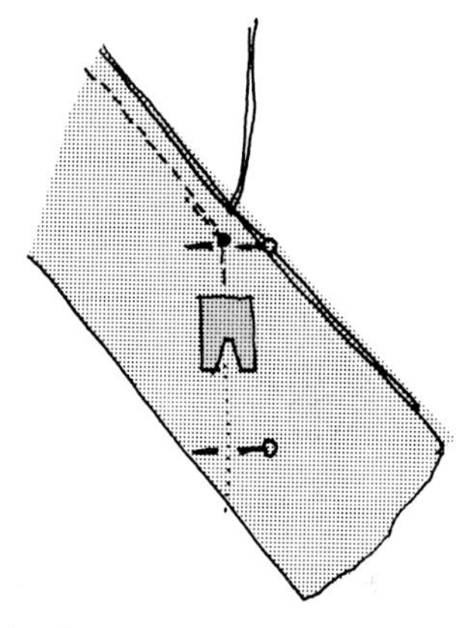

14-2 MITRING BORDER CORNER

FINISHING

Once your quilt has been tied or quilted, it is time to finish it, but how you trim the wadding and backing depends on how the edges are to be finished, and the corners dealt with.

CURVED CORNERS

These may be used on any quilts but particularly on those bed quilts that are planned to reach the floor. Curving the corners prevents them trailing and getting soiled. Mark the curve with a yard (metre) stick swung from the top-of-bed corner (14-3).

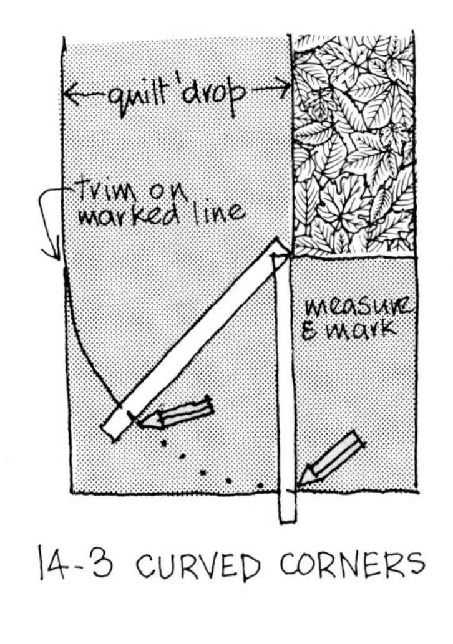

14-3 CURVED CORNERS

TURNED-IN EDGES

This is the simplest method. Do not quilt nearer than 1in (2.5cm) to the edge of the top. Trim backing and top the same, wadding ½in (1.2cm) smaller. Turn top fabric to back, enclosing wadding, and turn backing in on itself. Pin, hem and do one or two lines of quilting round the completed quilt (14-4).

14-4 TURNED-IN EDGE

RUFFLES

Ruffles (or lace frills) are inserted in a TURNED-IN EDGE. Cut ruffle at least 1 ½ times the distance round the quilt, and add a little extra for the corners. Allow for seam allowances and double fabric (for a finished ruffle 2in [5cm] wide, cut it 4 ½in [11.2cm] wide). Join lengths of ruffle into a huge loop. Fold in half, lengthwise, wrong sides together. Run a gathering thread ¼in (6mm) from raw edges. Mark

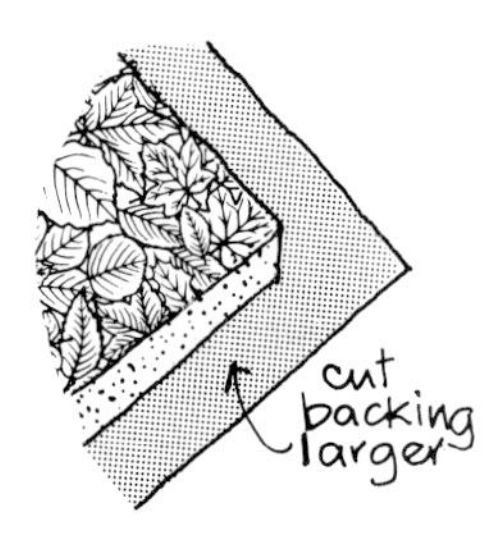

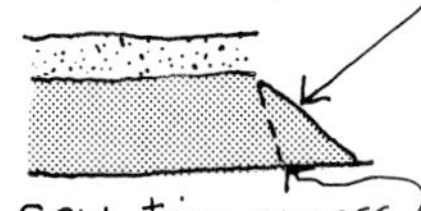

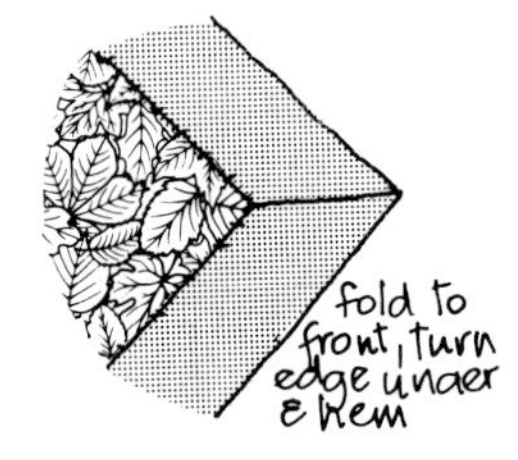

14-5 BACK BROUGHT FORWARD, MITRED CORNER

the centres of the sides of the quilt top, and quarter points of the ruffle. Pin through markings, with raw edges together. Draw up gathering threads, and distribute fullness evenly, but allowing extra at the corners. Tack [baste] all round. The quilt may now be LAYERED normally or ALL-IN-ONE LAYERED.

BACK TURNED FORWARD

Trim wadding to size of top. The back will be left larger, but how much larger depends on how wide a border of the backing you want to show on the front. Allow an extra ¼in (6mm) for turning under, and another ¼in (6mm) for the thickness of the wadding. Mitre the corners (14-5).

FRONT TURNED BACK

This is done just the same as the BACK TURNED FORWARD, but the other way round. Trim backing and wadding smaller than top.

SINGLE BINDING

Trim backing and wadding even with top. Cut binding. The width again depends on how much you want showing on top or back, but add ¾in (2cm) to that amount to allow for two turnings and the thickness of the wadding. The binding may be cut straight or bias. If there are any curves to bind, cut bias. For straight binding, it is best to cut across the fabric as this is stretchier than the length. Whether you cut straight or bias, join lengths on the diagonal, to reduce bulk. So, for a binding to finish ¾in (2cm) wide, cut it 2 ¼in (5.8cm) wide. Press ¼in (6mm) under along each edge. Pin in place on quilt top and sew on line of fold. Turn binding to back and hem over previous stitching line (14-6).

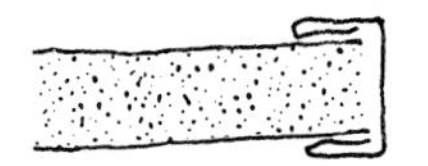

14-6 SINGLE BIAS BINDING

DOUBLE FRENCH BINDING

This is my favourite. It makes a nice firm binding and is extra-easy to sew. I make it finish ¼in (6mm) wide, but it could be more. For this, cut bias binding 2in (5cm) wide. Fold it, wrong sides together, and raw edges matching. Pin onto quilt top, matching raw edges. Stitch on with ¼in (6mm) seam. Turn fold to back and hem through stitching line (14-7).

PLAIN CORNERS

Bind two long edges of quilt, finishing binding flush with quilt at top and bottom. Turn under ¼in (6mm) of binding end, before sewing binding on top and bottom edges; when approaching the last corner, cut binding overlong by ¼in (6mm) and turn that in too before stitching down. After folding binding to the back and hemming down, stitch the 4 corners closed (14-8).

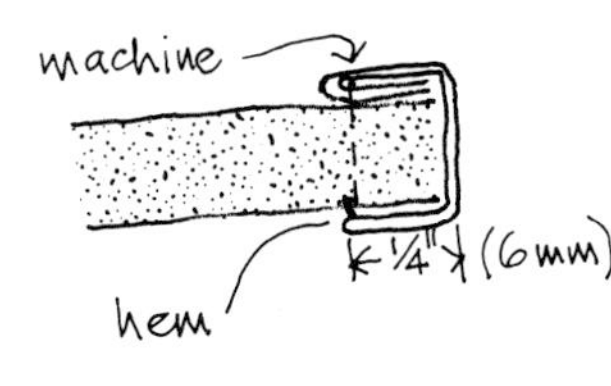

14-7 DOUBLE FRENCH BINDING

MITRED CORNERS ON BINDINGS

Mark a point at each corner, where the binding seams will meet. Start sewing on binding at least 8in (20cm) from a corner, leaving a tail of binding 4in (10cm) long. Sew to first corner mark and reverse a few stitches (14-9). Fold binding upwards (14-10) and then downwards (14-11) and pin fold. Reverse stitch up to corner mark, and then forward to next corner, where the manoeuvre is repeated. When approaching the end, estimate how much binding will be needed to complete the circuit (including enough for joining the two ends of binding). Cut off excess length, join the two ends on the diagonal, and complete sewing on binding.

INSERTING A ZIP FASTENER

The zip is inserted into a seam. First, machine stitch the two ends of the seam (seam allowance ⅝in [1.5cm]), leaving a gap the length of the zip fastener. Press the seam and the unstitched length open. Close the zip. Lay it under the seam. Pin in position, and then tack. Stitch ⅜in (1cm) away from seamline, all round zip, using a zipper foot.

QUILT-AS-YOU-GO

It is difficult to know where to put this useful technique. It is used when single quilt blocks or parts of a quilt are made and quilted before assembly. The techniques for making and quilting are the same as usual, but the quilting should not extend nearer than 1in (2.5cm) to the edge of the block. The backing may happily be a little oversize. Once the quilting has been done, sew the quilt tops *only* together, with ¼in (6mm) seam allowance. Press with the point of the iron, but avoid pressing the wadding. Trim both pieces of wadding at the same time by overlapping them, and cutting through the overlap. LADDER STITCH (14-12) loosely together. Finally, lay one backing piece over the seam (trim if necessary) and fold the other over and hem down (14-12).

LABELLING

Labelling is the last step in making a quilt. You owe it to yourself and the recipients of your quilts, now or in the future, to sign your work. This could be done with embroidery on front or back, or on a label stitched on afterwards. It could be a laundry-marker-written label, or even typed (try running a piece of fabric bonded to Bondaweb® through the typewriter). As a minimum the label should have your name and the year you finished the quilt. More information, such as the name of the quilt, recipient and your home town would be better for future historians. Have you ever thought how frustrating it is to look at an old quilt, 'provenance unknown', and wonder where it came from, who made it, and why? Now project your quilt 100 years into the future and understand why it needs signing.

And so on to the next project. *Happy quilting!*

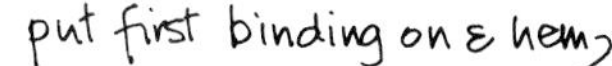

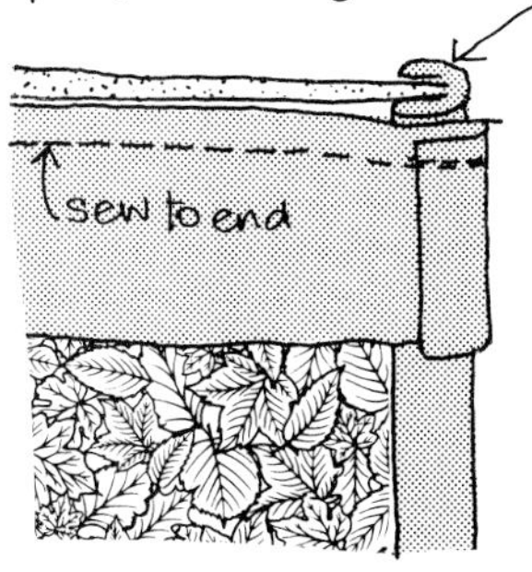

14-8 BINDING WITH PLAIN CORNERS

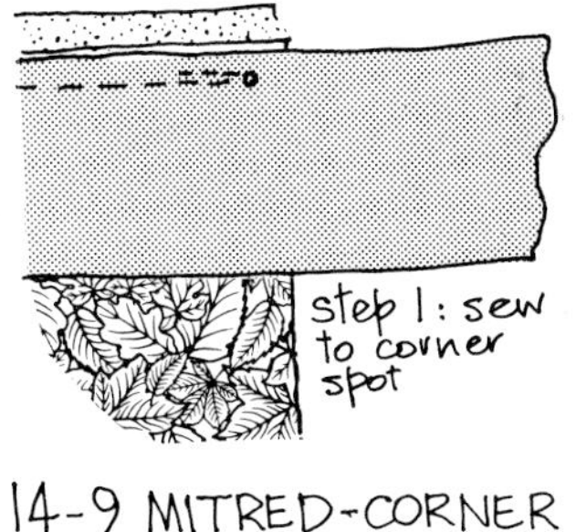

14-9 MITRED-CORNER BINDING

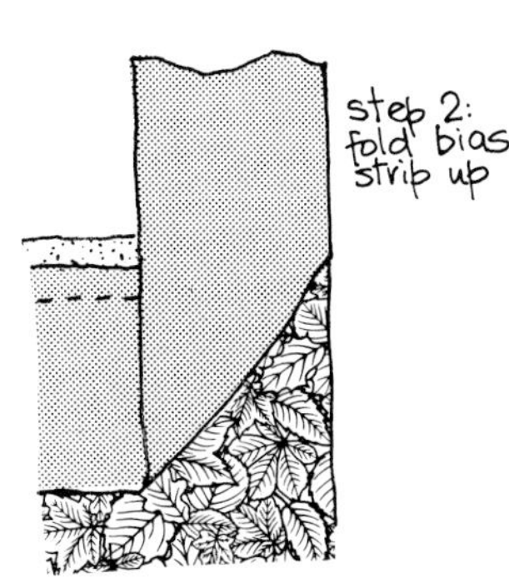

14-10 MITRED-CORNER BINDING

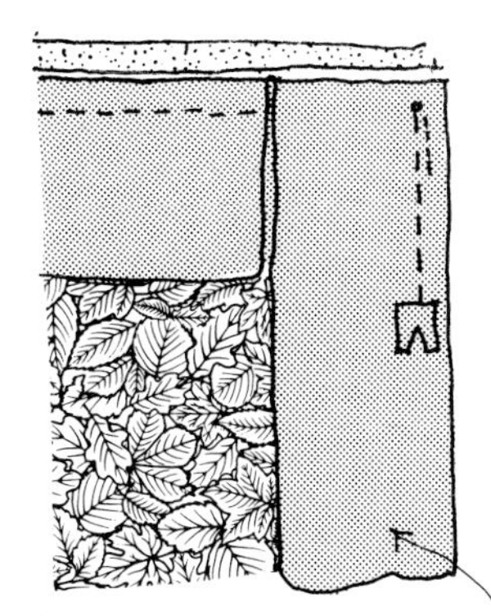

14-11 MITRED-CORNER BINDING

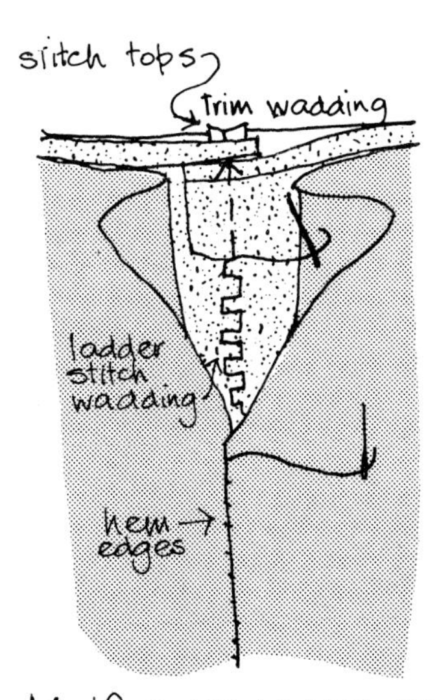

14-12 QUILT-AS-YOU-GO BLOCK ASSEMBLY

GLOSSARY

ENGLISH	AMERICAN
Bath	Tub
Calico	Muslin
Caterpillar	Inchworm
Cotton print	Calico
Cushion	Pillow
Cushion pad	Pillow form
Fraying	Ravelling
Filling	Batting
Muslin	Ecology cloth
Plain (colour)	Solid
Tack	Baste
Tone (colour)	Value
Unpicking	Ripping out
Wadding	Batting

REMINDERS

Here and there in the text are useful bits of information. I have gathered them here to save difficulty in looking them up.

STANDARD SEAM ALLOWANCE — For all straight strips and general piecing, CALCULATE sizes of strips with a ¼in (6mm) seam allowance. SEW with a SCANT ¼in (6mm) allowance.
HALF-SQUARE TRIANGLES — add ⅞in (2.1cm) to the UNIT SQUARE size.
QUARTER-SQUARE TRIANGLES — add 1 ¼in (3cm) to the UNIT SQUARE size.
DIAGONAL of a square = side x 1.414.
SIDE of a square = diagonal divided by 1.414.
INCH FRACTIONS CONVERTED TO DECIMALS
⅛in = 0.125in
¼in = 0.25in
⅜in = 0.375in
½in = 0.5in
⅝in = 0.625in
¾in = 0.75in
⅞in = 0.875in

BIBLIOGRAPHY

Beyer, Jinny. *The Quilter's Album of Blocks and Borders*. EPM Publications, McLean, Virginia, 1980.
Bradkin, Cheryl Greider. *The Seminole Patchwork Book*. Yours Truly Publications, 1980.
Campbell-Harding, Valerie. *Strip Patchwork*. B T Batsford Ltd, London, 1983.
Fanning, Robbie & Tony. *The Complete Book Of Machine Quilting*. Chilton Book Company, Radnor, Pennsylvania, 1980.
Horton, Roberta. *Calico and Beyond: the Use of Patterned Fabric in Quilts*. C & T Publishing, Lafayette, California, 1986.
Ickis, Marguerite. *The Standard Book of Quiltmaking and Collecting*. Dover Publications Inc, New York, 1949.
James, Michael. *The Quiltmaker's Handbook* and *The Second Quiltmaker's Handbook*. Spectrum, New Jersey, 1978 and 1981.
Johannah, Barbara. *The Quick Quiltmaking Handbook*. Pride of the Forest, Menlo Park, California, 1979.
Leone, Diana. *Fine Hand Quilting*. Leone Publications, Los Altos, California, 1966.
McKelvey, Susan Richardson. *Colour for Quilters*. Yours Truly, Atlanta, Georgia, 1984.
Martin, Judy. *Patchworkbook*. Charles Scribner's Sons, New York, 1983.
Martin, Judy. *Shining Star Quilts*. Moon Over the Mountain Publishing Company, Wheatridge, Colorado, 1987.
Puls, Herta. *The Art of Cutwork and Appliqué*. B T Batsford Ltd, London, 1978.
Rae, Janet. *The Quilts of the British Isles*. Constable and Co Ltd, London, 1987.
Sienkiewicz, Elly. *Baltimore Beauties and Beyond*. C & T Publishing, Lafayette, California, 1989.
Walker, Michele. *Quiltmaking in Patchwork and Appliqué*. Windward Frances Lincoln, London, 1985.
Wright, Margaret K. *Mitred Patchwork*. B T Batsford Ltd, London, 1986.

SUPPLIERS

In Britain (please send stamped self-addressed envelopes for catalogues)

The Patchwork Dog and the Calico Cat
21 Chalk Farm Road
London NW1
Tel: 01 485 1239
(Shop and mail order — including antique quilts)

Pioneer Patches
The Store
Marsh Mills
Luck Lane
Huddersfield HD3 4AB
Tel: 0484 547031.
(Shop and mail order)

Quilt Basics
31 Batchelors Way
Amersham
Bucks HP7 9AJ
(Mail order — equipment and tools only, but including quilter's imperial rotary cutting mats and rulers)

The Quilters Patch
82 Gillygate
York YO3 7EQ
Tel: 0904 30448
(Shop and mail order — including quilter's metric rotary cutting mats and rulers)

The Quilt Room
20 West Street
Dorking
Surrey RH4 1BL
Tel 0306 740739
(Shop and mail order — including safety pins)

Strawberry Fayre
Chagford
Devon TQ13 8EN
Tel: 0647 33250.
(Mail order only — fabrics only)

Craft Publications
Unit 13
Marsh Mills
Luck Lane
Marsh
Huddersfield HD3 4AB
Tel: 0484 432598
(Mail order — magazines, books, freezer paper)

Crafts of Quality Books
Unit 8, Bow Triangle Business Centre
Eleanor Street
London E3 4NP
Tel: 01 980 3525
(Mail order — craft books)

The Quilters' Guild
OP66
Dean Clough
Halifax HX3 5AX

INDEX